# MISCONCEPTIONS

Naomi Wolf was born in San Francisco in 1962. She studied at Yale before going to New College, Oxford, as a Rhodes Scholar, and working for a time in Edinburgh. *The Beauty Myth* became an international success when it was published in 1990, and was followed by *Fire with Fire* and *Promiscuities* which were also published to worldwide acclaim. Naomi Wolf lectures widely on women's issues, gender and politics. She is married, with two children, and lives in New York.

D1342440

## ALSO BY NAOMI WOLF

Naomi Wolf

# MISCONCEPTIONS

Truth, Lies and the Unexpected on
the Journey to Motherhood

VINTAGE

Published by Vintage 2002

2 4 6 8 10 9 7 5 3 1

Copyright © Naomi Wolf 2001

Naomi Wolf has asserted her right under the Copyright,
Designs and Patents Act 1988 to be identified as the author
of this work

First published in Great Britain in 2001 by
Chatto & Windus

Vintage
Random House, 20 Vauxhall Bridge Road,
London SW1V 2SA

Random House Australia (Pty) Limited
20 Alfred Street, Milsons Point, Sydney
New South Wales 2061, Australia

Random House New Zealand Limited
18 Poland Road, Glenfield,
Auckland 10, New Zealand

Random House (Pty) Limited
Endulini, 5A Jubilee Road, Parktown 2193,
South Africa

The Random House Group Limited Reg. No. 954009
www.randomhouse.co.uk

A CIP catalogue record for this book
is available from the British Library

ISBN 0 099 27416 7

Papers used by Random House are natural, recyclable
products made from wood grown in sustainable forests.
The manufacturing processes conform to the environ-
mental regulations of the country of origin

Printed and bound in Great Britain by
Bookmarque Ltd, Croydon, Surrey

FOR MY MOTHER
AND MY DAUGHTER

# Contents

# Introduction

Being pregnant and giving birth are like crossing a narrow bridge.
People can accompany you to the bridge. They can greet you on
the other side. But you walk that bridge alone.

African proverb

The first time you give birth, the medical establishment calls you a
'primigravida'. *Primigravida* is the Latin medical term for 'a woman
in her first pregnancy'.

Every year, millions of women cross that bridge for the first time.
Every year, the same number of women find themselves in a paradoxical situation: during the time a woman is in the grip of one of
the most primal, joyful, lonely, sensual, psychologically challenging,
and physically painful experiences she can face, she is often overwhelmed by messages that infantilize who she is supposed to be, and
mystify what is happening to her.

This book will explore the hidden truths behind giving birth in
the developed world today. By looking at how a number of women,
including myself, experienced the journey to first-time motherhood
– and by examining what lies behind the standard landmarks along
the way – I intend to show how the experience of becoming a
mother, as miraculous and fulfilling as it is, is also undersupported,
sentimentalized, and even manipulated at women's expense.

So many of us face the journey filled with misconceptions. Many
women I heard from began their birth stories with the phrase 'I wish
someone had told me . . .': 'I wish someone had told me how
unbelievably bloody and violent it would be,' said one new mother.
'I wish someone could have let me know I would lose my self in the

process of becoming a mother – and that I would need to mourn that self,' said another.

Still others remarked:

'I had no idea my emotions would be so extreme during pregnancy.'

'I wish I could have been prepared for the fact that nothing happened the way I had hoped in the hospital.'

'I wish I could have been better prepared for the pain.'

Women pregnant for the first time often said to me, 'I feel something is being kept from me, and that is the scariest part.' The fact is, they are right. Indeed, as I discovered long after having given birth for the first time myself, quite a lot of important information is too often concealed from pregnant women.

Not only are we inadequately informed about what pregnancy, birth, and new motherhood really involve, we also lack the freedom to describe what we have seen for ourselves along the way. For complex cultural and personal reasons we are expected to keep the full range of our feelings and discoveries to ourselves.

Some of the last secrets kept in this tell-all culture are secrets about the white-knuckle struggle, as well as the triumph, involved in this passage. What are the secrets that new mothers whisper? 'I have never felt so alone in my life,' one new mother confided, a generous woman with plenty of friends and family support. 'I feel that there is this intruder in the house who is never going to go away.'

'Two weeks on, I wondered when I would bond with her,' a frightened new mother admitted. 'No one prepared me for the fact that I would be on a forced march of exhaustion for months. I wish I had known that it would take a while to bond with her, and that it would be okay.'

'I wish someone had talked about what having a baby can do to your sex life.'

'Nothing else matters to me as much as the baby now, but I feel I just can't say that to friends who are working.'

'I feel as if I'm not allowed to say to my friends or family that sometimes you just can't feel like nothing else matters as much as baby.'

'Nothing I ever felt for anyone compares with this; I am besotted – like an addict. I stare at her for hours. My relationship with my husband is just an afterthought, you know, a runner-up,' said another woman, who is devoted to her husband.

'When she nurses I sometimes just want to scream,' said a woman who has a patient temperament.

Giving birth and becoming a new mother demand great reserves of strength. But all too often, women are merely offered a collection of sugar-coated niceties, to guide them on the journey, misleading information, half-truths, and platitudes. Books, classes, and videos available to mothers-to-be, I discovered, frequently have hidden agendas. Many of them omit aspects of the birth experience, or withhold information to advance their cause, to women's detriment. Little that women are exposed to in pregnancy adequately prepares them for the first three trimesters and delivery, or offers them a grounding in the gut-wrenching changes of what has been called the 'fourth trimester' – the sometimes savagely difficult adjustment period that follows birth.

Today's American pregnancy bible (also available in the UK and elsewhere), *What to Expect When You're Expecting* by Arlene Eisenberg and others – a book that in my opinion is the intellectual equivalent of an epidural – notes disapprovingly that women who have gone through the birth experience tell other pregnant women horror stories. To my mind, what is most distressing is not the prospect of a woman hearing about some of the tougher aspects of labour and delivery honestly told, but, rather, the psychic cost to mothers-to-be of literature that is determined to focus on happy talk and sentimentality.

Becoming a mother requires a supreme focus, a profound discipline, and even a kind of warrior spirit. Yet our culture prefers to give women doggerel: it suggests that motherhood is simple and effortless. It calls motherhood 'natural,' as if the powerful attachment women have to their babies erases the agency they must show in carrying, giving birth to and caring for children. It casts maternity as a 'natural' biological unfolding, as calm and inevitable as calving in the spring or peaches ripening and dropping from a tree. There remains a powerful social imperative to maintaining our collective belief in the 'natural bliss' of new motherhood. The American cliché 'Mom and apple pie' is a telling one. Birth is viewed through a softened lens of pink haze: the new baby and radiant mommy in an effortless mutual embrace, proud papa nearby, solid and supportive, but just slightly out of the picture.

Because of the power of that image, many women feel permitted to ask few questions; we too often blame ourselves, or turn our anger inward, into depression, when our experience is at odds with the ideal.

But to what extent does reality conform to this ideal? American new mothers are a particularly sad group in the months immediately following birth. Our country has the highest postpartum depression rate in the developed world.

To examine what women go through on the journey to motherhood, I went back to a journal I kept during my first pregnancy, visited new mothers' groups and asked various women – women whom I knew or who were referred to me by others – to tell me their birth stories.

What emerged again and again was a picture of pregnancy and birth that is much more dramatic, more true to life, and at times more dire than anything I had read elsewhere. Pregnant women and new mothers are grappling with questions about identity – their own – that upend assumptions they have made about themselves all their lives, and with questions of life and death.

Many women were compelled at an early stage of the pregnancy to ask themselves what kind of baby they could 'accept' and what kind of mother they could be. Others were shocked at the birth experience itself within a hospital setting. Still others had a harder time recovering, physically and psychologically, from the birth than they had expected. And many had a tougher time than they would have liked negotiating time off with employers to care for their new babies. Moreover, there was a realization on the part of many of the new mothers that the balance of power in their relationship had shifted after the birth. It was the kind of profound transformation that the women I spoke to, many of whom had been used to controlling their lives, had scarcely expected. Finally, the women I spoke with shared a sense of the profound accommodation they had had to make – as well as a realization of how much that accommodation had changed them.

From the interviews and research, I discovered many insights about first-time motherhood today.

Women on the whole are not adequately prepared for the extremes built into the experience of birth and new motherhood. A decade after Jessica Mitford's exposé of troubling birth practices, *The American Way of Birth*, and almost a quarter of a century after

*Introduction*

Suzanne Arms' exposé of high-tech birth, *Immaculate Deception*, alerted women to problems in the birth industry, the reforms these books sought are far from realized. The medical establishment too often determines their birth experience in a way that can be physically and psychologically harmful to the women involved, even by its own standard of measurement. And American women in particular are profoundly undersupported – by their families, their workplaces, their medical care, and society in general – in coping with the strains of new motherhood.

Many women I spoke to learned with surprise that new mothers are not born but, through a great effort, made. Bonding fiercely with your baby may be natural, but good day-to-day mothering, as few seem publicly to acknowledge, is no more 'natural' than is any painstaking, exhaustive, difficult work that is both biologically driven and deeply willed. As anthropologist Sarah Blaffer Hrdy shows, nurturing is most likely to be good when it is continually reinforced. Giving birth is natural – but 'becoming a mother' is not necessarily natural. It is a far greater work of stoicism, discipline, patience, and will than the ideology of 'motherhood' allows for.

It is not biology alone that drives women to find the will and grit and creativity to put their own impulses aside to serve the needs of a tiny creature around the clock – especially in an environment in which that heroic choice is only casually acknowledged, much less honoured, cherished, or assisted.

I believe the myth about the ease and naturalness of mothering – the ideal of the effortlessly ever-giving mother – is propped up, polished, and promoted as a way to keep women from thinking clearly and negotiating forcefully about what they need from their partners and from society at large in order to mother well without having to sacrifice themselves in the process.

These silences and myths, working together so severely, white-wash women's experience of first-time pregnancy and birth, and keep them powerless to improve the conditions of becoming a mother in our society.

When you have a new baby, what you get is a whole world; it's a world filled with gifts but also with losses. While the gifts new mothers receive are well-documented, the losses are often hidden. This is one truth that we are not told.

Many cultures explicitly pair the potency of fertility with an awareness of loss. Our own grandmothers and great-grandmothers recognized that pregnancy and birth had a foreground that was joyful and miraculous and a background with strokes of dark and traumatic moments. Although few women in the West actually die in childbirth today, we deny the many symbolic deaths a contemporary pregnant woman undergoes: the end of her solitary selfhood, the loss of her prematernal shape, the eclipse of her psychologically carefree identity, the transformation of her marriage, and finally, the decline in her status as a professional or worker.

When I spoke to new mothers, it seemed to me that although a child and new love has been born, something else within them had passed away, and the experience was made harder because, at some level, underneath their joy in their babies, these women were quietly in mourning for this part of their earlier selves.

Indeed, the greatest loss for many new mothers is the loss of self – a very old phenomenon, written about by women long before the women's movement began. In *Misconceptions*, I explore, through my own experiences as well as those of my peers, the death of the old identity – the independent, youthful self – and its rebirth into that hard-won, messier, more inter-dependent new maternal self and new love. I also wanted to explore some of the new costuming in which that old dilemma is clothed.

It was one thing to experience a loss of self in a prefeminist culture that at least assigned a positive status to motherhood itself; it is very different to lose a part of one's very sense of self to motherhood in a world that often seems to have little time, patience or appreciation for it or for parenting in general. This is especially hard for women who have struggled to be independent and self-reliant. At the birth of a first child, the expectations of our generation can collide with what is too often a radical social demotion in a culture that is dismissive of mothers and babies and contemptuous of what they really need.

For many women faced with this, new motherhood can seem at once a total joy and a devastating experience of sliding downward. This collision between expectation and reality creates a kind of statelessness for many women of my generation; we are no longer the brave, free girls we once were, nor are we the easily subordinated mothers that women once were expected to be. Yet in this nameless new country there is also, underlying the spilt-milk comedy, the hitches and adjustments and rueful smiles, an unarticulated rage. The shock of new mothering for women today is in some ways the shock our grandmothers and great-grandmothers experienced; but there is a doubled disappointment in the startlingly constricted circumference of our lot.

*Misconceptions* is also about love between couples who are turning into parents, and how it changes. Most couples I heard from went into childbirth without realistic preparation for how it would change their lives. I saw many marriages suffer, as younger women, raised to expect equal parenting, found the equality of their supposedly trusted modern partnerships shipwrecked on the rocks of childbirth. One source of difficulty in many women's lives upon becoming new mothers is the radical renegotiation of their hitherto equal romantic relationships into ones in which they have less power, less choice, and less say.

Some of the stories I recount show how, incrementally, rippling out from one couple to another, that renegotiation of the woman's role comes about – generally to her surprise and without her full consent.

Are we bad women, bad mothers, for exploring such issues? Should pregnancy and birth remain such sanitized rites of passage that we can't speak graphically or honestly about them? I think not. This book delineates some of the drastic, absurd and sometimes painful changes women go through in the transition to new motherhood, but it is still a book about love.

Motherhood, good motherhood, motherhood in the real world, from conception through birth to caring for an infant, is an epic commitment of the will to work in tandem with the heart and the instincts. It is far from an idealized, impossible love. It is a tough slog.

I want to record and do honour to the real thing, not the fantasy. More impressive than the fantasy of it is real mother love: that *actual,* specific, fierce maternal love that grows in the wake of the immense psychic and physical tremor that is pregnancy and birth should inspire awe not sentiment. I wrote this book to explore the genuine miracle, not the Hallmark card; to trace the maternal bond as it forms heroically and poignantly, in spite of, rather than because of, the obtuse and unnatural ideology of motherhood we labour under.

The idea of family will not be less precious when women are provided with a more realistic view of what happens to them in the process of becoming mothers. Rather, if we speak more honestly about the darkness as well as the light on our journey to motherhood, family life will be better understood, and can therefore become better supported.

Only by listening closely to the full spectrum of stories that women confess to one another, including stories that cultural reasons dictate we must not speak out loud, can the taboo against voicing our fears and bowdlerizing our experiences be broken. And when the stories emerge in their light and their darkness, we will be closer to honouring the real victories involved in the tough, sweet work of making ourselves into mothers.

We know very well that having a baby is a miraculous event. I wrote this book in the hope that we may realize that 'becoming a mother' is not just something that happens to women who have babies but is also a truly miraculous achievement – of the will as well as the heart.

*Part I*
Pregnancy

# First Month
## Discovery

'A dream . . . tells the . . . woman herself that she is about to be with child.'

M.F. Ashley-Montagu,
*Coming Into Being Among the Australian Aborigines*

For us, how did it start?

In an improbable place. My husband and I were surprised ourselves at our surroundings: Italy, in a farmhouse outside a Renaissance town made of stone the colour of baked bread.

In these surroundings we felt a bit like Mark Twain's Connecticut Yankees in King Arthur's court – except that in this case the court was a wedding celebration of a friend of ours whose fiancée was the doyenne of a certain group of hard-living glitterati.

The wedding preparations that we watched from the sidelines involved a ragtag carnival of New York's disaffected – pale young people with dark sunglasses who populated the edges of the art world. The old sweetness of the beds of lavender and dusty thyme, and the bending olive trees, made a strange contrast with the wedding party. Everyone seemed still sweaty from the plane trip and acrid smelling from too many Marlboro Lights.

Behind the small veranda where we sat, ex-models dressed in black bikinis and the white high-heeled hiking boots that were having a brief vogue were making pasta in the kitchen. They were chopping fresh basil on a century-old slab of white, grey-veined marble. The groom paced the sloping lawn where the ceremony would be held, looking pleased and scared.

During a lull in the conversation, I gazed at my coffee and then at the line of distant hills. A guest at the wedding – a part-time photographer, perhaps, or a gallery employee – with lank over-processed blonde hair and sharp features – a woman who had said nothing remarkable in my hearing for three days – suddenly leaned over toward me. She looked with surprising compassion into my eyes and, still smoking ravenously, said, with absolute conviction:

'You're pregnant.'

Was this some sort of conversation starter? Were these the New Age ramblings of someone who did not have much to say without resorting to the *faux* intuitive?

Nonetheless, something was going on. Was my cycle disturbed by travel? By the rich food we'd been eating? By the medicine I was taking to ease a sore knee?

When I went to wash my face some time later, my eyes in the mirror looked like nothing I'd ever seen before: yellowish and blurred, as if I were drunk. That must have been what the wedding guest had seen. I thought maybe this had been caused by too much red Montepulciano wine, by jet lag – by anything, I half-prayed, but that thing.

After the pied-piper band scattered to make its way back across the ocean to Manhattan, my husband and I stayed on for a week to see a little of the country. But even as I waited, day by day, the question always at the back of my consciousness as we went sightseeing or napped in our high, white-plastered rooms, I felt something indisputable: a sickness in my gut. It was a kind of nausea that was entirely new to me: it had a richness to it, as if I had gotten sick by ingesting pure gold. If a mountain of sweets had been touched by Midas, I felt, that's what I had in my belly.

Ordinarily, when I've had scares, I've felt panic. This time, though, I felt far away from concern. Every time I realized I might indeed be pregnant, I experienced, in spite of myself, a little thrill of joy.

We were in Perugina, the town of candy. There were whole streets devoted to varieties of nougat made from an ancient recipe. And still I felt that sick sweetness, surrounded by sweetness.

We asked a pleasant young woman pharmacist for a pregnancy kit. She leaned over very patiently and showed us the instructions in Italian, a language we did not understand at all: '*Questa . . .*' she said, speaking as if to a two-year-old and pointing at a picture of the strip with one line, '*SÌ. Questa . . .*' she said, pointing to a picture of the strip with two lines: '*NO.*' I recall a sense of absolute peace coming over me as we left with the packet in a small brown bag; a sense of fatalism; something that people in my cohort scarcely ever feel – a sense of events moving beyond one's control.

The thought was something like: *What will happen will happen.* Or even: *What will happen has already happened.*

When we knew for sure, we were in a smaller, neighbouring town, which had been built up around a dark, cool bath that a medieval woman saint used to swim in.

We looked at the results and gazed at one another – 'in wild surmise'. Then we reacted very differently. My husband, David, needed to go for a run – and think; and I needed to sit still and not think. Male and female, after our first amazement we reacted spontaneously, like different elements.

I went out to sit by myself, perfectly, uncharacteristically becalmed.

I sat on an old stone bench looking out over a deep, green, shadowy valley that the sun had saturated for days without number. My first thought was this: Thank God I travelled a lot in my life when I was young.

Because now I will have to sit still.

For who knows how long.

For 15 years birth control had never failed me; and then, when my heart and body longed for a baby, when I was newly married, when it was finally safe – birth control failed me. Was this baby 'planned'? Technology did not plan this pregnancy; indeed, technology planned against it. It seemed that my heart planned it. Like many women I would hear from later, I had the strong intuition that will and longing had somehow altered chemistry; that mother love, the mother wish, had created a different alchemy, more powerful than the alchemy of the lab or the product trial.

We returned to Washington, DC, where we were living in a small apartment in an old leafy neighbourhood. I soon lost the quiet confidence I had briefly felt when newly pregnant on a bench in the Italian sun. Being home meant that I was inducted into a medical system that had very clear expectations of me – but little room for me to negotiate my expectations of it.

I visited a highly respected practice and endured a brisk, efficient pelvic exam with a cold-handed OB-GYN (obstetrician-gynecologist). His focus on 'me' (though, in fact, his attention seemed focused on an interchangeable 'it') was entirely waist down. I felt slightly irrational for being bothered by his manner. I was clearly in good medical hands. Did it really matter that the doctor did not look me in the eye? Did it matter that this man, a heavy set fellow with a middle-European accent, had reminded me of Helmut Kohl attending impatiently to a routine briefing? When I left, I had the sad, sinking feeling of someone trying to summon the energy to do something creative within a rigid regime.

A few weeks later I met another of the obstetricians in the practice. The obstetricians rotated their duties and I wondered at the reason for this – did it help them to keep a professional distance? Was that good?

I was glad to know that this one would be a woman. I had a lot of questions to ask. I had just finished reading Jessica Mitford's *The American Way of Brith*, the terrifying investigation into medical intrusiveness in the birthing profession in America: soaring Caesarean-section rates, needless forceps interventions, routine epidurals and episiotomies, the technique of forcing labour into a pre-ordained bell curve – all practices that were performed far less frequently in Europe, while Europe, she said, had better outcomes.

My obstetrician that day was a glamorous woman with perfectly coiffed suburban hair, a tennis-toned figure, and an office full of gleaming French country-style furniture. Her husband was a powerful local figure; I had seen their picture in the society pages. She gazed at me as if she were the president of a one-woman bank and I was a high-risk loan applicant.

She said curtly that I could go ahead and ask my questions.

'Can you tell me what the Caesarean-section rate for our hospital is?' I asked politely, respectful and curious.

She looked uncomfortable. 'I think it's about thirty per cent, but that figure is misleading. A number of those Caesarean-sections are high-risk. Since the hospital gets the difficult cases, you can't judge from the number with any accuracy.'

I had read that this was a standard response, one of many that make it hard for parents to judge the Caesarean-section probabilities in any given hospital for themselves. I tried another tack.

'What about the rate for this practice?'

She flushed. 'Maybe nineteen per cent. I'm not exactly certain. But all of the Caesarean-sections we perform are done for a good reason, you can rest assured.'

'Is there any way for us to find the figures? Does the practice keep records?' In my innocence, I thought perhaps she didn't know where to find the data I was requesting. I had not yet done the kind of reading that I would do long afterwards, so I did not know that an ideological war was being waged over delivery methods in mainstream hospitals. I did not know that these seemingly innocent questions of mine were, to my obstetrician and virtually everyone else in the medical profession I would encounter, part of a complexly negotiated minefield of litigation, politics, vested interests, money, and beliefs about who holds the power over the delivery room. I thought I was asking about a biological process. More fool me.

'Believe me,' she replied, like a politician on message, 'an OB-GYN at this practice is only going to recommend a Caesarean-section if it is the medically called-for solution to a problem.'

'Okay . . .' I said, taking a silent step back. I saw I was going to get no further with that question.

'Well . . . what is the rate of epidurals?' I continued.

At this she laughed. A note of casual contempt for my naiveté seemed to filter through her otherwise well-bred, well-modulated voice. 'Everyone wants an epidural. You may think you can do without an epidural, but, my dear, one good contraction and you will be begging for the injection like virtually everyone else.' Her reaction astonished me, although in retrospect I shouldn't have been surprised.

'So epidurals are routine in this practice? I've read that some nurse-midwife practices find that they only need epidurals in about sixty per cent of the first births.'

'I didn't say they were routine,' she snapped. 'I said everyone wants one, and we are not about to go against that preference. Just about every woman here gets an epidural block.' I did not yet understand why she sounded like a politician under scrutiny.

'What about the episiotomy rate?' I pressed on, feeling increasingly uncomfortable.

'Again, I don't have numbers, but it is part of the standard of care at this practice to give episiotomies just about every time.'

'I read that in Europe, the episiotomy rate can be as low as six per cent.' (In Britain the average is now 15 per cent, but with regional rates ranging from 4 per cent to 30 per cent.) One reason Jessica Mitford gives for low numbers is that practitioners in certain parts of Europe have avoided the need for episiotomies by using a gentle massage of the perineal area; some use olive oil. (A Belizean midwife told me that a steady application of warm oil on the perineum had allowed her to deliver over 800 women without anesthetic, without one of them tearing.) It was hard for me to imagine the woman in front of me massaging anyone's perineum, let alone with a condiment.

'That can't be right. I've never heard of that.'

I was slowly getting angry, as well as feeling humiliated and diminished. Not only was she dismissing my questions without addressing them, she seemed to be dismissing my right to ask. She was acting as if it were irrational of me to request hard empirical information. She clearly saw my questions as an attack. But this doctor held my baby's well-being in her hands. Infantilized by this new relationship of dependency, I said nothing. Why should her professional status suddenly strip me of my lifelong assumption that a woman has a right to know? I wondered. Yet I felt intimidated.

'We do episiotomies on everyone,' she continued. 'Especially for first births. We do them because it is easier to mend a straight, sterile cut than –' and here she fixed me with her eyes – 'a ragged, bloody-edged *tear*'. She paused. 'Some tears extend all the way from the vagina into . . . the *anus*.'

And that did, indeed, shut me up.

As I would eventually find out, the glossy, efficient practice, and many in the medical establishment behind it, had a vested interest in not informing me more fully. What I did not know then was that my first gynecologist's assumption of high medical intervention – one that a first-rate Washington practice takes for granted – is part of a standard of care increasingly prevalent in the developed world. My friends and I, and the women I would later interview as a way to find insight into the trauma of my first birth experience, were all prepped and directed into this self-same journey with the self-same landmarks. Yet each of us was encouraged to think – and, indeed, did believe – that this was our unique experience, with hardships unique to our babies and ourselves.

But when you listen to women talk about birth, their horror stories about the medical profession are about something deeper and more fundamental than too much intervention; the thread that unites many is the experience of a telling, subtle, but distinctive lack of compassion.

My friend Yasmin, who lived upstairs, was five months ahead of me, vastly pregnant when I was still just queasy and struggling to get into my clothes. When I confided in her my qualms about my icy gynecologist, she told me about a similar experience. Early in her pregnancy, she had called her gynecologist about spotting. She got back one of those enraging, condescending, *What-To-Expect* kinds of answers: 'It's nothing, it's nothing – but nonetheless, don't do any physical activity.'

The doctor's answer to Yasmin's question about spotting had only confused her further and, scared, she had begun to cry.

'Oh . . .' her gynecologist had said, with ill-disguised horror. 'You're *upset*.'

Another new mother told me that after she had delivered twins by Caesarean, her doctor had come in to to check the scar. She had gained 50 pounds during her pregnancy because of a nausea that had restricted her food choices and was feeling self-conscious about it. The doctor checked the vertical incision, explained that it was too bad she could not have had what is called a 'bikini cut', but then went on to say that she didn't have to worry because she did not look like a candidate for a bikini anytime soon.

Soon after my encounter with my own 'Stepford' obstetrician, I called her receptionist: 'May I speak to the doctor? I'm bleeding, and I'm spitting up blood.'

'Well, you can't talk to a doctor. And Melanie, the nurse-practitioner, is eating her lunch right now. I'd have to disturb her.'

I remember holding the phone and feeling not only anger at her lack of response, but danger as well; it was not that, on the whole, I thought I was getting bad medical advice from the group – in fact on some level I knew that I was probably getting good medical advice – but that it was coming from people who lacked compassion for me. On some primal level that I did not yet understand, I knew that to be so dispassionately cared for was dangerous.

Indeed, most of the unhappy stories I heard later from other mothers-to-be involved some signal failure of compassion on the part of the medical personnel. As I discovered later, this lack of compassion actually has a medical impact. Your doctor's or midwife's or medical institution's level of compassion, and the amount of control you feel you have as a pregnant woman, can directly affect the physical outcome of your birth and your recovery from it. Your caregivers' emotional support and compassion can be as important as the right choice of instruments or medication in terms of a good outcome.

When I was pregnant for the first time, I did not know – nor did my friends, or the many women I interviewed – that we were entering a tunnel of experience dictated in large measure by money and institutional politics that presented itself as the medically objective best practices of prenatal and childbirth care. We thought that the birth stories we recounted to each other, whether easy or difficult or even traumatic, were ours alone, just fate or the luck of the draw.

Shortly thereafter my husband and I changed practices – to one that advertised itself as being very different, ideologically, from the high-tech practice from which I had fled: a midwifery team that was paired with an obstetrical practice. The 'midwifery' part of the practice had all the markers that reassured me: soft-spoken women who spent an hour on each appointment, as opposed to ten minutes at the obstetricians'; a decor that included photo albums with the names and portraits of all the babies they had 'caught' (rather than the less woman-centred 'delivered'); even big banks of leafy ferns. The obstetrics part of the picture offered efficient yet kindly doctors with prestigious degrees and the latest high-tech equipment. This last was represented to us as backup in case of emergency. The two kinds of caregivers were represented as equal partners. The practice boasted an affiliation with a major hospital that offered a relaxed, low-tech Alternative Birthing Center. I thought we were getting the best of both worlds.

Little did I know.

# Second Month
## Experts

'To treat motherhood as something that just happens denies a woman's participation in conception, her decision to carry a child to term, her nurturing and sacrifice for nine months, and the labour of birthing.'

Catharine MacKinnon, 'Can Fatherhood Be Optional?'

Faced with something new and unclear, I turned to the experts: I went to the bookstore and began to read. Like pregnant women all over the country, and 80 million women worldwide, I reached first for Arlene Eisenberg et al.'s *What to Expect When You're Expecting*.

I quickly developed a love–hate relationship with that book; I found it often obfuscating and condescending, yet I needed it. This particular pregnancy guide, with its cosy line drawings of suburban white women in rocking chairs, annoyed me more than did any of the other books. Moreover, the reason it annoyed me was the same reason that, when in physical distress, I returned to it again and again – I and all the other expectant women in our millions. Why? Because beyond the studies, science, statistics and probabilities, it reassures.

As my own pregnancy journey grew more profound and challenging, the book added ever more sunny infomercials to counter or paper over any dilemma I encountered. The book seemed set to reassure me about every damn thing under the sun. Birth defects? Probably not in your case, never mind, don't fret was the tone. Been mainlining heroin? Not good, but why not stop today! Hard candies can ease those cravings! To my mind, its tone reassured at the expense a full array of hard data – to the point where I began to feel a sort of shameful addiction to it, like a secret penchant for drinking. It made me feel worse, and better.

For example, its 'Best-Odds Diet' offended me even as I tried to follow it. It offended me because it was just as unrealistic and controlling as any patronizing weight-loss system aimed at women. ('Green Leafy and Yellow Vegetables and Yellow Fruits: Three servings daily, or more . . . Vitamin C foods: Two servings daily . . . Other Fruits and Vegetables: two servings daily . . . Whole Grains and Legumes: Five servings daily, or more . . .') You might as well just sit down with a crate of kale. According to a midwife I later got to know, it overstates the amount of nutritious food you're supposed to eat, because the goal is to get you to eat *some* healthful foods.

Why do this?

Because, I guessed, we are considered too dumb, with only the facts presented to us, to moderate our intake like sensible bovines. I felt manipulated by the authors as I gazed, dumbfounded, at the sheer mountains of roughage prescribed day by day. I tried to imagine eating five servings of bran or other unmodified grain product before nightfall, servings of leafy green vegetables with every meal, and for between-meal snacks, a mound of citrus fruit. If you eat a muffin, you have 'cheated'. You cannot have even half a glass of wine 'except for a celebratory half-glass of wine on a birthday or anniversary, *with* a meal', because, though the studies on moderate alcohol intake show statistical insignificance, studies also show that pregnant hard-core alcoholics deliver compromised children. We can't be trusted with moderation. So drop that glass of white wine. Now.

I understood the authors' motivation. I simply resented what I guessed to be their core assumption: that, given the facts and left to draw sensible conclusions, a pregnant woman would veer like the sense-glutted harlot she really is into the slough of sugary desserts and the dark forest of wantonly emptied bottles of Baileys Irish Cream.

With each of the pregnancy books I'd started to read, the cultural subtext grew clearer and clearer, and it did not make me comfortable. I could see it blinking red-on-black in my mind's eye like a Jenny Holzer slogan:

YOUR BABY NEEDS TO BE PROTECTED
FROM YOU

Relatively early in my pregnancy, my friend Cara had a Caesarean, giving birth to a six-pound, nine-ounce girl named Daisy. Another friend, Yasmin, delivered a boy, Amos, after only a five-hour labour – thank God her baby was small, she said. Our friend Minnie also had a Caesarean-section, giving birth to a boy she and her husband named Luke.

Yasmin seemed to sail through her vaginal birth radiantly into motherhood; she put her career on hold and settled down on the green couch in her living-room to nurse her baby, looking sleek and glowing. When I ran into Minnie or visited Cara, however, I was unsettled: both women had been hardworking professionals, both had had surgery, both had husbands who went back to work after two weeks off, and both looked stricken and dazed. They were evasive when I asked how they were. Both looked as if they had just straggled out of the ruins of an earthquake, in shock, clutching their baby, the prize.

Woman after woman I encountered had Caesareans, woman after woman seemed to have a hard time recovering, psychologically as well as physically. Each had a story of some drastic emergency in the birthing room. We all silently thanked heaven for a medical establishment that could save us and our babies.

In spite of all the evidence before us, my friends and I still believed that those 'emergency' or Caesarean-section births were the exception. I would flip past the chapters on Caesareans in *What to Expect When You're Expecting* with slight irritation; that was for unusual emergencies, or for women with frail constitutions, I thought. I am strong and healthy; that won't happen to me. Some of the books I was reading supported me in my denial. A few even seemed to suggest that one reason women don't 'let go' enough in labour to avoid a Caesarean is that modern working women, 'used to controlling their lives', don't like to relinquish control.

Hell, I thought, I know how to lose control. So I dutifully ate my greens and took my folic acid, and my belly grew, and I skipped those pages.

# *Third Month*
# Baby Values

'The perceived need for ritualized medical care during pregnancy is more cultural than medical.'

Thomas H. Strong, *Expecting Trouble*

I went for my first ultrasound scan at a monolithic medical building that sprawled over a part of Virginia that not so long ago, my cabdriver told me, had been a stretch of apple orchards and dairy farms. Passed from one smiling, absent-faced, white-coated woman to the next, I ended up stripped to a gown under the cold hands of a technician. We were in the bowels of a vast, squat, 1980s concrete medical facility, as atomized architecturally as the profession itself. There were no windows anywhere.

Scared, I focused on the blonde confection the technician wore on top of her head. Pert and professional, she wiped a chilly, gelatinous substance on my belly; I was filled with trepidation at who or what I would encounter on the screen as she began to move the sensor over my abdomen like a computer mouse. It felt odd to be the informational field. On the black-and-white screen were grey-blue tumbled clouds, like the primeval clouds of creation.

An oval emerged at length out of the chaos. 'There, you can see the top of the fetus's skull,' she said, without inflection. This was, after all, a routine part of her day, though to me it was the introduction of a lifetime. My heart started to race.

She moved the mouse mysteriously over my abdomen, guided by some information that was unclear to me. 'There you can see the back of its skull. Perfect,' she remarked as coloured digits and a measuring graph superimposed themselves over the image. My eggshell, my tiny chalice, the magic habitation of my child's sensibility. 'Right on track – just as big as it should be.'

The skull vanished, lost in the fog. 'See that string of pearls?' she asked in her practised voice. I squinted at the screen. Out of the formlessness appeared a sinuous X-ray serpent. It could have been a strand of pearls, but the pearls of a fairy tale: a living, luminous thread. It shot, undulating, through the darkness. I cannot recall ever having seen anything so beautiful. 'The spinal cord: see, each vertebra is there. Again, perfect. No visible defect.'

Now the creature assembled itself against the mouse, manifesting its parts seemingly at will, as if it were battering against the membrane between us to make itself blindly known to me. A hand appeared, a forearm, the fist utterly relaxed. There was nothing to grasp at yet. A foot, a footprint, white against the blackness, a thin ghostly shank, oddly clumsy toes.

As I saw that hand and that foot, something irrational happened: a lifetime's orientation toward maternal over fetal rights lurched out of kilter. Some voice from the most primitive core of my brain – the voice of the species? – said: *You must protect that little hand at all costs; no harm can come to it or its owner. That little hand, that small human signature, is more important now than you are.* The message was unambivalent.

The technician pressed harder into what I would have guessed was some vital organ of mine: the baby – annoyed? playing? – shot away from the sensor, and we lost sight of it. 'It's turning over,' she said. 'Somersaulting.' Then we found it again.

I could scarcely breathe. Now it was reclining on its back – practically resting on its elbows, knees bent, in profile, like the reclining gods in Mexico. Its face was in profile too, a perfect, eerie, conventional snub-nosed baby profile.

Then slowly, as if it were looking straight at me – as if to warn me not to ever take its seeming familiarity for granted – it turned its face fully forward. The sweet baby profile dissolved and reconfigured itself. The down all over my skin rose in chills: the eyes were not human eyes, but the overscale almond eye-shields of space invaders in cartoons from the 1950s, the vast, sightless eyes that contemporary 'alien' abductees report: eyes that fix and nearly drown you in their flat depths. The overscale eyes, the flat skull-nose and delicate nostrils, the bulging brow and the thin line of the mouth – was this where that mythology came from? In a way, I thought, it was not surprising: we've lit up the dark regions of our world with electricity. The fairies have fled. In Malaysia they say that after the electric lights came on, the ghosts vanished. There is nowhere left for us to imagine alien beings, except within the dimensions of the womb and its inconceivable processes.

I tried to regain a sense of normality. 'Do all three-month fetuses look like ET?' I asked the technician in a voice that tried for levity. I would have to love this child whether it came out looking like ET or not.

She laughed. 'Oh, sure. I should have told you ahead of time. They all look like that. We get so used to it, we forget to mention it, but parents are often spooked when they see the face for the first time.'

Wiped off, dressed in my street clothes, wrapped against the cool suburban air, I hailed a cab back to the real world, holding a tinted printout of my baby, the photo taken of it facing sideways in a sweet, reassuring profile. I wondered if that must be the convention for those images – to hide the alien helmet discreetly away from the camera's eye. The technicians presented it to me already framed in a cheap plastic cube, suitable for hanging on my kitchen wall, for all the world like a souvenir snapshot from Disneyland. Fetuses all look like that, I comforted myself, but even as I reassured myself, I knew that I could make only the most superficial of efforts to remember this baby's face as more familiar, less 'other'.

Of course my baby looked like an alien because it *was* an alien. Its true face was the one that turned the eyes of a whistling cosmos right at me and through me. This was a baby in my belly, but it was also a time-glider hanging poised in inner space, ensouled already, or to become ensouled at some moment that I would be wholly unaware of; as I was steaming broccoli or reading the morning paper. Emergent from God alone knew where, suspended on a journey that I could never fathom, of course it was an alien: it hailed from another world.

I hung its sweet profile on the nail on our kitchen wall that held a Maurice Sendak calendar. As I looked at it from time to time, I knew that while this was the guise the newcomer would assume so I could love it and take it through this life, its first face was older and stranger by far.

What was this new life – new life *form*? Pearl, kernel, gem, nugget, faerie, night rider? The weirdness was intense. Years later, I was to read British academic Lorna Sage's powerful and haunting memoir, *Bad Blood*, in which she describes her shock on finding herself pregnant as a teenager in 1959. 'I wanted my body back,' she says. 'I'd never until now thought of it as mine, really, now that it wasn't. Pregnant, I was my own prison . . . I was an outsider, harbouring an alien, an alien myself.' This is how it was for *me*. There was something *in* me; nurturing itself *from* me; what was the difference between this inner inhabitation and a kind of benign possession, or gentle succubus? The strangeness of it was reflected only in the oldest of folklore: when they are born with a caul, they see the future; if they lactate on arrival from the birth hormones, the substance is called 'witches' milk'.

'Oh, look at its sweet nose!' exclaimed Yasmin. 'Sweet, sweet little hands, all cuddled up!' I looked often. I cherished that nose and those hands. But I felt: I am not fooled. And I could swear that, when it had looked at me, it had conveyed this directly to me: *Yes, I will be a human baby eventually, small, helpless, new, and wholly lovable. But not yet.*

When I was just visibly pregnant, I was interviewed by a conservative commentator. A subject he raised in passing was abortion. 'Is that not a baby?' he asked, gesturing at my belly, in a cheap but, I suppose, un-pass-uppable shot.

'Of course it's a baby,' I answered. 'And if, God forbid, I was not able to care for it or feed it or raise it; if I had to face the terrible decision to end the pregnancy, that decision would be between my conscience and God.'

Did my baby lurch against my lungs?

On another day, I found myself in an argument with my friend Peter, an abortion rights lawyer, about a programme that required cocaine-addicted mothers-to-be in South Carolina to enrol in medical drug treatment if they were to receive welfare benefits. From his point of view as an abortion rights activist, Peter saw the case as opening a theoretical door to penalizing women who wanted abortions: treating the fetuses as having enough 'rights' to ask their mothers to get drug treatment to protect them was 'a slippery slope'. I agreed wholeheartedly with the theory; yet I suddenly saw it from the point of view of someone who was thinking more about babies that would be brought to term than about the abstract importance, to those with our pro-choice views, of resisting fetal rights. In a way that was new for me, I thought very concretely about these actual fetuses that would surely be brought to term – and about whether a baby had a right to develop in a safe environment. My wondering caused me acute discomfort: once a pro-choice woman starts thinking about whether a seven-month fetus should be spared being bombarded by crack cocaine, it can indeed be a slippery slope.

Yet I had to face my new conviction: I could begin to see some point in policies that encouraged – but didn't force – drug-addicted pregnant women to get treatment in order to help babies who could not help themselves.

'You are compromising those women's rights!' Peter warned. He thought I was becoming a reactionary.

But with every day of my pregnancy dragging me into closer awareness of the being in my body, I began to think that his views were based on an abstract ideal of the self and its rights – constituted by men – that simply could not account for pregnancy. I was still passionately pro-choice, and yet I was beginning to wonder whether a pregnant woman was an implicit challenge to the idea of the autonomous 'individual' upon which basic Western notions of law, of rights and even of selfhood were based. 'There are two people inside me now,' I thought. 'Everything is different.' Pregnancy, it seemed, required a different kind of philosophy, even a better pro-choice language.

A few weeks later, at my new OB-GYN's office, I overheard a slackery teenage girl on the phone to her friend. 'Her test is positive,' she whispered confidentially to me as I waited for her to relinquish the phone. All at once I wanted to shake her, recognizing all too well that almost gleeful sense of high teenage melodrama, of making incursions on the grown women's territory. This, I wanted to tell her, is not a game. My attitudes about abortion were shifting like magma under the ocean floor, caused by upheavals too deep to see.

As I read the newspapers over the following few days, I was haunted by an escalation of the violence in the abortion wars. It tore me up in a new way. Wanted and cherished though this baby was (I did not yet truly think of it as 'my baby'), my wish sometimes to escape brought home to me as never before the feelings that must, multiplied a thousandfold, accompany an unwanted pregnancy. At the same time, my sense of being at the front lines of the species made me newly judgemental of those who skimmed this awesome edge of life and death out of nothing more consequential than carelessness.

Being a pro-choice woman, pregnant in a country in which almost a quarter of all pregnancies end in abortion, presented a conundrum so uncomfortable, I could hardly stand to think about it, yet I could not ignore where my thoughts led, either. Was being pregnant in a pro-choice world like being a greenhouse, in which some strains of what you grow are clipped back and some are propagated? Was being pregnant in a country with such a high abortion rate like going to the hairdresser's, in which something sort of alive, but not really, is either allowed luxuriantly to grow or else is shorn away?

It was, as the pro-choice slogan asserted, 'my body'. But did I own this baby the way I owned my possessions, my hair and my fingernails?

It began to become clear to me that babies were part of a currency system. And I began to wonder: What is this baby *for*? That is: what is its meaning, its value? I thought we were just having a baby, but it seemed that fetuses and babies stood in for so many other things, many of them abstract: freedom, wealth, values, lifestyle, identity.

An acquaintance told me a story about an educated, sensitive couple in their early thirties who wanted to have a baby. The woman's family had an unusual medical history: the men, who were otherwise healthy, carried a gene that led them to go deaf in adolescence. This had happened to her father, her uncle and her brother. Some relatives had been made so distraught by this onset of deafness that they had suffered severe depressions. One had killed himself.

Each male fetus the woman carried had a 50 per cent chance of bearing the defect. The sex of the fetus could be identified only by amniocentesis in the fourth month. The woman had gotten pregnant three times. Each time she had discovered in the fourth month that she was carrying a boy. There was no test to identify if the boy carried the defect, so each time the couple had decided to have a fourth-month abortion – not knowing if the baby boy would have borne the gene for deafness. The fourth fetus was also a boy.

Again they scheduled an abortion. But a friend of the father's had told him that a research lab had just developed a test for the gene in question. A sample of three cells was taken from the fetus and delivered to the lab.

On the day of the scheduled abortion, the researcher, who was not an expert at the procedure, botched the slides with the first two cells. On the slide bearing the last remaining cell, he found that the baby was not a carrier. The father raced over to intercept his wife two hours before she was to undergo the abortion. As a result, they are now the happy parents of a healthy son.

'That's such a lot to go through,' I told my acquaintance. 'Why didn't they consider adoption instead?'

'They really love each other, and they felt it was an important expression of their love to have a baby of their own who looked like both of them.'

'But lots of kids who are biologically related to their parents don't look like them. Or they look like one but not the other. Is that really enough of a reason to go through three abortions?'

'How can you make a judgement about their reasoning?'

'Well . . . it seems narcissistic to me. I mean, where do you draw the line? It's a terrible thing to lose your hearing. But that couple was willing to terminate four advanced pregnancies rather than risk a son being born with a fifty per cent chance of becoming deaf.'

'She saw what deafness did to the men in her family.'

'But not all deaf people are depressed or suicidal. Most would probably say they are leading good lives.'

My friend got angry with me, just as Peter had done. Looking at me with pity and outrage, she called me judgemental. It was true: I was making new judgements.

I later read a newspaper article about a group of women ministers with disabilities who had started a prayer service called 'Healed By Our Wounds'. Their premise is that disability can be a call to spiritual understanding. Who was more right, I wondered, the couple who hoped for perfection, and a reflection of their own faces in a child – or the women who wanted to teach that their disabilities helped them to identify, as they put it, 'the truth of who we really are'?

That 'truth' about who we are is distilled for contemporary pregnant women in the technological crucibles of pregnancy: amniocentesis is one. The three-to-four-month point in pregnancy – the time at which a woman, especially if she is over 35, may be offered an amniocentesis (analysis of amniotic fluid, removed via a needle inserted through the mother's abdomen, to detect abnormalities) and must then decide, based on the results, whether to go through with the pregnancy – is the point at which many couples begin a gut-wrenching examination of 'how perfect' they need their child to be. Other couples take the test without fully thinking through what they will do if the result is bad – only to find themselves blindsided by the terrible choice they must make if the baby is shown to have an abnormality. It was a subject that was treated lightly in the shelfload of books I read.

At the end of my first trimester (three months into the pregnancy), we received an 'abnormal' alfaprotein (AFP) test result, which could have indicated birth defects such as spina bifida. This terrifying experience, I subsequently learned, is not uncommon. This test is usually offered routinely to patients with little discussion of the common false-positive results. Out of every 1,000 women who take a triple screen test up to 100 will have an abnormal result. However, only 2 to 3 of these 100 women will have a fetus with a birth defect. 'Bad news with AFP screening is very common,' writes Barbara Katz Rothman in *The Tentative Pregnancy*, her book about amniocentesis and other screening tests. An abnormal test result means that additional testing (ultrasound and maybe amniocentesis) is needed.

Why do the screening? To give couples more information, of course. Which then comes down to a decision on their part if the information suggests bad news: whether or not to keep the baby.

But behind this routine push for testing there is also an unspoken agenda. Screening tests and amniocentesis account for a great deal of the total American birth revenue. As one presentation in the Second World Congress on Controversies in Obstetrics, Gynaecology and Infertility, a conference for obstetricians and other specialists held in a Paris luxury hotel in September 2001, sponsored by 14 pharmaceutical and medical procedure companies, baldly put it, 'Fetal Malformations. Capsule: the cost of fetal screening for anomalies is not optimized yet . . . Screening: Can We Still Increase Cost to Diagnose Down's Syndrome?'

'With so much false reassurance and so many false alarms, why have these screening tests become the standard of practice?' Rothman asks. '[M]arketing,' she concludes, by drug companies and labs, which profit from every test. Indeed, amniocentesis adds revenue: in 1997, the test cost $398 in New York, $343 in Chicago, $315 in Philadelphia. But the costs of litigation are a stronger pressure. Pulled by marketing and pushed by litigation fears, many doctors like the tests: for the tests provide protection for them and their hospitals against lawsuits on the basis of 'uncaught' abnormalities, thus determining the level of malpractice insurance the doctor will pay. Every baby born with a defect raises the risk that a doctor will be sued. Every lawsuit raises a doctor's malpractice insurance fees. The record of an amnio is a useful defence for the doctor in the event of a lawsuit. Hence, many women feel that their obstetricians subtly encourage them to have the amnio done, in spite of their own possible reservations; and hence the subtle bias of many 'amnio' presentations, such as the one I observed at a major New York hospital, which spoke reassuringly about how the great majority of pregnant women whose fetuses showed abnormalities chose termination, but which offered little information or resources for those who might choose to keep a baby with a birth defect.

But while the women with fetuses that actually do have birth defects wrestle with what to do, the routinization of amnio follow-up causes many additional women whose fetuses turn out, in fact, to be fine, to agonize. Some birth activists – even psychologists, such as Michelle Asher-Dunne, who specialize in restoring the bond between mother and baby if it has been damaged – believe this two-to three-week ambivalence about accepting the baby complicates bonding between mother and child. When taking AFP tests, tens of thousands of women must call a kind of time-out as they wait for the return of the results, which can take up to three weeks. Carrying a developed fetus that for up to 21 days you must consider aborting – and for women who have already given birth once, the fetus is often palpably moving at that stage of the pregnancy – is an emotionally fraught experience. It forces a woman who has not ruled out termination to decide what she can or cannot accept in a child; who she can or cannot be as a mother.

An interesting new development to have emerged from the UK is the nuchal fold test, which detects chromosomal abnormalities by measuring the thickness of skinfolds in the neck of the developing fetus by ultrasound. Developed by Professor Kypros Nicolaides at the Fetal Medicine Centre in London, the test is non-invasive and, when used in combination with a blood test measuring the levels of HCG and Papp hormones, is claimed to be 90 per cent accurate. The main advantage of the test, other than its non-invasiveness, is that it can be done at 11–13 weeks of pregnancy and the results are available to the parents within a couple of hours. In the UK it is available privately and, in some areas, on the NHS, but it is being increasingly adopted in many other countries of the world. There's no doubt that nuchal fold testing dispenses with the agonizing wait that is associated with so many other forms of antenatal screening, but its false positive rating is still to be determined.

In the days before ultrasounds and amniocentesis, that moment when you first felt the baby move was taken to be the start of life. It has a lovely name: 'quickening'. After four months, you quicken and quicken and quicken: 'It's like having a sackful of ferrets in your stomach,' Minnie remarked, quoting Virginia Woolf she thought.

Today, many women have amniocentesis at four months – after quickening. In other words, advanced technology, combined with obstetricians' and hospitals' financial interest in avoiding lawsuits, encourages women to suspend their attachment to their developing child for a month or so after the baby can first be felt to move but before the amnio results are in.

In addition to the emotional upheaval, what are the medical risks of amnio? Should we take the test so casually?

Many women are under the misconception that amniocentesis is fairly safe. Here is what *What to Expect When You Are Expecting* says about amniocentesis:

'How safe is it? Most women experience no more than a few hours of mild cramping after the procedure . . . Although fewer than 1 in 200 women experience an infection or other complication that may lead to miscarriage, amniocentesis, like most other prenatal diagnostic tests, should be performed only when the benefits out-weigh the risks.' What does that mean to the lay reader? Essentially, consult your doctor. We are in the subsequent section given the risks, but not their probability. Before a woman has an amnio she is given a routine hospital form to fill out that lists all risks. But, as with so many medical procedures that uniquely affect women, she is not given data to help her make an informed choice about the real probability that those risks might occur.

*What to Expect* reassures some more: 'Although complications with amniocentesis are rare, it is estimated that following about 1 in 100 procedures there is some leakage of amniotic fluid. If you should notice such leakage from your vagina, report it to your practitioner at once. The odds are very good that the leakage will stop after a few days, but bed rest and careful observation are usually recommended . . .' Sounds comforting. The 'odds are very good' that nothing bad will happen. But others claim that the odds that something bad can happen are significantly higher.

The risks of amniocentesis, according to Ruth Wainer Cohen, author of *Open Season*, are 'still horrendous . . . infection, hemorrhage, fetal damage (including puncturing the baby), miscarriage, embolism, premature labour, abortion, damage to uterine and placental vessels, and sudden deaths, to name a few.'

According to Dr D. Barrere's 2001 explanation of amniocentesis, the risk of miscarriage related to amniocentesis is 1 in 200; the risk of infecting the amniotic sac is 1 in 1000, and the risk of fluid leakage, which can also harm the baby, is 1 in 100. Another 1996 study confirmed a 1 in 200 chance of losing the baby secondary to an amniocentesis.

These concerns were borne out for me by Caroline, an English Further Education teacher, who told me about her experiences under the British National Health Service. Now in her fifties, Caroline had the test in the 1980s – a time when no serious alternative to amniocentesis was available, and when there was a lack of sufficient data, she felt, to enable her to make an informed choice.

'When I first became pregnant at thirty-five,' she says, 'it seemed both logical and responsible to opt for amniocentesis. I was extremely anxious about the increased possibility of Down's syndrome – the papers at the time were full of stories of increased risks for over-thirties. I was also certain that neither my husband nor I could deal with the realities of caring for a child with this or any other severe handicap. Friends within my approximate age group had made the same, what seemed to me to be routine, decision to go for the test as a sensible "precaution".

'My consultant, a nice woman, warned me of the risks, but they seemed so low that I thought, "Well, the chances are so slim that anything will happen . . . I'll be fine." Given my anxieties – which, I now see, were vastly exaggerated – she agreed that it would be a good idea for me to have the amnio, so I went ahead. The test was unpleasant and worrying, but not traumatic. It was done by another doctor – one of my consultant's team, I think.

'After a couple of days, I started having contractions and was rushed into hospital. I remember not just the pain and fear but also the anger and helplessness of being left for at least an hour on a trolley after I was taken to hospital in an ambulance. I felt no one cared and that it was all the hospital's fault, even though they tried hard to save the baby. It died . . . This, at the time, was diagnosed as a "very unfortunate event". I was, the doctors said, part of a statistical minority who had a sensitive uterus. I can't help wondering, in retrospect, why there hadn't been a way of testing my uterus before I got pregnant. My consultant also admitted privately that the doctor who had carried out the test was relatively inexperienced. I was astonished – I had no idea that people with little experience could do the test unsupervised, or that this could affect the result.

'The miscarriage devastated me and my partner. I couldn't eat or sleep for weeks and was crying constantly. Six months later I became pregnant again, and, for reasons that seem impossible to explain now, agreed to go through the whole process again. All I know is that I was even more terrified of having a Down's syndrome child – I think I was still so distraught from the first time round, that I wasn't thinking clearly. The consultant agreed to do the test herself this time, but didn't attempt to dissuade me from having it, which I now feel she should have done.

'Within a few days I had miscarried again. Perhaps I should have sought private medical care. Who knows? I remember thinking this in desperation after both miscarriages, when I was recovering in a ward of mothers who had just given birth to healthy babies. I found this unbearable, as well as the guilt that it was all my fault, and that neither of the miscarriages need have happened if I had just trusted that things would probably be okay. I was told that both babies I miscarried were normal – a horrible irony.

'When I eventually became pregnant again, I did not have an amniocentesis, and carried full term. I now have a healthy teenage daughter, but I always think about the babies I lost, and feel angry that no one talked to me properly when I wanted to have the amnio for the second time. I really feel the doctors should have realized how distraught I was, and offered me special counselling. If I had been given the information I needed at the time, I would never have agreed to have the test.'

Caroline's experience of isolation and denial of information is one that many women share. When I went to the hospital prep session I mentioned for women about to undergo amniocentesis, I was told – as were all the women present – that the risks to mother and baby were 'minuscule'. But in spite of my repeated requests, I was refused statistics to back that up. When I asked what could happen to the fetus during amnio – knowing that standard research pointed to a 1 in 200 incidence of losing the baby – I was told, 'It might get a little nick. Some babies come out and you can see a little scratch on their cheek.' When I asked for that hospital's data on miscarriage or other negative outcomes for the baby related to amnio, I was told 'The hospital doesn't keep such statistics.'

'Why?' I asked. 'How else can women make an informed decision about this?'

'We are understaffed,' the hospital spokeswoman insisted. 'And it's hard to follow up – we can't keep track of everyone's address.'

I looked around at the bustling, richly endowed hospital and the enormous office filled with data processors, who were busy doing the detailed paperwork that went into billing.

'You are able to keep records in great detail about how much your patients owe the hospital,' I said. 'Don't you need addresses for all these patients in order to bill them? How hard would it be to keep a note in the hospital records of the outcome for amnio?'

'Look, the hospital does not keep statistics,' she said curtly, ending the exchange.

Critics have suggested that many hospitals do not keep statistics for poor outcomes for amnio because they do not want women to know how frequently poor outcomes for amnio occur.

When my husband and I got our abnormal AFP test, I was paralysed with fear and indecision. Like women everywhere, I prayed. I respected and admired women who could give their lives over to caring for a severely disabled child, but I knew I could not do it myself. In an obsessive mental video of caring for such a child, I watched the things I loved in my life being stripped away; I witnessed vivid scenes detailing the exact nature of my own callowness. On the other hand, having heard that heartbeat racing like a little runaway train, there was no way I could imagine the alternative.

In the end, I made a decision by making no decision: I let the date by which I could get an amnio 'elapse' and clung to what the midwives had told me – that many AFP screening tests deliver false positives.

Most women accept the tests as standard. Certainly Caroline did. My friends and I did. Had we to do it over, we might well undergo the tests again. But we would have been better served had we been told the entire truth about the gravity of what we were doing. We would have been better served had we known all the interests that were involved. In my case, and in the cases of other women I talked to who went through prenatal testing, we were ill-prepared for how momentous the soul-searching that resulted from those tests can be, nor did we understand how serious the risks can be to mother and baby.

Around this time, the media began to report on a wave of infertility among what one doctor called 'yuppies who just waited too long'. ZIFT and GIFT and other procedures that artificially assist women to get pregnant were becoming increasingly popular as more and more women waited before starting a family.

Sarah, a travel agent in her mid-thirties, offered me one story illustrating the kind of humiliation many women experience in trying to get pregnant and the lack of compassion on the part of many doctors who treat them.

Sarah grew up in California. Although she studied English at a California state college, travel became her passion and she went into the field. At 31, she moved to New York, where she met her future husband, Alan, a contractor. Relaxed and earthy, she seemed to be a woman sure of herself and what she wanted.

Sarah made sculptures, in her spare time, of joyful pregnant women: around her small apartment were displayed images of pregnant women in the basins of fountains, pregnant women in the branches of trees and pregnant women standing on rock outcroppings, all apparently triumphant. It was a shock to see these huge-bellied women exuberantly posed. The beauty of the settings made each sculpted woman seem like a kind of archetype celebrating victory.

As the interview progressed, it was clear why this might be. 'In October of 1995,' said Sarah, 'we started trying to have a baby. Lo and behold, I couldn't get pregnant. I tried for one-and-a-half to two years naturally, but at thirty-nine decided to see a fertility specialist.

'The fertility specialist was like a little Doogie Howser – he looked twelve years old. You go for a two o'clock appointment and hopefully see him at four. There were twenty people in the waiting-room, and the tension was unbelievable. Nobody was talking. They kept to themselves, looking ashamed. I thought to myself, This is when everyone should be opening up.

'I had a laparoscopy – the test to check for fibroids – and after surgery I was discharged from the hospital that same day. After the anesthesia wore off, my upper body felt as if I'd been hit by a truck. I couldn't stand straight. I took a deep breath; it was killing me. I thought something had gone wrong, it was so painful. I was taking half-inch steps. If I'd been prepared, it would not have been so painful and shocking.

'I said to my doctor, "You might have told me, because this is unbelievable." He feigned surprise: "I've never heard that before." My girlfriends, however, said, "You had abdominal surgery and they let you go that *same day*?" I was projectile vomiting. Other women I heard from were in the hospital four and five days. It was major surgery.

'Following the laparoscopy, we went to a couple of specialists for four to five months of tests. Afterwards, my doctor said: "You have 'anticardiolipins.'" "What does that mean?" I asked. He proceeded to explain it to me in even more complicated terms. When I told him I didn't understand what he was saying, he chuckled as though he were humouring me. He couldn't be bothered with a clearer explanation. My inability to conceive was unexplained. They said it could be age. They said it wasn't Alan: "His boys are great."

'One time when I was up there in the stirrups, being examined, there was something wrong with the mechanical seat you have to climb into. There I was with the doctor, who was having a conversation with the interns about something unrelated to me, right in front of my crotch; two nurses, the interns – while two maintenance people were working on the seat I was lying on! The exam had apparently long been over, because the nurse said, "Doctor, are you done?"

'He said, "Yeah . . ."

'She said, "Can she put her legs down?"

'Inseminations involved them shooting me in the butt and leg two times a day for three weeks. I would go in during ovulation. I put all my hopes on the *in vitro*. When my period came it was heartbreaking. I had ten or eleven viable eggs. They do the *in vitro*. You wait two days. The doctor put three or four eggs back into me. "It looks terrific, two look good and one's not so hot." Then I got the call telling me I wasn't pregnant. Alan cried. The person who called me to tell me I was not pregnant wasn't even the doctor. It was a nurse. Not even a nurse I knew. I wasn't surprised by that callousness. Every time I saw the doctor I needed a reintroduction. He was like, "Who are *you*?" The cost? Twenty thousand dollars. My insurance didn't cover it.

'Alan said, "Honey, don't worry, we're gonna get pregnant. Let's forget this guy."

'So we went to see another doctor, who does things more holistically. He took a swab to see how fast Alan's sperm were moving, and he discovered they were slowed down by the Prednisone which thickens mucus. He looked at the whole context, not just the tests' numbers.

'Just talking to him made such a difference. He's reassuring. In his waiting-room, which has only five seats, you felt like a person, not a number. With the other doctor, it was all a numbers game. He simply filled your body with eggs.

'The nurse who helped us was so sympathetic and so lovely. She had gone through it herself. She explained exactly what was going to happen and what it would feel like. I felt totally confident.

'A few days later she called to say, "Congratulations." I got pregnant just three months after seeing him, after just three visits. I had felt so miserable at the other practice, and those emotions have to affect you, biochemically. I felt so good about the experience, and that may have affected my fertility.

'I just knew it would be good news.'

Marina, a drama therapist, told me the story of her struggle to become pregnant. What interested me was that Marina reached conclusions about the importance of compassion in the treatment of infertility that were similar to Sarah's, though the women had no connection to one another.

Marina is a 34-year-old Irish-American from Long Island with dark, curly hair and an engaging grin. Her husband runs a small post office box business. They have been married four years.

'We started to try to have a baby in July of 1998, after I got sick with an immune system problem. They did a hormonal workup – it was not good.

'Depending on whether your FSH – follicle-stimulating hormone – is low or high, your fertility is okay or not. In one and a half years of trying with no baby, my FSH doubled. It was now at a level at which I could only use egg donation. The number was so high, it was if I were in menopause.

'When I found I could not get pregnant, it was the *secretary* who gave me the results. Not even a nurse. I was crying.

'So I started on my way through the whole system. My hospital – the best in New York for infertility – turned out to be a barbaric factory. At the clinic, I had to walk naked in one of those little hospital robes that don't close, down the hall and through the waiting room.

'My husband would have to bring his sample from home, or do it there. They make it comfortable for the men. The rooms where the guys provide the sample are cosy. The guy doesn't have to even press a button, a movie simply comes on for him. They have sex magazines on a rack for the more literate! Chairs have cushioning, doors lock to give you privacy, they provide lubricant. The guy does this thing, and a dumbwaiter comes and *takes the sample*! He doesn't even have to go through the embarrassment of handing it to someone. It was such a positive experience for my husband, he joked he wanted to have a bachelor party there. It's nothing at all like what the women go through.

'One morning I went in at seven to get blood drawn. I found all these depressed women; some were crying. They were getting their results. A number found out they didn't do so well, and their cycle was cancelled. But there was no counselling. There were no *tissues*!

'Ten women were having their blood drawn side by side. The nurses would yell, *In vitro* or insemination?" And they would shout out instructions as they drew blood: "Tonight you will have intercourse," or, "Do your Betadine douche" – in front of everyone. Later they take you into your room, where they do a vaginal sonogram to see how your ovaries are being "stimulated". They tell you, "Okay, come back tomorrow and we'll inseminate you." Like a cow.

'Another specialist heard my medical situation. He said in front of everybody, "I am so sorry, there is no possibility of you ever having a biological child."

'There were a series of moments when they were insensitive or worse. I complained to the doctor that the drugs made my breasts painfully big. He told me, "Don't complain. Many women wish they had that problem."

'They put things in a way that made me feel helpless and hopeless. This doctor, who said my prognosis was very bad, said, "Well, I'll put you on the shots, and we'll see if you *even stimulate*."

'At one point I asked him, "I'm so little, do you think I could safely carry twins?" I knew multiple pregnancies were common with fertility treatments. He looked at me condescendingly and said, "Marina, let's see if you can even get pregnant." And then he laughed.

'Dr X, who is on the "Best Doctors of New York" list every year, came in and stuck the vaginal probe in. I was thinking, Maybe it's my eggs that are wrong. I've failed. You are primed for self-hatred at this point or at least a sense of being defective. I was waiting to find out if I could ever get pregnant. And he said, "What's goin' on here, there's nothin' happening! What are we, growing grass here?"

'My condition was diagnosed as "premature ovarian *failure*". I walked around feeling as if I had sixty-year-old eggs and was a failed woman.

'I had been on Clomid, and it wasn't working. I had to go on to Pergonal – which is a serious step. Yet Dr X broke it to me offhandedly, saying, "Looks like it's time to graduate to vitamin P." When I had been on Clomid, I had serious side-effects. Headache, double vision, which can result in lasting damage. The next month, however, Dr X forgot who I was. He didn't bother to look at my chart and prescribed a *double dose* of Clomid.

'The effect of all this was that I didn't know what sex was like anymore without trying to make a baby. We had sex according to "the kit". I don't know how we stayed married. I felt stripped of my femininity and sexuality. I felt so beaten down. We fought a lot. I would say, "We have to have sex!" and my husband would say, "I'm going to sleep." He resented being on call and couldn't stand that it wasn't romantic. Your lovemaking starts to come from such a negative place, a place of deficiency.

'The drugs made me crazy: I would cry uncontrollably.

'When I told the doctor I was crying all the time, he said, "Marina, you are clinically depressed. We have to put you on Prozac. And proceed with *in vitro*". He told me, "Seventy per cent of my patients are clinically depressed and on medication." He was willing to write a prescription then and there.

'I decided at that point I had had it. I quit the drugs and stopped crying immediately. I found the one doctor in this field in this city who believed that the mind and body work together. When I saw him, he said, "When you are ready, we should start. You are not ready. Go relax and feel better. I want you to feel a hundred per cent better before we proceed."

'I stopped testing my FSH. I worked with a therapist, who asked me to imagine that my ovaries were blooming. Hearing messages such as "I can open my body to receive" is so much more positive an experience than hearing, "Your eggs are old, your ovaries are all shrivelled up." Before, I had the physical symptoms of going into menopause. Now I felt like a million dollars. And my numbers went down to normal.

'It was Holy Week, and I was in church Thursday, Friday, Saturday, and Sunday. My friends, my sister, my sister-in-law, were all pregnant. I said, "God, I cannot bear it if I can never have a baby."

'I was thinking about Jesus rising from the dead, that whole miracle. I thought, "Miracles can happen."

'I threw out the kit. We made love the next three days. That month I conceived.'

Indeed, these women may be on to something by intuiting that the stress they experienced as patients harmed their fertility: researchers Dobson and Smith found that stressors interfered with endocrine activity that affected the release of reproductive hormones. The research team of Clarke, Klock, et al., found that psychological stress even has an effect on sperm quality – as stress goes up, sperm quality goes down. Dobson and Smith point out that in animals, stress often results in failure to reproduce. The fertility industry would serve its own purposes as well as that of couples by supporting the mind as well as interfering with the body.

*

As my pregnancy progressed, I spent a lot of time with Yasmin. She had a low-slung green couch that was easy on my back and supported my growing heft. She usually offered me Indian delicacies to eat with our tea. Her little guy, Amos, was a tiny princeling of charm. We would play with him and slip into baby time, that languid, slightly harassed, limpid time when the heater hisses and the baby burbles and sometimes howls and nurses and sleeps and the sun rises and crests and goes down through the big windows looking out over the avenue. In that dimension of time, a golden light can touch the wall and the baby's soft hair, and you think, There is nowhere else that is better to be; everyone who is not here is missing the point of it all. Time had no meaning but a baby's pleasure. It was a sweet maternal bubble Yasmin let me into, and I loved it while I feared it.

An acquaintance of Yasmin's named Stephanie, a woman I had met once, was in the hospital; her triplets, at seven months' term, had all died. She now had to deliver all three babies dead. I felt heartsick at the news. I remembered Stephanie dropping off some groceries for Yasmin one day when I had been there. Yasmin and her husband had recently taken on a Jamaican woman our mothers' age, Bernadette, to help her once a week with the baby. Bernadette was a sharp-eyed woman with an acerbic wit; she stood by the sink in the kitchen where we had all gathered, bathing Amos in a little tub while we put the groceries away.

Stephanie's belly had been enormous at the time, and I had asked her when she was due. She had told me how, at 41, she and her husband had wanted desperately to conceive. They had tried everything and finally decided to try an experimental fertility drug, which had the frequent side-effect of producing multiple embryos. She had become pregnant with triplets.

Her OB-GYN had warned her that her babies were at risk; they could face problems unless she 'selectively terminated' one of the fetuses. By choosing to abort one, she could optimize the health and survival of the other two. If she refused to abort one of them, she might jeopardize the health of all three.

This situation is a uniquely American phenomenon. Because we lack universal health insurance and pay exorbitantly by the cycle for fertility treatments, many fertility specialists in our country raise their chances of producing a pregnancy before the couple's resources run out (while also raising their own profile for success) by harvesting many eggs and implanting a number all at once, in the hope that at least one of them will 'take'. This is one of the causes of multiple pregnancies – including the five-, six-, and seven-baby pregnancies – that are now becoming weirdly famous.

I discovered later at a global conference for fertility specialists that most other countries consider this practice barbaric. Few doctors outside our borders will implant so many eggs at a time precisely because of the risk of multiple pregnancies. Research by C. Chang shows that multiple births place relentless stress on families. Moreover, doctors in other countries consider 'selective termination', which is practically a necessity when implanting high numbers of eggs at once, to be too traumatic for women to have to undergo. Australia, for instance, treats women faced with this prospect as medically traumatized, and offers counselling, as does the UK. In the United States, it is a practice dictated by market pressures, so women undergoing the experience are generally expected to treat this risk simply as business as usual.

Stephanie only knew she was desperate, and she started spilling out her misery to me, a stranger.

'What have other mothers in this situation done?' I asked. 'Do you know?' I was aware of Bernadette listening intently as she shampooed the baby's little head, hushing him gently as he whimpered.

'I'm at a loss,' Stephanie admitted. 'I know one woman who selectively aborted one, and had the twins, and they were fine; and now she's consumed with anger at her doctor and feels that the abortion was a mistake. She feels she has a missing child. I also know a woman who decided to have all three, and they are doing poorly; she's depressed and almost suicidal, they're wiped out with medical bills, and she's thinking of suing her obstetrician for not advising her more strongly to abort one. And I know another woman who selectively aborted, and her twins are fine and she had no problem with it. She said I should just terminate. I have no idea what I'm going to do, and I only have three weeks left to decide.'

As I looked at her belly, I thought of the three siblings swimming in her amniotic fluid like intertangled trout, curled, developing, growing. And then I imagined being the mother, seeing images on the ultrasound screen: this brother's hand, this sister's arm, this brother's shoulder – and being forced to choose. Which one was to go? I imagined a woman standing by a pool, a lance in hand, waiting to spear one sentient fish from the three, as they moved in still water. It was like a gruesome fairy tale.

How could Stephanie decide? What sort of violence might the surviving siblings remember in that place below memory?

'I'm so sorry,' I said. I knew that if I were she, I could not make the decision to choose one; I would be too weak. Yet out of respect for the difficulty of her choice, I was careful not to show that in my voice.

Bernadette was less circumspect. She wore a slim gold cross around her neck, and I could see that she had little patience for us and our treating this decision as if it were ours alone to make. I felt her watching us and judging us, seeing us as if we were choosing between double or triple Peg Perego Italian strollers, as if the outcome had only a measure more weight than the weight we assigned to our tastes and schedules. We were comfortably off and we were young; other than in this journey toward birth, we had rarely faced anything outside our control. Fate, let alone grim fate, rarely intruded into our world. 'Choice' was our usual dimension.

She glanced at us as if we were children, before looking directly at Stephanie. She gave the counter a firm wipe, hefted Amos on her hip, and declared, in a strong, musical voice, 'I don't know how you could ever look at those babies in a monitor and decide to kill one. Maybe this is just a choice God is giving you, and you'll feel best if you just make the right decision and trust yourself and your babies' well-being to God.' Then, her shoulders squared and her posture tall, she turned away and strode into another room.

Yasmin looked into her teacup. Stephanie grew very quiet. But Bernadette's certainty had filled me, paradoxically, with a sense of relief. Surely Stephanie will be okay, I thought; surely her babies will be okay, if she trusts this situation to a higher power.

That was my inadequate greetings-card thought at the time.

And now she had done so, cast her lot and her children's on mother love and divine providence, and as a result, all three babies were dead. And what, dear Lord, was the message in that?

The struggle to become fertile and bear one's own biological child is a heartwrenching one. But it takes place in a context in which women are made to feel as if that way of becoming a mother is by far the 'best'. As women I knew or heard of were trying desperately to get pregnant, babies and children of the 'wrong' typology or colour yearned for families. In private adoption agencies, I discovered, white babies often cost more to adopt than black babies.

I was struck by a picture I saw in the paper of a party held regularly by a New York children's services organization, a kind of matchmaking event whose intent is to bring together potential parents with difficult-to-place children who need homes. The picture was of a little girl whose hair had been carefully braided, looking up hesitantly at adults whose faces were cut off by the photo, who seemed to be moving on like couples at a cocktail party to mingle with a more promising guest. I thought about how terrible it must feel for that little girl to get dressed up for this event each month.

Babies born in the 'wrong' circumstances seemed to be accorded little value at all in our society. Winston Churchill once said that the best investment a nation could make would be to put milk in babies. Yet now Congress was targeting prenatal care for cutbacks. While black babies in DC were already born *two pounds* lighter on average than white ones. I thought to myself: How can our government explain taking away calcium and protein from a pregnant woman?

In New York, a 17-year-old girl threw her newborn baby out of the second-storey window of the apartment in the run-down neighbourhood where she lived. The baby fell on to the grating just below, where she sustained fractures to her skull. Some teenage boys found her and brought her to the police. The baby's cord was still attached. The story got only a passing paragraph.

With my big belly before me, I felt outrage at the girl's desperate circumstances, which I would have responded to before; but I also now felt outrage at the girl herself for her actions. If the teenager didn't want her baby, why couldn't she pick up the phone and dial 911 and tell them anonymously where to find it? Or leave the baby in a basket outside a church? My politics were rebalancing around my belly.

Yet: if she *had* left the baby outside a church, it would have found no home among the people I knew. At dinner in a local Greek restaurant, a husband and wife who were both reporters regaled us with stories of infertility and adoption. Minnie, who was pregnant again, described a seeming epidemic of infertility among her friends, co-workers and acquaintances, couples who had been trying for years to conceive. She told us we should be grateful for having managed to get pregnant without going through such contortions. When I asked her what these affluent, well-educated couples – almost all of them white – were planning to do now that biological conception seemed hopeless, she answered, 'Adopt.'

'Where are they going for their adoptions?' I wondered aloud.

'Chile,' she said. 'Romania, some of them. But overwhelmingly, Latin America: Paraguay, and countries in the ex-Soviet Union.'

As she described these couples' exhaustive searches, night was falling in Washington. Washington is one of the most segregated cities in America. In the southwest and southeast quadrants of the city, babies and small children who could not be cared for by their biological parents needed parents. Unless they found adoptive parents, these babies would grow into toddlers who risked getting lost in the foster care system.

I thought about the white couples who would rather adopt a light-skinned baby from a faraway mountain village than a dark-skinned baby from a neighbourhood in our own city; and of the motivation of such prospective parents. Did they hope for racial 'neutrality' for their family in a country torn apart by race?

One highly paid professional woman, a southwestern colleague of a friend, told me the following story.

She and her husband, both white, had wanted to adopt. They did not want to adopt 'what was out there' – you never knew who the mother was, what the problems were, she said. A white baby was very hard to find. They found that people in their situation put ads in certain newspapers for a mother who suited their description who was already pregnant.

They found a pregnant white woman. She assured the prospective parents that she had not done drugs, was drinking no alcohol, and her health and that of the father was good. She assured them that the baby was Caucasian. She was scared and grateful for their willingness to take and raise her baby. They befriended one another for the remaining five months of the pregnancy, building up a bond of trust. But the pregnant woman kept saying, 'I'm not sure you'll follow through – I'm not sure you'll be there for the baby.'

Then in the hospital, as the labouring woman was about to give birth with the adoptive couple present, she 'admitted', in the words of the teller, that the father was Mexican.

When the woman related this, her voice shook with anger – at the pregnant woman's *duplicity!* 'Of course,' she said, 'we stormed out of the hospital.'

I was unable to speak. The woman took my shocked silence as a shared sense of outrage that she and her husband had been 'cheated' out of what they had planned for.

But my head was crowded with the scene: the woman in labour, watching as the people whom she had chosen to raise her baby, had trusted to love it for life, walked out on her and on the baby coming into the world, because of its colour.

While I knew that bearing this whole assortment of judgements about people looking for a baby of their own was cheap from where I sat, my midsection full of my own genetic offspring, I couldn't help but wonder why we could not see babies for themselves, rather than seeing them as extensions of ourselves, our lifestyle preferences, our heritages, our fantasies. I became scared by what appeared to be a distorted value system in which fetuses and newborns were mere commodities.

And if they were commodities, who 'owned' them?

A couple of years before, I had sat in on a course at Yale Law School taught by feminist theorist Catherine MacKinnon. The hot topic of the moment was the 'Baby M' case (the surrogacy case where the biological mother wanted to keep the baby). Many in the class supported the claim of the biological mother, arguing that because of the structural social inequities that apply differently to women and men, a contract between a surrogate mother and the would-be custodial parents cannot be said to be just. In their view, a biological mother's rights win out over those of a non-biological mother, and certainly over those of a father.

Another story was in the news at the same time: a woman who had divorced her husband had been granted custody of the dozen fertilized eggs that they had prepared while in the process of trying to conceive five years before. After the divorce, the father had tried to block the implantation because he did not want to pay child support to children conceived and born to a woman he had divorced long ago. A similar case was decided several years before in favour of the father, who donated the eggs to scientific research. But the judge in this case ruled differently, granting sole custody of the eggs to the woman, because of the precedent set by an earlier case, *Roe* v. *Wade*: in his view, if a woman could terminate the life of the embryo *in utero*, she had custodianship of the eggs in a petri dish as well. The mother, ecstatic at the ruling, had all the eggs implanted at once, a gesture that, to my mind, suggested a kind of conspicuous consumption directed at her ex-husband. The woman's lawyer said, 'We will be seeking funds from the father so that he will be responsible for the support of his children.' The father was enraged.

I started to see eggs, fetuses, and babies as little coins, chits used in a modern currency system; they had the meaning and value we assigned to them. Healthy or unhealthy? Mother's or father's? White or black? Related to you or unrelated? The baby's value seemed to shift, to rise or fall accordingly. The economy was based on what adults longed for and needed.

But what about the babies? I thought. What about what they needed?

It seemed to me that there was wreckage everywhere from the way we projected on to the babies our notions of valuable or less-valued. Newspaper features described the hyperanxiety of affluent, first-time, older mothers who were saying, in effect: 'I want my life to be perfect: my baby has to be perfect.' How can such conditional love foster in even those 'perfect', highly valued babies and children a true sense of security? It is easy to imagine that such 'trophy children' sense the expectation placed upon them: that they add a gratifying dimension to their mothers' 'self-esteem' and, perhaps, to their fathers' sense of achievement, rather than being accepted simply as their squalling, needy, oblivious, developing selves.

My friend Alex told us about a new mother, an actress, who confessed that she had tried and tried but, she said, 'just didn't much like her baby'. In a culture that actually valued babies for their own sakes, and supported new motherhood, one would not need to 'like' one's baby the way one needs to 'like' the shade one paints one's bedroom wall.

A baby needs to be born securely into a safe net of committed relationships. It seems as if we, as a culture, are cutting those strands, one after the other, and leaving babies with an emotional lifeline made of very few threads – or none at all. The possessiveness of the woman who appropriated her ex-husband's paternity against his will; the expectations of the couple who tried and tried to create a baby that was just right; the impulse of mothers and fathers to say of a baby, mine, mine, mine – what was lost in the culture in which I was pregnant was, I feared, something profound: a sense of the sacred 'otherness' of the child. After all, the child is not there to meet our needs and expectations. What is lost in a market economy of 'best' and 'seconds', in a society where babies are a form of currency, is the central paradox of true parenthood which should be defined as our absolute commitment to a creature of whom we can claim no rights of possession.

Is there any other relationship in which we have to love not for ourselves or the return on our investment, but for love's own sake? Is this what we are talking about when we refer to 'the leap of faith'?

I went for a walk with Alex, who was carrying her three-month-old girl, Kirsten, well wrapped up against her bosom in a Snuggli. It was an icy day, and there were large patches of blue-white ice on the streets. Kirsten lay nestled against Alex, sleeping.

As we walked, Alex put forward a booted foot and suddenly started to slide. I watched helplessly as she pitched forward – the baby could have been crushed. Then I saw something that seemed a marvel to me at the time; of course now, as a mother, it is as obvious to me as breathing.

I understood then how the body really works when in danger and the reflexes kick in. I saw Alex somehow twist to pitch herself, with lightning speed, forward, face and hands down, on to the sheer face of the ice, throwing the most vulnerable parts of herself without hesitation full force against that rock-hard surface – in order to protect her child. And she landed hard, on face, knees, and open palms, hurt but thankful that the baby was safe.

The baby kept sleeping.

I was amazed at what Alex had done. She had not wasted an instant trying to go down one micrometre more easily. There, on the ice, I saw a physical manifestation of faith. What amazed me even more, as she got shakily up again, was that she thought nothing of it.

That, I thought, was it: that was a mother. That was what it meant to be a mother, a true parent. To defy self-interest, to the level of your very bones, your very reflexes.

But how, I asked myself as the days passed and the stakes grew higher, would I ever manage it myself?

# Fourth Month
## Losses

'The cultural idiom of motherhood, and the only one that people find bearable, is that once a woman has produced a child she bonds with it in utter devotion, forgets her own wishes, and sacrifices herself for her baby. When she does not slip easily into this role, she risks the accusation of being a bad mother.'

Sheila Kitzinger, *The Year After Childbirth* (1994)

As the days passed and I grew, I felt a growing sense of excitement at my pregnancy. I also felt more than a little trepidation at what lay ahead. But I felt guilty over harbouring mixed feelings, as if my conflicted emotions were somehow not permissible and must be kept hidden.

One day I accompanied Cara and her seven-month-old girl, Daisy, to a 'playspace', that modern-day innovation that is a substitute for the safe neighbourhood streets of our childhoods. The place made my heart sink. It was a big room with a dozen separate 'areas', filled with dress-up clothes, sandboxes, crawlspaces, and pretend treehouses. There was a sort of raised balcony overlooking the sea of toddlers, where the moms and nannies could have coffee. You needed an adult in order to unlatch the gates, and there was 'security' in the form of a young woman who checked everyone's name tags at the downstairs door where Cara parked her stroller. The moms' name tags read: 'I am CARA. I'm with DAISY. And the kids' read: 'I am DAISY. I'm with CARA.'

I thought: Is this what lies ahead? 'I am NAOMI. I'm with . . .' Who? What?

For perhaps the first time, I had an inkling of the radical loss of privacy that lay ahead. I remembered the new mothers who had told me, 'I'm not able to go to the bathroom alone.' I realized that my identity was about to be cloven in two, my independence cut by half. It was the first time I could see it spelled out for me in all its sweetness and regret, in all its ambiguity.

The books and experts that were supposed to explain what I was about to go through seemed to trivialize my real concerns – losing my identity, for example – and condescending about the momentous physical and emotional changes I was undergoing. Other women I spoke to felt similarly. We knew we were missing information, we just did not know what it might be.

Everything I read seemed to suggest that the universe of solutions for pregnant women was just one big 'Bed, Bath and Beyond.' Nothing was so scary that a little potpourri and bubble bath couldn't soothe it.

Jennifer Louden's *The Pregnant Woman's Comfort Book* told me that when I experienced anxiety, I needed

> bubble baths, country music, historical novels, solitude – whatever makes you feel contented and cozy . . . Take a shower by candlelight. Read a meditation in *Being Home* by Gunilla Norris. Locate a farmer's market or wholesale market, buy a mass of flowers, and arrange them while listening to Vivaldi's Flute Concerto in D . . . Float in the ocean . . . Buy or make a special oil or lotion . . . Rub the lotion on your breasts . . . say to yourself, 'My breasts can nourish life'.

Such books' frequent suggestion that women take the initiative to nurture themselves seemed terribly poignant and important to me; women had to nurture themselves in these trivial ways, it seemed to me, because we lived in a culture that was not bothering to nurture us in substantial ways as we went to childbed. Pregnant women were asked to keep their eyes on the lotion and potpourri because the realities of the medical establishment and the demands of the workplace were too big, and too intractable, to bear looking at.

'Encourage moments of stillness in your life,' the *Comfort Book* exhorted. Vomit carefully into a sink or other handy receptacle, I thought to myself, silently imitating the Martha Stewart-like voice of the experts as waves of nausea hit me.

Like many women, I was sick every morning. I soon found that my illness was not my concern, but my fault. One relative, worried about my vomiting, asked, 'What have you done to yourself?' My grandmother remarked, meaning it kindly, and referring to my work schedule, 'Sensible eating and lots of rest – that will be a first for you!' My otherwise supportive mother announced, 'I have to talk to you about the fat in your diet.' I felt for the first time the experience of being addressed as a good or not-so-good vessel for someone else's well-being.

It turns out that 50 per cent to 80 per cent of all pregnant women feel some nausea, according to one medical textbook; according to another study, between one- and two-thirds of women feel sick all day long. The 1991 edition of *What to Expect When You're Expecting* put forward the notion that the stress of modern life is an important factor in morning sickness (and, oddly enough, that women who are highly suggestible are more likely to suffer from it; the authors proposed that the suggestion that morning sickness exists, a view common in our culture, could cause the problem).

I begged my obstetrician for relief of the condition and was told that there was essentially no treatment beyond the anecdotal remedies of ginger ale and Saltines. Was I too highly suggestible? I would be sick daily until my child was delivered.

Morning sickness tends to hit women between five and twelve weeks' gestation. Some women experience symptoms in the afternoon, and some in the evening or throughout the day, though most who suffer from it do so in the morning before getting out of bed. The exact cause of nausea and vomiting is unknown, though most experts claim that the sickness is either hormonal or psychogenic in origin – or some combination of both. Interestingly, pregnancies complicated by nausea and vomiting often have a more favourable outcome than do those without.

*What to Expect* suggested that some morning sickness could be in the pregnant woman's mind, whereas when I went years later to independent midwife Ina May Gaskin's house in the woods, I saw the hand-lettered manual of homeopathic and herbal cures, drawn from centuries of hands-on midwifery experience, for various pregnancy conditions: in the section marked Nausea there were a dozen careful descriptions of different *kinds* of morning sickness, observed in a depth of detail that can only be called respectful, down to the colour of the bile and the emotional component associated with the experience. Pregnant again and sick again, I tried the cure proposed for the kind of morning sickness that was recognizably 'mine': Arnica. My six months' nausea was gone within two days.

New research suggests that morning sickness is both a reaction to stress and an important defence of the body. According to a hypothesis by Flaxman and Sherman, pregnant women are more vulnerable to serious, often deadly, infections; and morning sickness causes women to avoid foods that might be dangerous to themselves or to their embryos, especially foods that, prior to widespread refrigeration, were likely to be heavily laden with micro-organisms and their toxins. Perhaps that is why meat is one of the most likely foods to turn a pregnant woman's stomach. I wished I had known this about morning sickness when I was suffering from it. Knowing the very seriousness with which some researchers were investigating the condition might have made it easier to bear the first time around. But when I was being treated by the standard medical care recommended by my obstetrician, my nausea was seen as something between a mystery and a routine, trivial complaint.

When I talked about how nauseated I felt or about other minor wretchednesses of pregnancy, I felt guilty in a whole new way. For the first time I was haunted, when I did something as banal and human as complain about how I felt, by the feeling of being a bad mother: which in my value system was about as close to the bottom as I could get.

There is an impossible expectation placed on pregnant women in our society: that we're supposed to get on with everything and express only a blossoming sense of joy and anticipation, even as the person we have thought ourselves to be is transfigured and reborn. It was an expectation that made me feel I was particularly difficult and perverse, in a specifically female kind of way that I had never felt before, in my ambivalence toward what was happening to me and within me. The suppression of the darkness that is also part of pregnancy I think actually muted the experience of what was wonderful and affirming about it.

I would think to myself: I am a bad woman because I am not continually blissful at the imminence of the being in my belly. I am a bad woman because I am not perpetually floating on air, radiant as someone in a shampoo ad, beaming.

I felt I was a bad woman because I was throwing up five times in seven hours and feeling upset about it; because I snapped at my nurse-midwife when she asked me whether I had done something that had created any stress that might have led to my vomiting; because my life was not without its stresses, which I did not do enough to avoid because I still cared about 'selfish' concerns like my career, even though I feared it was bad for the baby.

I felt a terrible sense of guilt about possibly doing something that might hurt the baby. Yet I was angry that I had to feel guilty for caring about my career. In addition to feeling guilty, I felt angry, and guiltier still *because* I felt angry, and angrier still that I had to feel still more guilty. I resented the authority figures, relatives, and medical advisers who made me feel ashamed about what the stress I was experiencing might be doing to the baby, instead of wrapping me in their arms and encouraging me for being such a trouper. After all, I thought defensively, I was managing to meet my commitments, even though I looked like a globe of the world and moved like a Land Rover.

In the midst of this funk, I went to a 7-Eleven one day to pick up a soft drink. The cashier who took my money was a woman in her twenties, who was six or seven months' pregnant. She had been standing all day. As she stood every day, all day long. My silent litany of grievances stopped short.

So my workplace did not give me slack time I thought to myself. Her workplace would not even give her a chair.

I had to travel to give several lectures. A pregnant woman may feel like the same person, but she sees others' perceptions of herself change. The bigger I got, the more preoccupied my audiences seemed to be with my belly. As the lectures wore on, I could feel people become less and less able to focus on what I had to say. Finally, by the end, I could feel their ability to comprehend me as lecturer rather than as mother-to-be soften and shift as my belly overtook me.

My usual talk had not changed: parts were confrontational; parts focused on sexuality, ego, and ambition. But I could feel audiences recoil from such confrontational topics the closer to motherhood I visibly was. I sensed that those listening felt that mothers – or mothers-to-be – were not supposed to be interested in such things.

'So,' one interviewer said. 'You're pregnant. Your hormones are running wild. Are they changing everything you believed in?'

'Yes,' I replied irritably, 'I'm insane.'

From the nature of the questions I was getting, it seemed that impending motherhood was taken to mean losing one's mind.

I could sense the social space given to my personality shifting, and certain rooms – some of my favourite rooms – being quietly, indeed lovingly, but nonetheless very firmly, closed. It was a loss of my former self that I felt very keenly.

Finally, there was the loss of my physical shape.

In a word, I gained a lot of weight. I began to feel jealous of slim, agile, prepartum younger women. In a culture that does not celebrate pregnancy and birth, sharp indeed is the loss of one's prepartum body.

As we changed in the gym one day, Yasmin showed me the stretch marks on her otherwise smooth and tawny belly. They were so blue that they were almost black, a blue-black net criss-crossing her lower abdomen. I said something reassuring and turned away, dumb with fear. Was this ahead?

Even at four months I felt I was startlingly big. My size began to make people I knew react to me in ways that could range from the embarrassing to the offensive. Some men I knew blurted out remarks that revealed their own acute discomfort. Other pregnant friends said that men who had once found them attractive were especially prone to such comments. It was as if their superegos had scarcely had time to throw a towel at their panicky ids which were rushing, naked, out of the burning building of the subconscious. 'Sex. Attraction. Mothers. *Yaaaaah!*'

Some comments were remorseless: 'Soon you'll look like the Venus of Willendorf,' said one friend in the presence of his fashion-model-slender wife.

'You remember Naomi?' asked one political activist of her novelist husband. 'Yes, of course,' he said. 'I remember you at half the size you are now.'

'You're hardly showing much,' said a biographer I had only just met. 'You have no idea,' interjected a literary critic who had known me for a while. 'She used to be a mere slip of a thing.'

When I said to another male acquaintance, 'Nice to see you again,' he replied, 'And you – so much of you.'

Another person had remarked on my 'matronliness'; his face showed his unease when someone else pointed out, in the veterinary terms I was reluctantly becoming accustomed to, that I was 'carrying high'. I felt some sort of emotional switch turn off in other men's reactions. Was it because I was so clearly another man's property?

'Relax,' said my friend Rhonda. 'There are men in Paris who only get turned on by women in your condition.'

As my pregnancy advanced, I started feeling a kind of defiance about what my gravid body did to alarm people. On good days, this made me wear black maternity jumpsuits that unapologetically thrust the line of my torso into the room. On bad days, it made me bundle up in heavy sweaters and glare at the young woman in my building who, when I picked up my mail at the front desk, insisted on glancing meaningfully at my belly and smiling that fatuous Oh-how-cute-you're-going-to-reproduce-yourself smile.

I thought of my friend Susan, a beautiful African-American historian who had gained 50 pounds before moving to a new city to teach at a think tank there. A tall, sensuous woman, a dancer in her spare time, she revelled more than ever in her sexuality and wore bright, flowing clothing, refusing to hide herself. But there was a continual bubbling current of rage underlying her relationship with most of her male colleagues, for she felt that in their dealings with her, they could not get over their discomfort at the size of her body. 'I feel like they are constantly thinking, "Big butt, big belly, big tits, black woman," and can hardly hear me talk over the static in their pea brains,' she said. 'But I'm the same person I was before. I just want them to deal with their issues around this and leave me out of it.'

I now knew a bit about what she had meant. As a heavy woman in society (I hoped temporarily, but who knew?) I felt as if I'd slipped several notches down in the social hierarchy of the world. My self-image had gotten skinned on the fast slide down.

Along with every other woman I knew, I had conflicting feelings about getting so darn big. Some women were happy to be 'permitted' to eat normally for the first time in their adult lives. 'It's not like going off your diet,' I recall overhearing one such mother reassuring a newly pregnant woman. 'It's okay to eat, because it's for the baby.' (A doctor I knew commented that he wished all his women patients would be willing to eat, on their own behalf, the way they ate when they were pregnant.) Others, however, feel a sense of being out of control as their weight shoots up. My friend Andra said people would ask her: 'Are you okay about being so big?' and 'Are you sure that's all baby?'

This fear of the change in our appearance can be dangerous: a report from the University of North Carolina shows that women fearful of changes in their appearances run a materially higher risk of incurring birth complications.

Rhonda told me about a co-worker of hers, a chubby girl who had become, with the most stringent discipline, a sleek-limbed woman. Pregnant, she could not bring herself to gain the weight that the baby needed. So the child was born underweight, its lungs ill-developed; and his mother was back at the Stairmaster and on her usual subsistence diet, even though she was breast-feeding. The woman feared having a fat baby so acutely that she fed him only when he screamed.

But the greatest loss I experienced as I grew more heavily with child was the loss of the young woman I had been. Moreover, I lacked role models to help me make the transition. Pregnant women and new mothers, I discovered, had few real role models to turn to.

What do pregnant women see when they cast about for guidance, when they look for heroines to help them walk through this transcendental life crisis? Demi Moore, chicly protuberant in lacy black déshabille on the cover of a national magazine? Courtney Love, rocker dilettante, her toddler dazedly in tow?

Where is the sexy mother, or the triumphant, battle-scarred mother, or the mother who is her own person while still being responsive to a child? Whom do we turn to who is good both to herself and to her little ones?

A number of other cultures have women who are not just sexual goddesses, but powerful, sexual mother-goddesses too. In America, we do not.

I know because I went to the mall. When I wanted to find something a little racy in a maternity outfit – not a bustier, but something – I had no luck. Everything I saw in Washington in the mid-1990s seemed to be designed as if all pregnant women wanted to look like 1960s flight attendants wearing pillows.

It seemed to me that you could not be a cowgirl and a mother.

You could not be a heartbreaker and a mother. You could not be a rock-and-roller and a mother. Nor a lonesome traveller and a mother. You could not, in our culture, easily pair motherhood with many other alluring archetypes or descriptions.

As a writer, I was haunted by images of all the bruised kids of women writers: Mary McCarthy's neglected son; Sylvia Plath's abandoned toddlers; Colette's wan-faced daughter left with the au pairs; Zelda Fitzgerald's tough, self-sufficient daughter; Anne Sexton's despairing daughter. And yet, I reminded myself, there are plenty of unhappy kids of women who drove them dutifully around to soccer practice every week of the year.

I found myself desperate for positive maternal role models with whom I could identify. Yes, I thought, there are any number of good mothers who have been women of accomplishment. But the wild ones, the chaotic spirits I liked best – to have been good mothers, would they not have had to give away their majestic instability? What women in the past had made real art or real revolution not only in spite of, but even because of, their lives with their children?

They were there, I knew. But I counted them in the dark, on the fingers of my hands.

At around four months, fetuses can squint, frown, and make grimacing expressions. They start to suck when their lips are stroked; they can discriminate among tastes, preferring sweetness and rejecting bitterness. But even while they are little bundles of simple responses, the outer world is placing complex expectations upon them.

For years now, women and men had asked me, with their hearts on their sleeves, 'How do I raise strong daughters? How do I protect them from the undermining influences of this culture? Again and again I had felt inadequate to that question; my own childlessness had rendered me ignorant: 'Be sure your daughter sees women treated with respect in the home.' 'Explain sexism to her . . .' I realized now why so many mothers of daughters looked sceptical at such blithe advice. For now that I thought I might have a daughter, I felt as helpless as they did to change the world that would bear down upon her.

When I could not imagine my baby's gender, I could not imagine what to wish for it. But when I thought it would be a girl, I saw a clear train of wishes and associations.

I longed just as fiercely as any of those parents for a 'Fairness Tsar' who could magically sweep pernicious influences out of her path. I knew quite well that her father and I were almost powerless in the face of the allure of what older girls do and are asked to do. Why should a teenage daughter believe me more than she will believe *Tiger Beat* magazine or any more than daughters have ever believed mothers?

I saw parents trying to inoculate their daughters against self-doubt and self-hatred, and my heart contracted at the meagreness of their – our – magic and the impotence of our wishes.

My brother Aaron is a hands-on father. He would take Yardena, his two-year-old girl, to a city park where the grass falls away in all directions. He would put her down on the top of a hillock and say, 'Go and conquer! All this is yours!'

And oh, how she believed him, tilting back her little head and crowing with victory. He called her 'Mastodon Girl', and she staggered upright and roared, her power travelling from lungs to throat to outstretched limbs, the primeval forest of her imagination shaking at her approach. He lifted her up and swung her around. 'Fly free, little dove! Fly free!' And she would zoom out her arms, navigating the air.

Already at two she was as tough a little sabra as you would ever hope to meet. My brother played hard with her, roughhoused with her, accustomed her to loud noises and harsh surfaces, and her demeanour showed it: she was resilient and good-humoured as a little all-terrain vehicle.

She did not yet know this was unusual.

She would soon learn, I knew. Aaron told me that when he took her to the pediatrician's and put her on a floor that was scattered with toys, Yardena crawled at once to the corner where several five-year-old boys were playing with Tonka toys. Intrigued, she joined in. She was in no danger: she was equal to the situation. But a mother, wordlessly, bent down, scooped her up, and deposited her back on Aaron's lap as if correcting his lapse in judgement, in taste, were the most natural and neighbourly thing to do.

How quickly it begins; how helpless, I thought, I will be to protect my own daughter, if I were to have one. Of course, I was open to discovering that boys and girls were innately wildly different; but from the interactions I saw, I felt it would be impossible to tell what 'innate' might look like.

The most common thing I heard grown-ups say to little girls was, in a goony, Mickey-Mouse hyper-admiring voice: 'I like your *shoes*!' At first the two-year-olds would look down at their feet, bemused: What's that about? But by three, they have accepted that a normative social greeting involves some adult admiring their footwear. By three-and-a-half, they refuse to wear anything but Mary Janes. Then we say, 'What a girl!'

I noticed that when little girls played 'guns', the grownups ignored it, or told them, 'That's not nice'. The same grownups tried hard to distract their little boys when they attempted to carry their mother's handbag, or play with shiny necklaces. The parents certainly did not comment on their behaviour to other adults admiringly: 'Look at that!' But when the girls preened or flirted and the boys engaged in combat, grownups commented loudly to those around them about what 'girls' or what 'boys' the children were – and called attention to the 'innate behaviour'. You don't have to be a genius, at the age of three, to figure out that if you're a girl, you'd better act in ways that the grownups identify as girl-like, and vice versa.

Suddenly, in looking at babies, I found myself imagining what was in store for my child. I watched my friend Liza's daughter, Nellie, a force of nature at the age of one. She was sitting in her stroller in the park one afternoon, when a sour, fortyish woman, attracted by her beauty, actually reached into the stroller to try to embrace her. When Nellie, naturally enough, started to wail, the woman retreated, stung by the rejection. She said defensively: 'You're much less pretty when you cry.'

What I wished for my daughter, if I were to have a daughter, did not yet fully exist: the tools of an intact imagination. I wished her a medieval castle set with soldiers like the white-walled, red-roofed, turreted castle set; actually, a version of the set that my brother had played with when we were children, and that I had longed somehow to take part in. But his toy figures were all male knights on horseback, in silver-painted plastic armour, with pennants looping from their halberds. I wished my daughter the same castle, the same clever drawbridge, but, oh, I wished her knights and ladies, too: ladies in Joan of Arc armour, ladies on horseback with quivers slung over their shoulders; wenches positioned on the battlements, tipping vats of boiling oil on to the siege, wenches down below hoisting a mighty pine trunk horizontally against the bolted, arched wooden doors; wenches with slingshots and wenches with crossbows. I wished her a roistering plastic figure of breast-plated Boadicea, queen of the Britons, and an army of well-equipped Roman centurions to vanquish; and I wished her a stealthy, strategic plastic figure of Zenobia, Warrior Queen skilled as Mark Antony; and I wished her figurines of a dynasty of poisoner-queens, each of whom was more deceitful than the last. I wished her villainesses as well as heroines.

But that was not all. I wished her a science kit with a girl on the cover, and a lab coat, and a picture book about Marie Curie. I wished her a firefighter uniform with a girl on the package driving a fire truck. I wished her a version of *Where the Wild Things Are* with Anna, not Max alone, roaring her terrible roars. And more than anything I wished her a Hans Brinker and the Silver Skates in which it was a strong-legged, feisty Nina or Nora who swept across a frozen Dutch river, arms clasped behind her, from village to village to village across the landscape, friend to threat and challenge, as night fell around her exerting, capable body.

# Fifth Month
## Mortality

A Beriba proverb states, 'A pregnant woman is a dying person.' An often-told tale depicts the ancestors in the act of digging the woman's grave throughout the pregnancy. If she survives the days after the delivery, they begin to shovel the sand back; forty days after the delivery, the grave will finally be closed without her.

In my fifth month, I sustained another panic, this time during a weekend excursion.

My husband and I were eating in the communal dining hall of an unusual dilapidated holiday resort a few hours from our city – one that offered only high-fat, high-salt foods and plenty of alcohol.

'When are you due?' asked our waitress with a certain inevitability. She was a virtuous-looking, dark-haired woman in her late forties. One could hear in her West Virginia pitch the voices of generations of women before her who had probably been more used to clearing elm saplings than stacking boxes of Celestial Seasons herbal teas on a polished service counter.

When I told her, she leaned against the service ledge, her back to the coffeepots and clean glassware, and placed both hands, palm down, forefingers pointed to indicate a triangle, on her pubic girdle in a gesture that seemed timeless but also oddly proud and brazen. 'Aren't children a blessing?' she asked rhetorically. Then, before I could answer, she plunged into what she wanted to say all along – not necessarily to me and my husband, passing tourists in her enclave, but to the world at large.

'When I had my first, just before, my mother sat me down,' she said. 'And looked at me' – and the waitress's face took on the heavy jowls and the deep scowl of an older woman with a harder life – 'and she said to me, "Daughter" – she only said "daughter" when she had something real serious to say – "Daughter," she said, "women don't cry."

'I believed her and I tried. I tried my best. And in the delivery room there were half a dozen women and they were screaming and shrieking, and they were sobbing and asking God for mercy. But I remembered what my mother had told me and I kept my mouth closed like this.' She pressed her lips in a tight line. 'And even when I could not bear it one more minute I just whimpered a little and all I said was – her voice dropped to a tiny girl's stoic, plaintive wail – "I can't do this anymore." '

She paused, and looked at us significantly and triumphantly. David took my hand under the table. 'Because I believed my mother: that women don't cry.'

I stared into my teacup, thinking, 'Women don't cry.' 'Real women,' as opposed to mere girls? What rough rural wisdom was this that this mother's daughter had just recounted so proudly? It was an example I already knew I would never be able to live up to. Women don't cry. Why not? I asked myself. Why shouldn't we cry?

I wanted to cry just listening to her, whether for the howling wardmates, or for the young, scared West Virginia girl of 20 years ago clamping her mouth shut, or for myself, I didn't know.

Clearly, I was not going to prove myself in the enduring hardscrabble female value system the waitress had just recounted, one that probably descended from a century or two before when the mother's ancestors made their way from Ireland or England to set their hands against this unyielding valley. I felt the weight of their judgement in the waitress's brief account. Suddenly it felt to me that I was immature past my age, an imposter in the brutal country where true women reigned. In their imagined company, I was nothing but a fainthearted and silly superannuated girl.

A day or so later, I made my way down the walkway beside the pool, in an 'aqua-aerobics' class at the same resort, balancing my belly carefully to guard against slipping on the slickness of the tiles underfoot. A sentry marked my path: a handsome, white-haired elderly man with an aquiline nose, who held a blind person's red-tipped cane out before him so that it just blocked my way. The foot and leg that rested in my path were inflamed with phlebitis.

But I could not step around him unless I risked falling into the water.

'Excuse me,' I said. He was impervious and did not budge. 'Sir, pardon me,' I repeated more loudly.

'He can't hear you!' an immense grey-haired woman exclaimed in a jovial tone from the water. 'Jonas! Jonas!' she bellowed. 'Let the lady pass!'

With a start he drew back, letting me make my way down the aluminium steps into the water.

The other members of the class were either elderly or middle-aged women, and each possessed a body that showed every sign of lassitude and gravity. The exception was the instructor, a bouncy young woman who was a fit four months' pregnant. As she called for questions before class began, I approached and asked quietly what modifications I needed to make, given that I was in my second trimester of pregnancy.

'Five months!' she exclaimed. Her voice echoed off the damp tile walls. The female council of elders in the water turned toward us as one. 'I'm tempted to ask you to get out of the water and show yourself to us! Be sure to let me look you over when the class is done,' she said. I slinked down a little further in the water, which suddenly felt cool and made my skin clammy.

'Do you know what it is?' bellowed an old woman from the corner of the pool, referring to the instructor's baby.

'Not yet,' the instructor yelled back. All at once, the conversation bounced loudly from grey head to grey head, bobbing in the water.

'How much did you gain?' shrieked one elderly lady toward the instructor.

'Twenty pounds,' the instructor shouted back.

'I had twins, I gained fifty,' her questioner declared proudly.

'Boy or girl?' another woman shouted in my direction.

'She's got a girl,' asserted one more, pointing at the instructor, 'and she,' the Sybil said, pointing at my abdomen, though I was trying to crouch underwater, as if that could provide me with some privacy, 'has got herself a boy!'

'Really? How can you tell?' called out another.

'Well,' replied the woman with what could only be called a squawk, 'because she's so *pointy*!'

As the class got under way, I seemed to be in a frenzy in the water, bending lower, leaping higher, doing my submerged jumping jacks with more push and agitation against the resistance than the other members of the class. I was annoyed at the complete abandonment of my personal boundaries – and 'pointy', no less! But it was more than that: I thrashed, I churned, I sent myself flying through the waves, while my classmates took decorous steps alongside me. I felt myself trying to assert my strength – my youth, my health – against the dreamlike sense of submersion that had begun to overwhelm me.

For all at once, the watery interior had become a kind of nightmare. I looked up at the healthy instructor, who was still more maiden than matron; and I looked around at the universal grey heads and loosened bodies of the women in the water – women who had done their job and given the world their births – and I realized: Now I was one of them.

I felt as if I had slipped; I had fallen into a primordial soup of femaleness, of undifferentiated post-fecundity. In my heightened state of anxiety I felt myself standing on the slippery slope into ageing and mortality, the universal slope I'd been able to ignore for so long. My very individuality seemed to loosen and melt away in the slow warm water. *Don't you know*, the little waves seemed to lap at me, *that no woman is unique? Don't you know that* that *is your delusion?* We are all liquid, all deliquescence; the unbounded, unidentified matrix out of which new life comes endlessly creeping. I was drowning in the Lake of Fecundity. I, a woman, was also experiencing for the first time the feeling of misogyny, and understanding why the fear of women is grounded in the fear of death.

My throat seemed to close up. Out through the sliding-glass windows, pass the instructor's feet, I could see the hard wintry world of commerce and ambition, politics and debate, that I used to inhabit before I slipped into this luxurious water-world of pregnancy, procreation, and passing away. That was what I wanted, I realized with a biting nostalgia, as I became more and more the servant of my developing child: the world of reason, individuality, selfishness. I wanted to climb up and out, to rejoin the clash and parry of the world occupied by, owned by, men. My lust for that universe, where I had lived all my life, was suddenly more poignant than I could bear.

What flashed through my thoughts was a set of movie stills of lives I imagined were beyond me now. I wanted to be addict-thin, smoking a harsh Gauloise, bending over a marble-topped table at an outdoor café in Les Halles. I wanted to be able to drink wine and smoke brown-black tobacco and flirt with strangers. I wanted to wear a scarlet suit cut as sharply as a diamond. I wanted to brush ashes off my blood-red cuffs and argue with a smart man, and win. I wanted to speed up the parched sheer drop of California's Highway 1 in a fast car with the top down, the fierce wind pushing against my face, as I shifted into the next gear. I wanted to shoulder my back-pack with its few possessions at dawn, opening the door on to a desert road. I wanted to glance down at a lovely sleeping back and leave without saying goodbye, and let the white heat of the desert swallow me up and obliterate my footprints behind me.

'You can do laps now around the pool,' said the instructor, bringing me back to my reality. 'If someone is in your way, just go around them.'

I began to run through the water as if there were Furies chasing me down. I overtook one white-haired mortal after another, passing each in a burst of water and speed, as if running for my life.

When I was worn out, I lumbered, ludicrous in my flippers, my belly preceding me by a foot, through the water toward the ladder. A woman squatted at the top of the ladder, blocking my way. Grinning with gapped yellow teeth, she asked me to wait until she could get down into the water.

As I hurried away into the dressing room, I could imagine her smiling at my retreating back.

*Run*, she might have been saying; *there is no hurry. You have entered the great wheel. I am in you already.*

Suddenly death seemed everywhere. It seemed to step lightly beside me during my pregnancy. Other women felt the same, but we somehow sensed we were not to discuss it.

Thoughts of death entered where I would have least expected them. The bigger I grew with my child, the more clearly did I detect that fatal chuckle in the wings.

From the very onset of my pregnancy I had been cursed with what felt like a sixth sense to detect death and decay. I'd felt preternaturally revolted by images of death in news magazines; I had had to bury my face in my hands during death scenes in movies, and when I even half-recalled such images – the blood welling up out of an actor's mouth – I retched. Roadkill made my stomach turn, and I suddenly seemed to see it everywhere: squirrels and rabbits and unidentifiable creatures. I was so spooked by what looked like a fat dead grey maggot on the carpeting of my new office that it took me days to bring myself to pick up the thing with a dustpan, only to find that it was a piece of plastic wiring.

Why was I so surprised at this new sensitivity to the loss and decay of things? Many cultures pair birth with death and treat women's fertility as the gateway to both states. But our culture, by insisting on revealing only the life-affirming aspect of pregnancy and birth, seemed to make the darkness more palpable.

Certainly, Mimi Maternity had no aisle among the bath salts and flowered smocks for Mourning. *The Pregnant Woman's Comfort Book* and *What to Expect When You're Expecting* had no index listing, after Castor Oil but before Diarrhea, for Death. While Ina May Gaskin's *Spiritual Midwifery* lists Death, Fetal, none of the books I looked through indexed Death, Maternal – if not death itself then 'fears of', or 'intimations of'. *What to Expect* cheerfully noted that 'Fewer than 1 in 10,000 women die in childbirth . . . you stand a lot better chance of surviving labour and delivery than you do a trip to the supermarket in your car, or a stroll across a busy street.' But on the facing page, an anxious pregnant woman can see for herself that the risk of dying in childbirth is four times higher than the risk of contracting hepatitis B or C from a blood transfusion. From such cues that are so dismissive of one's fear, it seemed that it was acceptable to express fears of one's baby's death but impermissible to talk about or contemplate the not entirely unrealistic fears we had for ourselves.

Indeed, contrary to these assurances, the US National Vital Statistics Report asserts higher numbers: maternal mortality in America was 8.4 deaths per 100,000 live births in 1997, and 7.1 deaths per 100,000 live births in 1998. These figures include only those deaths reported on the death certificate with complications of pregnancy, childbirth, and the puerperium assigned as the cause of death.

Midwife Ina May Gaskin believes that hospitals are not held accountable for the real risks childbirth can pose to mothers. 'Compliance [by hospitals in reporting deaths] is voluntary,' she notes. 'There is no accountability.

'Not unless you live in Massachusetts [or New York] are you able to find out about the outcomes for your hospital or practice, and then only because state law requires it. I was shocked to hear a gynecologist who gave birth at our facility say there had been five maternal deaths in four or five months at [the hospital where she worked]. No such numbers had been reported in her local newspaper.'

Of course, I realized the chance of death – either mine or the baby's – was still small. Yet not enough time had elapsed in women's history to break that long association. To think of birth without acknowledging the familiar presence of death as attendant seemed like one of those contemporary half-experiences: safer, cleaner, wholly more desirable, yet somehow not quite real, like a 'safari' in which you peer out at wildebeests from behind bulletproof glass.

One difference I would find between midwives and traditional obstetrics is that midwives allow women to express their fears of dying in childbirth. In some alternative childbirth advocates' classes, the instructor will line up a row of grey-painted shoeboxes to create a cemetery: 'Rest in Peace, Little One', the shoeboxes read. The exercise, which allows pregnant women to mourn an old miscarriage or abortion, or release fears of their own or their child's death ahead, proves cathartic.

When I was five-and-a-half months pregnant, my husband and I were invited over to a meal at Minnie's. When we arrived, she was sitting on her back porch in a white-painted Adirondack chair. Her guests were milling around the suburban yard, its wintry foliage softened by an unseasonal burst of heat; her husband turned hamburger patties over a grill. There seemed to be an unspoken agreement among the thirtyish new parents that the men at a social event like this would be spared any overt diapering or nose-wiping in public. The men stood side by side together with their arms crossed, rocking slightly, their weight balanced. The women, holding glasses of white wine, talked in quiet, urgent tones, all the while alert to the peripheral sounds and sights of their children. Minnie's six-year-old daughter conferred with friends on the couch, her three-year-old daughter looked at the knees of the adults in a dream, and Minnie's one-year-old baby sprawled on her lap. Nothing could have been more ordinary.

'How are you feeling?' she asked me.

'Oh, pregnant,' I said with a laugh, as I used my hands to ease my big self down into the chair beside her.

Out of nowhere, she remarked with a sigh, 'There are two times when you are completely alone. When you're pregnant. And when you die.'

How odd, and yet by now how unsurprising, her remark sounded to me. In one sense I'd never been less alone; on the one hand, this sense of slowly being doubled was like my spirit cleaving into two. Yet on the other, this was the most solitary journey I'd ever undertaken. No one else could carry this baby for me or take my place at my appointment with the birthing table.

While it was socially out of step for Minnie to talk to me about death at her ordinary suburban brunch, she was right to do so. For I was getting ready for a momentous meeting in which death might no longer wait at childbed but could still be sensed watching from another room, held imperfectly at bay. I *knew* it, just as other pregnant women around me knew it.

The guests that afternoon were couples in their early thirties, as secular and commonsensical a group as you could imagine. Several of them were expecting children or had recently had children.

Sally, a newsletter editor who was soon to give birth, was talking to a friend who was standing beside us. She said, loud enough for us to hear, 'I thought I was the only one going through this kind of loss at a time like this: but I've heard half a dozen stories.'

Minnie explained to me quietly, 'Her younger brother has lung cancer. He's been hanging on for a couple of years doing pretty well, but now he's in the hospital and it looks like this is it. Sally just came back from Alabama, where she had gone to be with him for as long as she could, but she's due in seven weeks. The doctors say her brother won't last that long.'

We had recently been touched by two similar accounts. The previous week, a friend had called from New York to tell me that mutual friends of ours, whose baby, like Sally's, was due in a month, had had a terrible shock: the man's parents had been driving north the day after Christmas, and a car, trying to pass, had crumpled in the driver's side. His father was dead. The expectant couple had taken the last flight the mother-to-be was allowed on, and now she would have to deliver her child where she was, surrounded by mourning.

That same night, there was a quiet message on our answering machine. A relative who had been living stoically with her emphysema for years, bone-thin but elegant in her tailored suits, had gone into hospital and was not expected to come home.

The following day, I came down with a friend's cold symptoms, which turned into bronchitis. As I lay, wheezing and coughing, on the sofa, I thought of how close we all were to the ancient juxtaposition of life and death: how infectious diseases and bacteria could skip merrily into our bodies. In the nineteenth century, before the very idea of bacteria had been discovered – and life-saving antibiotics were a century away – doctors attending women in labour would carry the germs that transmitted puerperal fever from childbed to childbed, bring women a death sentence with the touch of their ungloved hands. When Oliver Wendell Holmes, an obstetrician who helped to identify the cause of puerperal fever in the mid-nineteenth century, urged his colleagues to begin washing their hands with antiseptic between attending each case, he was vilified, ostracized by fellow physicians who were affronted that he dared suggest they might be harbouring contagion. In some hospitals, as the lag continued between his discovery and his peers' willingness to accept their role in transmitting the epidemic, a third of the women who had come to give birth would die of puerperal fever. I thought of how, in my grandmother's time, before the invention of antibiotics and antiseptics, bronchial fever – or scarlet fever, or puerperal fever – could so easily have been fatal.

Later, over the phone, I told my father about the curious frequency with which the pregnancies of women I knew had been accompanied by the deaths of relatives. He laughed. 'All that means, Naomi, is that people are born and people die. You're just noticing it in a new way.'

# Sixth Month
# Birth Class and Hospital Tour

'Most Lamaze teachers continue to teach in hospital settings and
are paid by hospitals or groups of physicians.'
Suzanne Arms, *Immaculate Deception I* (1996)

What I wanted from my birth experience was not so complicated:
simply the chance to give birth in a safe, supportive environment,
according to my own body's clock, in a culture determined by those
who had given birth or knew about birth, with my mate and skilled
care-givers there to help me, with pain managed realistically and
well, with the best technology available, if it was medically necessary.

During my pregnancy, I read whatever I could find on the topic.
I wanted to be informed about the experience in a way that was
realistic, respectful, and honest. Most of all, I longed to be taught
about the coming challenge by people who could share their
expertise with me without an agenda of their own distorting what I
was to expect of myself or what others were to expect of me.

I did not know until long after the birth how much the
information we sought out to guide us through the birth experience
had been manipulated by others.

Our OB-affiliated midwives, seconded by *What to Expect When
You're Expecting*, urged us as a couple to write up a birth plan.
Naively, we specified that we wanted for me to be able to avoid
episiotomy if possible, avoid IV drips, try to postpone medication,
move around during labour to facilitate birth, dim the lighting for
the baby's arrival, and so on. Our midwives nodded affirmatively
and accepted our 'plan' – though they did caution us that sometimes
decisions had to be made in the urgency of the birth itself that might

depart from it. They described the birth plan as 'a means of communication' about the kind of birth the couple wants. And, in fact, the very act of writing the birth plan – dreaming about the kind of birth we hoped for – was exciting and felt empowering.

We did not know that our 'birth plan' was, in the words of a midwife from the Elizabeth Seton Birthing Center – one of the few institutions that provides truly independent midwifery – 'not worth the paper it is written upon'. Hospitals and obstetrical practices that deal with demanding clients such as our educated cohort encourage couples to write such a plan, as it gives us a sense of consumer choice. We are not told outright that it is hospital protocols that determine what will happen in the course of delivery, usually regardless of what the plan might say.

'The nursing staff laugh at birth plans at the nurses' station,' various midwives would inform me later. 'They pass them around for entertainment: "Get *this*." Or they say, "She has a birth plan? Get the operating room ready." The joke is that you would believe that you have any power in the hospital to change the outcome.'

Having no such insight at the time, we worked on our brave little birth plan religiously.

My husband and I also attended childbirth classes, another rite of passage on the journey to parenthood. These were held in an uncomfortable room in a downtown office building. We had no way of knowing that there was a hidden agenda behind what was being taught to us.

The hospital had recommended this childbirth class to us. It was represented as an independent course, led by an instructor whom the hospital objectively thought highly of. It was not clear to me that the course was developed and overseen by the hospital itself, and that the childbirth educator was *employed and compensated by the hospital*.

The instructor prepared us for Lamaze breathing, 'husband-assisted coaching', and what to expect in terms of 'routine' interventions. The women in the class were trying to get their partners to feel involved. The men were there, some clearly uncomfortable, trying to show their support.

The husbands sat next to their wives, who lay supine on the carpeted floor, and spent six weeks practising something that independent midwives will tell you is virtually useless if you are trying to help someone manage the pain of real labour: timing their wives' breathing. 'Hee-hee-huh!' we were supposed to pant, lips slightly apart. The men were advised to sit decorously beside us, as if beside our hospital beds, rubbing our necks occasionally. Then they were supposed to change the rhythm a bit to keep our minds focused on the task before us: 'hee-hee-huh-hee!'

Where did this ultimately inadequate panting exercise come from? The Lamaze method was part of a wave of 'natural childbirth' awareness that gained momentum in the 1950s as women themselves began to experiment with such methods, in an effort to make maternity more meaningful.

As a result of the popularization of the natural childbirth movement through books and classes, hospitals and obstetricians eventually began to incorporate childbirth education into the standard care of pregnant women. What most parents-to-be don't realize until it is too late is how little effect on pain such breathing is likely to have in a hospital setting: such natural childbirth techniques were not designed for high-tech hospitals that place time limits on labour and seek to speed up contractions. As Sheila Kitzinger points out in *Ourselves as Mothers* (1995) '. . . In the United States . . . it has become increasingly clear that what parents learn in childbirth classes does not prepare them adequately to deal with the highly medicalized environment and crisis atmosphere in the hospital.'

While Lamaze had its roots in the natural childbirth movement, many birth industry critics go further and argue that the versions taught in hospital-sponsored classes today are used for institutional convenience, and to create docile patients, rather than to support more natural births. These commentators argue that hospitals have co-opted Lamaze methods in order to 'domesticate' birthing women – essentially to teach them above all not to inconvenience the staff in the birthing room.

According to independent midwives, less 'ladylike', more socially disruptive methods of managing pain are actually far more effective. Midwives in birthing centres, who do not need to accommodate their patients to the hospital's expectations, teach women to manage labour pain and even to get through the pain without epidurals by using techniques that are highly effective but also socially inappropriate for women in semi-public settings: groaning like a tiger, moaning like a woman in the throes of lovemaking, or grunting as if making a bowel movement. They encourage women to move about freely as the impulse arises and to assume what may be undecorous positions: squatting, lunging on to all fours, and pulling on the furniture, on support staff, or on a husband, boyfriend or relative. They know that if you are flat on your back or even lying still on your side – as birthing classes teach you – you will be in agony and call quickly for the anesthetist.

Yet American hospitals in particular set a premium on patients' silence and immobility and generate higher fees with every epidural requested. From the hospital's point of view, it makes far better sense to have women in labour lying down quietly in agony, occupied relatively meaninglessly with panting and counting till the longed-for epidural kicks in, than to have women in labour trying to manage pain effectively without major medication by lunging, squatting, pulling on the underpaid attendant nurses, or worse, on the obstetrician, while guttural female sounds reverberate down the corridors like the howls of jungle cats.

In our birthing class, the guys looked dutifully at their watches as we made our little huffing noises, lying flat on our backs on the floor. We lay inert in our huge mounds, resembling nothing so much as the diorama of elks at leisure that I saw in my childhood at the Natural History Museum.

For weeks the guys fidgeted while the childbirth instructor told them everything they needed to know about vaginas (or rather, 'bagidas', as she pronounced it during her frequent allergy attacks). David and I collapsed in nervous laughter so often during the class that we had to excuse ourselves. Between classes, he would turn to me and say, 'Hee-hee-huh!' apropos of nothing, and I would keel over with a mixture of hilarity and terror.

The classes were sweet – and seemed educational; it seemed like a fun, tender, silly rite of passage. What I didn't realize was that under the surface, there was a hidden agenda.

At one point the instructor showed us a video of three births, escalating from an 'easy' birth to a 'difficult' one. It seemed very reassuring: as I recall, it showed us an epidural-assisted vaginal birth, as well as a Caesarean birth. We thought it was an 'objective' representation of different birth experiences. Later, I would find that it was a representation of the kind of birth hospitals gear women to have. What I didn't realize at the time was that the births depicted showed often unnecessary medical interventions that actually slowed or impeded labour, and that could ultimately increase the odds of women having a Caesarean. The video, however, portrayed these steps as if they were part of the natural standard of care.

In went the IV drip, on went the fetal monitor belt; as a result, the woman could no longer walk around. In came the anesthetist with the epidural needle, because the woman, now unable to walk around, could no longer bear the agony of labour while lying on her side restricted to a bed. Snip went the scissors performing a 'routine' episiotomy during delivery. Snap went the gloves on the hands of the surgeons before slicing open the abdomen during a Caesarean conducted behind a discreet little white curtain.

In one birthing sequence, we saw a contented-looking, working-class couple in the planning stage before the birth, hopeful and confident about managing the pain. Their instructor recommended that they bring to the delivery room a favourite object upon which to focus. (This, like the shallow, ladylike breaths that I was being taught, was supposed to help the woman transcend the 'discomfort'.) The couple decided that the father would hold up a Polaroid snapshot of their black-and-white cat for the woman to stare at.

Several scenes later, as the woman was in early labour, she emerged from the hospital shower, where she had retreated, with no midwife or birth attendant insight, to try to deal with what looked like intolerable pain, while her husband stood helplessly outside. She was clutching her belly, naked, practically crying. Nothing about that scene looked tolerable. Her husband frantically waved the Polaroid of their cat in her face. With a look of pure venom, the woman took a swing at the cat photo, muttering something that looked very much like 'Get that thing the fuck out of my face.' The message conveyed by that scene? The pain of childbirth without an epidural was clearly unendurable, and modern drug intervention was the only humane solution.

The final scene of her in the video showed her happily anesthetized, attached to an IV, chatting pleasantly with her husband while labouring – a far less disturbing image, and in fact highly reassuring of what the hospital could provide if one were willing to utilize its resources.

One thing the birth class did not explain to us effectively was the pain of childbirth and what to do about it other than breathe helplessly in its grip or take major drugs simply to cut off sensation.

In the past, people understood that childbirth hurt. Genesis 3:16 hides behind no euphemism: 'Unto the woman [God] said, I will greatly multiply thy sorrow and thy conception, in sorrow thou shalt bring forth children . . .' In the nineteenth century, doctors described labour pain as one of the most agonizing experiences known to medicine, more painful than the suffering of soldiers on Civil War battlefields.

Yet in the videos we were shown and the books we read, we rarely saw or had described to us how intense the pain of childbirth often is, nor were we clearly instructed about the many ways to handle it that depart from hospital expectations. (*What to Expect* mentions non-drug approaches to handling pain at the end of the Pain section, and calls them 'sometimes effective', but does not mention in this or in the Pain Risk Factors section the highly effective, but institutionally troublesome, techniques of hydrotherapy, changing position or vocalizing.)

Lisa, a news magazine journalist who had been posted in the Middle East, later told me, 'I was completely unprepared for the level of pain. As a younger woman I had had a lot of problems with menstrual cramps, throwing up, being in extreme agonizing pain. I thought I was prepared for anything. Then when I went through it I thought, Why didn't anyone prepare me better? But as one friend explained to me, "When at the end of *The Wizard of Oz*, Dorothy asks, 'Why didn't you tell me?' Glinda the Good Witch replies, 'Because you wouldn't have believed me.'"

'When I was going through delivery, which lasted forty-five minutes, I had to push for a really long time; Cory's shoulders got stuck. I remembered thinking while I was in labour about an article I had done for a news magazine about torture techniques. The worst thing I had ever read about was a torture device Syria uses called the Assad chair. It involves stripping a detainee and forcing him or her to sit on a hot conical piece of metal, basically shoved up his . . . you know.

'And that was all I could think about during the delivery: the Assad chair. I had read *What to Expect* – and it certainly didn't say anything about the Assad chair.

'I truly felt I was being tortured. I was in such intense pain, it felt like I would be haunted by it forever.

'The second birth was much easier. If you could measure the

pain, I'm sure it was no less painful, but I was prepared for it. It didn't frighten and shock me the way the first one did. A friend who is a psychologist said the most important thing for people in pain to know is that it is going to end. With the first I remember thinking, "I will never be the same". While I learned that that's not true – I am the same, to the extent that you can be after becoming a parent – with the second I was prepared.'

As one guide to pain management in childbirth puts it: literature about birth 'often avoids the "p" word altogether, describing it instead as "discomfort" or "pressure".' Gillian van Hasselt, the anesthetist who wrote *Childbirth: Your Choices for Managing Pain* described her birth story, 'Nothing could have prepared me for the agony-deluxe I experienced in childbirth . . . I felt as though I was being ripped apart. . . . The epidural did not help the intense burning low in my groin. I felt like a gourmet chicken being spit roasted . . .'

A rural Central-American midwife, who spoke at the New School Midwifery Conference in New York in 1999, claimed that women in labour need to be told they will be going into battle: 'Be brave. This will be tough and you can do it. Be brave.' They need to be warriors for themselves and their babies.

No one informed me even remotely in our birth classes about the kind of courage you need to tap into during labour. Yet women who are prepared psychologically and physically for extreme pain – prepared, perhaps, to do battle – may well be better able to manage the trial of labour with less fear, and possibly with fewer medical interventions.

Not only did the video fail to show women in pain who were managing the pain with intense emotional and hands-on physical support, which I found later is the only analgesia that can compete with an epidural; but it showed the women in a state of passivity. All three mothers portrayed in the birth class lay on their sides or backs in bed. I didn't see a single image that showed us a woman walking during contractions to ease the pain and assist gravity, squatting, or being held on a husband's lap or a birthing stool. No one giving birth in the 'educational' birth class video yelled, grunted, panted, thrashed, nor was anyone massaged all over her naked limbs, stroked or kissed, during her labour. I would not see those elements of a good birth – elements that I would later discover were far better, physically, for mother and baby than the kind of passive, emotionally detached births we were being taught to emulate in our birth class – until years later, in a midwifery video that was far from mainstream.

The video we saw in class showed women hooked up to fetal monitors. I did not know that fetal monitors frequently give false readings that can hasten 'emergency' Caesarean-sections, and have no reliable statistical advantage in predicting true fetal distress. We learned in class that in many standard births the mother-to-be would be hooked up to an IV drip, further restricting movement; we were not taught that women doing what their bodies are meant to do in labour – move from position to position – is best for both mother and baby. The video had taught us that we would not be allowed to eat or drink during labour, lest we needed a Caesarean and had to be put under anesthesia, for there was, we were told, a risk of choking. We were not informed that the data showing a risk from a full stomach in the event of surgery dates from 1946, when anesthesia was far cruder than it is today, and has since been discredited. We did not know that if a woman is allowed to eat and drink during labour as she desires she is able to keep her strength up and push effectively, thus protecting her from other damaging interventions. We were told that episiotomies, which are convenient for obstetricians and hospitals because they are fast and easy, are safe and routine. We were not told that they carry the not infrequent risk of major complications or that less 'medical', more patient midwifery techniques which are more common in Europe gradually expand the birth outlet often without the need for cutting through perineal muscle. We did not know that the gentle, Birkenstock-wearing instructor, who looked the part of an independent birth advocate, was a member of hospital staff, who, common sense suggested and later sources confirmed, could lose her job if she gave us information, no matter how important she thought it was for us to know, that conflicted with the hospital 'line'. Nor did we realize that the class guided a labouring woman to see her proper role in childbirth as providing a prompt, docile response to a series of medical interventions and instructions, and guided her husband or partner to comply as well.

In fact, the whole touchy-feely exercise we experienced felt 'woman-centred' because we mothers-to-be were the centre of everybody's attention once a week, which was a lovely feeling. But the class was in fact an advertorial for the hospital's way of delivering babies.

In the midst of the series of classes, my husband and I took a tour of the hospital maternity ward – another standard landmark on the pregnancy journey. The hospital where I was due to deliver was a downtown state-of-the-art facility. Along with our classmates from the birthing class, we made our way past the gift shop to the gathering point of the hospital tour.

We were told about parking, and insurance forms; we were shown the nursery, where hours-old newborns were left in what looked like clear plastic shoeboxes, to cry under the bright lights while the staff – from what we could see as we peered through the picture windows – converged in a back room, chatting.

The entire hospital had been redone in colours that I was all too familiar with from my stays in chain hotels: the mauve-and-teal combination that I couldn't help associating with jet lag and bad food. The spokeswoman told us that almost all the birthing rooms were in use at the moment and took us, sheepishly, into one set in the juncture of a busy hallway, claiming that it was used 'mostly for demonstration purposes'.

I could see at once that she was not being straightforward: the dark, stuffy cubicle, which was windowless, held a stripped birthing bed. The bed, which was half-upright, showed all too obviously at the midsection the stains of many deliveries. The fluorescent lights hung down like the eyes of a robot, and the fetal monitor's screen was prominently displayed on a ledge. There was a folding door behind which loomed resuscitating equipment; the bed held stirrups and straps. There was no room around the bed to walk, kneel, or stretch out, and the dark, hot, uncirculating air was vibrant with the disturbances of recent deliveries.

'Yikes,' breathed a woman beside me, involuntarily.

I asked our guide, a hospital spokeswoman, what happened when the protocols of the hospital conflicted with the wishes of the nurse-midwives. I was given an answer that could have come straight out of Machiavelli: 'The nurse-midwives and hospital management have a genuine respect for one another, and work well together. No decision would be made that wouldn't be explained fully to you.' I pressed further, asking directly what happened when the nurse-midwives' wishes and the hospital's were at odds. I was trying to understand whose view would prevail in a dispute, who would win. I got no further. 'There is open and regular communication about all such decisions, and you can trust your practitioner,' the tour guide insisted.

Wondering why so many spokespeople for the industry seemed to communicate like Stalinist posters, I asked what the Caesarean rate was at the hospital. The spokeswoman hesitated. 'First,' she said, the hospital's rate 'was one of the best in DC. Second,' she added, the institution was 'not obliged by law to release statistics'. In fact, hospital disclosure is a state-by-state issue – New York and Massachusetts, for example, have laws that guarantee access to data – but there is no Federal law that requires hospitals to release information on maternity services.

Then taking me aside, the spokeswoman confided that the hospital had a 30 per cent Caesarean rate. She whispered that my question was one she was not supposed to answer. No hospital in our region was obliged by law to provide its Caesarean statistics to prospective patients.

By this time my husband and I had decided to move from the conservative obstetrical practice we had first chosen to what was advertised as a joint midwifery-obstetrical practice. In reality, such joint practices benefit from the midwives' services which can be marketed as a lure for people like us – people who want midwives' empathy and judgement, with a high-tech medical backup in case of an emergency. So what we had chosen was actually a high-tech, traditional obstetric practice – with a cosmetic overlay of midwifery in situations, such as leisurely check-ups, in which the midwife having authority did not matter. What we did not get was a practice in which the midwives had authority in the birthing room. Unfortunately, neither the hospital nor our obstetricians informed us clearly that when it came to the actual medical decisions involved at delivery, our midwives were not equal partners in any true sense of the word, but, rather, under DC and Maryland law, handmaidens of the obstetrical practice that employed them; nor that our midwives lacked admitting privileges to the hospital we would deliver in, could not challenge the decisions of the doctors or hospital administrators in a meaningful way, and were unable usefully to advocate for us if their decisions or pacing contradicted those of the obstetricians above them.

*What to Expect*, which had guided our decision, describes the option of the 'combination' or doctor/midwife practice in glowing terms, characterizing such care as 'midwife-coached delivery', where you receive the 'extra time and attention' that a midwife can provide even as you can be 'assured that if a problem develops, a physician is waiting in the wings'. Yet the book does not mention that the true power dynamic between these groups of professionals is typically very much the other way around. In most such partnerships the midwives are very much the junior partners, who must yield to the physician offstage at crucial points in the drama.

Even the hospital's architecture played a kind of shell game with expectant parents that we did not understand at the time. The tour guide showed off with a flourish the hospital's *pièce de résistance*: following a national trend, as women expressed a longing for a more nurturing and less clinical environment in which to deliver their babies, the hospital administrators had set aside a floor of beautifully appointed birthing rooms, with sunlight-filled windows, in what it called the 'ABC' or 'Alternative Birthing Center'. Each of the five large, airy rooms was furnished with polished mahogany, king size four-poster beds, deep upholstered armchairs in striped ticking, ruched Viennese shades, European shower heads, and Mary Cassat mother-and-child prints. A jacuzzi beckoned just a step away, a refrigerator in a family room was stocked with juices and soups, and the armchairs flipped open into recliners to let the 'coach' get a little rest. Here was an appropriately comforting, expansive, and celebratory setting for a travail that would culminate in birth. It was the Ritz-Carlton of birthing room facilities, compared to the lower floors' everyday motel.

I certainly was drawn to the Alternative Birthing Center; like many of the other couples in the group, we were excited to have chosen a hospital with such a facility. The guide walked us through the floor, to our sighs of delight, with an air of triumph, but I could detect some uneasiness in her manner as well. I also got a funny feeling about its big, shiny emptiness. None of the rooms was occupied. There was a lone nurse on duty. The surfaces were almost too sparkling.

'How many people give birth here?' I asked.

'It has been very successful,' I was told, once again evasively. 'If you have a problem, you get taken down to the ordinary birthing rooms.'

What we could not know at the time was that the proudly displayed Alternative Birthing Center was essentially what marketers call a loss leader. It was never seriously designed to get more than a small minority of women who checked themselves in there through their labour. As one midwife put it later – speaking, as so many midwives I interviewed felt they had to do, 'on background' so that they would not suffer professional ostracism for sharing information about what was wrong with the practices of the obstetrics profession and hospitals that employed them – 'There was this trend for hospitals to rent a recliner and call it an Alternative Birthing Centre. Hospitals are putting up pretend birthing centres because women are demanding them. They are showing them beautiful rooms but not changing any protocols.'

According to another midwife who insisted on speaking not for attribution, but who had delivered for years at the hospital in question, it was set up for cosmetic and marketing purposes, not practical ones: 'No midwives were asked about the design [the imposing decorative design of the beds got in the way of easy manoeuvring]. We had to sew people up who were hanging off the side of the bed; we had to sit on a chair with their feet on our shoulders.'

The hospital spokesperson would not, years later, give me statistics on how many women actually gave birth at the ABC. The midwife who had delivered there reported to me – again, not for attribution – that of every ten women who checked herself into the Alternative Birthing Center, perhaps two would actually manage to give birth there; the rest would 'fail' and get processed downstairs. Why? First of all, no epidurals were given there – you can't stay if you need anything stronger than Nubain for the pain – but, since it is still a hospital with a hospital's culture, neither are you offered many of the other techniques that truly independent birth centres use to help you manage the pain. In addition, the majority of women who tried to give birth in that lovely place were processed into the bowels of 'downstairs' for any number of other reasons, from the trivial to the serious. The Alternative Birthing Center was an attractive gatepost to an unattractive reality; it was far more seldom an actual destination than we were told at the time.

It was no accident that there had been few births at the new birthing centre at the time we visited. The lovely, empty centre was, for most women, an advertising draw that lured commerce but limited liability. Years later, when I repeatedly tried to contact the hospital marketing department, which had conceived the eye-catching ads touting the ABC that had so attracted us, my calls were not returned. I discovered only from my midwife informant that the ABC, so rarely used and so labour-intensive when someone actually did manage to give birth there, had been closed down.

At the time, though, it was a powerful symbol of the birth I wanted. The contrast between the two delivery floors seemed to sum up a failure to give women decent choices in childbirth. I did not understand why the polarity was so stark: the beautiful floor with its rigid set of options regarding pain, or the slaughterhouse atmosphere of the regular birthing rooms where I could receive medication for the body if I needed it, but nothing for the soul. My heart longed for the Alternative Birthing Center, its beauty, its openness. But could I stand the pain? And would my labour go so smoothly that no complications would arise to get me sent to the warrens down below?

Meanwhile, my husband and I – and our friends who were expecting babies – listened to the soothing voice of our birthing class instructor, read the standard books on pregnancy, thought with anticipation about the big double beds and the soft recliners in the Alternative Birthing Center, and learned huffy, ladylike breathing as if that would be the answer to what lay ahead.

# Seventh Month
# Mysteries

'Pregnant [women] share a similar . . . mysterious power.'
D.V. Hart, P.A. Rajadhon and R.J. Coughlin,
*Southeast Asian Birth Customs*

By my seventh month, I felt as if I had entered a dark, emotional tunnel. It was richer, deeper, and more mysterious than any transformation I'd undergone before. I became more inwardly focused, absentminded, irritable, peaceful, at once the travelling nautilus and the shell. But because I had nothing to reach out to that could explain this new state, there was a sense of unreality to the half-submersion I felt. I felt like a lodestone, possessed of something inexplicable and magical. My personality was changing; though everything sort of went on as it had before, on another level, nothing really mattered except the baby. Other concerns seemed to drop away. Was there something wrong with me? I wondered. Was I going mad?

Though I felt put off by some of the 1970s hippie birthing books I consulted, and their insistence on pregnancy as one long ecstasy, I did in fact experience moments of epiphany. These were brighter moments of that sense of interconnection with all women that I had experienced, in a darker version, months before, in the resort swimming pool brimming with mortality.

One morning, in a hotel room, as I was showering, I saw to my amazement milk mingling with the water. The sunlight streamed through the windows on to the bland wheat-coloured bedding, the pastel floral wall panels, and into the shower stall, like a visitation.

The steaming water, the sun caught up in the shower stream, and these incomprehensible rivulets of milk all mingled together in a cascade of light. I had the sensation that my body had broken down and I was returning into molecules; that I had joined the universe in a new way.

Walking out to my office on another morning, I saw a perfectly ordinary street scene resolve itself entirely differently. I knew somehow that whatever was going on in my perception that was unusual came from this mystery of gravidity. I saw connections I had never intuited before between the squirrels on the lawn, the sparrows on the fence, the crows in the elms, Mattie, our mail deliverer, whose daughter had just had a son, the tired-looking taxi driver who had pulled up at the light, the black-and-white cat that blocked my path, and even, somehow, people not present in the scene – my grandmother, my mother, my baby. We were all held, touched, interrelated, in an invisible net of incarnation. I would scarcely think of it ordinarily; yet for each creature I saw, someone, a mother, had given birth. Someone had succumbed herself to this endless yielding motion of the world, this cleaving, of which I was now a part. Motherhood was the gate.

It was something that had always been invisible to me before, or so unvalued as to be beneath noticing: the *motheredness* of the world.

A little later, I felt the baby's head under my ribs for the first time. At that moment, I felt as if I were but a shell, a pod for the next generation, less essential, less unique, than I had thought. I felt a wild sense of joy, and – of all things! – freedom in that realization. I was aware of how good it felt; personal goals and preferences seemed less urgent, and I came to feel how light were my values as an individual self. I also began to feel how heavy was my responsibility to the fetus I carried; how much I mattered in my role as the individual being tasked with mothering this baby.

With my increasing ungainliness, I longed for something tangible that could reflect or give voice to those moments of otherworldliness I experienced. I wanted some acknowledgement of what I sometimes saw as the sacredness of my state.

In some cultures, pregnant women are ostracized or sanctioned and at birth isolated or treated roughly. But in others, including many pre-industrial cultures, they are treated reverentially.

According to anthropologist Bronislaw Malinowski, among the Trobriand islanders of the South Pacific, female relatives of the father of the mother-to-be create two ceremonial pregnancy skirts and cloaks for her. The pregnant woman wears one outfit during the first celebration of the new pregnancy, and one is saved for the moment when the new mother is reintegrated into normal tribal life.

The women place the four finished garments on a mat and strew over them the white leaves of a lily. Then they breathe a prayer into the fibres of the clothing, exhorting a white bird to hover over the place where the pregnant woman will be ceremonially bathed before dressing. The women ask the bird to 'make resplendent' each segment of the robes and every part of the pregnant woman's body – from her head to her belly, from her buttocks to her knees – so that her body will be 'like the pallor before the dawn'. They asked that the community praise the pregnant woman for the achievement represented by her pregnancy. Then the women wrap the bundle tightly so the magic will not evaporate and then leave it for the pregnant woman as a gift.

Cross-culturally, women's pregnancy is marked by ceremony: a festive meal in China, a visit to a Shinto shrine in Japan, a blessing in Malaysia. The respect implicit in these ceremonies appealed to me; not that pregnancy was a greater achievement than any of the other remarkable things women do in the normal course of events. I just longed for some sense that it was an achievement at all.

A magic celebration of the 'great achievement' of pregnancy was a long way from the pregnancy culture I saw around me: the routine checks at my obstetricians' offices, where nurses would efficiently go over the baby's progress, the dispiriting assortment of maternity T-shirts and the cloying advice from paperbacks. Cautions about weight gain and creams for stretch marks conveyed a very different message from 'blessings for every part' of one's big old gravid body.

Some cultures attribute to pregnant women an altered, heightened spiritual state; some rural Catholic Filipino communities, for instance, see pregnant women as more open to the spiritual world and more attractive to its unseen entities. As a result, they are treated with great deference; the community is supposed to rush to fulfil a pregnant woman's least craving. As I observed the slowly emerging *linea nigra* of my belly, bisecting it like the two hemispheres of a new world, I did indeed feel at times that pregnancy put me into a state of heightened openness to altered insight: the kind of openness that ordinarily, I imagine, comes to us only in moments of extreme beauty or pain. Ordinarily, such moments last only long enough for us to say, Yes, Lord, that's it! I recognize it, I remember: how could I have forgotten? *That's* the inclining face of it, *that's* the white-hot heart of love. I will never forget it again. And then the fog rolls in, or the telephone rings, and it's over: we are once again our diurnal selves, curt with the ticketing agent, and we've forgotten again until we learn it again with a start, the next time, from the beginning.

But pregnancy, on the other hand – like, perhaps, a terminal illness or a state of grace – seemed to make that barrier between the mundane, fretful, everyday world and the luminous 'ground of being' that much thinner. It seemed to 'efface' the barrier, thinning it to transparency the way the barrier of flesh that separates the baby from the outside world is effaced at delivery. I did not imagine that pregnant women were 'naturally' any more sensitive or exalted than people in any other condition; only it seemed as if – perhaps only because we are in such a twilight state, a melting down and reconstituting of the self – there was more opportunity to hear strains from what must be the other side, the moral music of the sphere.

And with my celestial antennae tuned, this was what I seemed to hear through the static of contemporary debate: babies come with spiritual information encoded for us. I had begun to intuit earlier that a baby's need for its mother breaks down something in the personal ego that then gets reconstructed around service. Now I began to consider how the newborn baby's unmeditated need for family – any structure of family so long as that family is bound heart and soul to its welfare – calls us, on a spiritual level, to sacrifice; challenges us to be strong enough to weather the frictions of personal dislikes and temperamental differences in the interest of holding some kind of family together, even if ultimately a family of one, in order to meet the needs of that baby.

Babies, I speculated in that peculiar mystical state, are sort of leaky little understudies for God. With each baby the human species gets the chance to break out of the self into the service of something so 'other' that the reasons for conditional love can give way to faith in unconditional love. Most of us ordinary mortals can't manage that invitation to unconditional love on a daily, ever-renewed plane in the form of looking after the poor, the dispossessed, or the outcast all around us. But with babies, we get the chance to take one manageable baby step on the long hard path of the saints.

Although I am Jewish, when I was pregnant I could suddenly see the good sense of worshipping God in the guise of a human baby.

That was the bright aspect of the dismantling of self I was undergoing, but it had its dark aspect as well. Like so many of the feelings of pregnancy and new motherhood, it was paradoxical: sometimes I felt the brightness and darkness at the same time.

I would burst into tears at the slightest emotional nick – scalding, cleansing, perverse tears that are, to paraphrase Colette, lightly called hysterical.

I once read a feminist treatise on PMS: the author held that when women are at their most premenstrually 'emotional', they are most in touch with the deeper wisdom about their life situation. While this premise has its element of extremism, it also makes a kind of sense. It occurred to me that, even if they were 'merely hormonal', those convulsive tears were necessary, just as tropical storms are necessary when the barometric tension rises too high.

The tension was this: I was mourning, protesting a point of departure in the road that I could never retrace. An 'I' would go forward, swept irrevocably on by the tide of the natural order, and that 'I' would sit on the sofa hour after hour and be someone's Lithium, someone's Lethe, someone's Popsicle – someone who would come to be a love of my life, but whom I did not yet know. And the 'I' would reconfigure eventually around that need, and take joy in it, and spin a new identity. But it would never again be the 'I' it had been before.

So many older women kept advising me that the mother-self to come would be a better self. I found this less than reassuring. This ostensibly transformed person of the near future might indeed be kinder and more patient than my pre-maternal self, whom I was at least familiar with, shortcomings and all. But that maternal 'I' did not exist yet. I did not yet know if I could successfully transform my current self into her – let alone, given how fatuous descriptions of motherly qualities can sound, if I would even *like* her.

Meanwhile, the maiden 'I' sometimes had to weep with the sure, coming death of the maiden self, the self that could 'arise and go now' at will; the self that is not food for others, but eats and drinks the world.

Who was this being growing inside me? My husband and I had been told the baby was lying in a breech position, which was not good. Now, in my seventh month, I rested on the couch at my in-laws' house, wondering idly about whether our baby could communicate with me or I with the baby. For no particular reason, I thought of the baby as 'her'; I was worried about her being head-up; I had an image of her suspended there, as in an ocean, but dangerously. I wanted to tuck her under in the right way, to give her a proper sleep and awakening.

Before thinking, I blurted out to my relatives, 'Hey, what if we all take a minute and send a request to the baby to flip around?'

There was a beat of silence as my relatives considered my odd proposal. It was not the sort of thing any of us particularly believed in. I have no idea why I came up with the notion – if anything suggested the idea to me at all, or whether my mind, or the baby's, somehow triggered some mysterious biochemical signal that future scientists will later be able to explain. Nonetheless, half a minute later, I felt what can only be described as a great lurching in my belly, like a lava flow buckling and shifting far beneath the earth. And our topsy-turvy baby, after developing mischievously head-up for seven months in no particular hurry to shift anywhere, since no one had asked her to do anything about it, turned herself, properly, upside down.

What happened to my baby in my in-laws' house was not so unique: according to midwives' anecdotal reports, quoted in Ruth Wainer Cohen's *Open Season*, other women have seemingly 'turned' their babies simply by asking them to turn. Some mothers-to-be have done so by writing letters to them; or by swimming in a pool and showing the baby how to do a somersault. Research by Dr L. H. Mehl, published in a reputable journal, the *Archives of Family Medicine*, showed, almost unbelievably, that mothers with breech babies who were hypnotized had almost twice the rate of their babies' turning into an ideal head-down position than did the control group who were not given the suggestion. Eighty-one per cent of the fetuses in the hypnosis groups turned, versus 48 per cent of those in the control group. The author concluded that 'psychophysiological factors' – a mind-body connection – could have influenced the change from breech to vertex (head-down). Obstetrician Christiane Northrup notes that anxious women have a higher rate of breech presentation, and speculates that tension tightens the uterus; in that case, the relaxation of the hypnosis could theoretically relax the uterus enough for a baby to turn. In the UK some NHS hospitals – including University College, London – have introduced acupuncturists into their maternity units who are said to be achieving good results in turning breech babies naturally.

Did I believe that what I thought or saw could affect the baby? No way. But did I find myself covering my belly with two hands when something grotesque appeared on a movie screen? I did. I began to experience a strange sense of vulnerability as my irrational mind – what I had almost begun to think of as my 'pregnant mind', which was increasingly superstitious, and medieval – took seriously the possibility that my baby could be imprinted in the womb by expereinces outside of it.

Many other cultures take for granted that what the expectant mother sees will imprint her baby, psychologically and physically. The Old Testament describes matter-of-factly how Jacob produced speckled lambs in his flock by showing the fertile ewes speckled sticks. Other folkways recommend that pregnant women avoid looking at accidents, watching violent movies or thinking harmful thoughts. Some rural Southeast Asian communities have a long list of prohibitions and recommendations that pregnant women are advised to follow based on what is called 'sympathetic magic' – if a pregnant woman mocks someone with a deformity, her child will be born with the same condition; if she eats dark fruit, her baby will have a dark complexion; if she sees quarrels, her child will have a difficult temperament; conversely, if she keeps all knots loosened and drawers open in her home, and looks regularly at a snakeskin that has been easily shed, she will have an easy delivery. This principle of caution about what the pregnant woman should expose herself to, based on sympathetic magic, is common in cultures ranging from Ghana and Benin to Malaysia to Guatemala and Ecuador. Indeed, most cultures warn the pregnant woman to avoid disturbing scenes and events. It is because of this belief that the Chinese established the first prenatal centres a millennium ago to shelter women from alarming scenes, and still maintain prohibitions against pregnant women encountering stressful situations. Leonardo da Vinci believed that 'the things desired by the mother are often found impressed on the child which the mother carries at the time of the desire'.

There is now mind–body research that shows there is some basis for the cross-cultural belief that a pregnant woman's experiences might imprint her child. If you experience stress, your baby will become stressed. Some studies suggest that the mother communicates with the baby via the flow of her neurohormones. When the mother is upset, her neurohormones rise, heightening the baby's stress level. When the mother is distressed, her emotion triggers off activity in the hypothalamus gland, which controls the endocrine and autonomous, or primitive, nervous system; through this interconnection, neurohormones flood the mother's bloodstream, then pass the placenta to reach the baby. Such hormones, called 'catecholamines', include epinephrine, norepinephrine, and dopamine. These constitute the biochemical make-up of the emotion we call fear. These catecholamines circulate when the pregnant mother is anxious or afraid, and this affects the baby's environment. In other words, the fetus experiences the mother's anxiety in a physiological way. While short-term upsets aren't cause for concern, intense, long-term stress, which can alter the fetal environment, apparently can have a possible negative impact on the child.

Not knowing this when I was pregnant, I still found myself turning away from violent images in the news and shunning frightening movies. At a reading I gave in a bookstore in Berkeley, several people wanted to place their hands on my belly. Most, I knew, were kindly people with good wishes; the good fairies bestowing blessings. But what if one, just one, was not? A white-haired, well-intentioned, Women's March for Peace activist, her hand outstretched over the baby, might just as easily, I imagined, have been a conjurer. In a rush, I was convinced – or rather, my superstitious pregnant alter ego was convinced – that others' hands had power to send intentions, evil or good, straight through my skin, fat, muscle, and placenta, into my baby.

I became increasingly atavistic and almost primitive in my reasoning: hands, images, wishes, and dreams are not, I thought in a new way, simple things.

\*

Dr Thomas Verny and John Kelly, in their book *The Secret Life of the Unborn Child*, explore the admittedly ambiguous research into what the fetus experiences *in utero*. From looking at the field of perinatal research, Dr Verny makes the claim that the fetus is 'an aware, reacting human being who from the sixth month on (and perhaps even earlier) leads an active emotional life'.

According to Dr Verny, the fetus can 'see, hear, experience, taste and, on a primitive level, even learn *in utero*.' There is evidence to support this. In one experiment, researchers were able to teach 16 fetuses to respond to a vibration by kicking; they did so through associating the vibration, which would provoke no response, with a noise, which typically led them to kick. Later, the researchers withheld the noise, yet the fetus would kick upon feeling the vibration alone.

A 2000 study found that acute stress in a pregnant woman does affect the fetus heart rate patterns, which supports the theory that 'maternal psychosocial variables' – the mother's state of mind – can shape the neurobehavioural development of the fetus,' just as some cultures must have intuited in the days before medical technology.

Dr Michael Lieberman's research, quoted in *The Secret Life of the Unborn Child*, showed that a fetus may react in an associative way to mothers who smoke: experiments in which fetal reactions were registered by measuring heart rate indicated that a fetus grew agitated when its mother reported she had *considered* having a cigarette, before she had even lit a match. The authors hypothesize that the fetus learns to react this way because maternal smoking is so unpleasant to it – causing a drop in the oxygen supply in the blood passing through the placenta – and that it learns to associate the mother's smoking with heightened distress. How it can register agitation when the mother merely anticipates lighting a cigarette, even before the inhaled smoke has affected her bloodstream, is anyone's spooky guess.

The baby *in utero* has been listening to the world outside the womb for a long time before he or she is born. According to natural birth activist Frederick Leboyer, the noises of a mother's body reach a baby's ears; a baby *in utero* hears 'intestinal rumblings, joints cracking, and most clearly of all the beat of the mother's heart'.

Recent research indeed suggests that the mother's voice is the most intense sound the fetus hears – a fetus's heart rate decelerates in response to her speech and sounds.

By the sixth or seventh month, research shows, babies are sentient beings; studies suggest that from the twenty-fourth week on, the fetus is listening at every waking moment. Vivaldi and Mozart seem to lead fetuses to kick less and cause their heartbeats to steady; Beethoven, as well as rock music, makes them kick inordinately. One researcher found that 'the fetus will literally jump in rhythm to the beat of an orchestra drum'. A review of studies on fetal experience demonstrates that the fetus's sensory experience has short- and long-term effects – including possibly transnatal learning. Dr Henry Truby of the University of Miami points out that from the sixth month on, a fetus's body rhythm matches the mother's inflections and speech patterns. When the baby is born, the baby 'dances' to the rhythm of the mother's speech patterns, so well known to the baby is her voice. When the mother speaks to her newborn, the human eye cannot perceive the baby's subtle, rhythmical response; but when films have been taken of the interaction and then played in slow motion, anyone can see the mother's rhythm mappable in her speech – and the newborn dancing to it. In fact, once the baby is born, he or she may be able to recognize familiar amniotic fluid – the atmosphere of home.

The mother's powers are mysterious as well. Studies by Israeli researchers show that hours after giving birth, a mother can recognize her baby by smell. Researchers gave a number of women T-shirts worn by their own and other babies. Each woman smelled each T-shirt individually. All of the women could correctly identify their own babies simply by smell. In a different study, researchers blindfolded and stopped the ears and noses of the new mothers allowing them to two-finger stroke the back of the newborn's hands. A large percentage of women knew which baby was her own just from the sense of touch.

Given these new findings about the interconnection between a pregnant mother's emotional state and a baby's well-being, it would make sense that the happiness of pregnant women should be of paramount importance in the medical care given them. Yet hospitals and doctors (not to mention policy-makers) seem to ignore or downplay the possibility that the mother's state of mind is important in determining the medical outcome of a birth.

The evidence suggests that the mind–body aspect of pregnant women's wellness is neglected to our physical peril. Several studies conclude that one of the most basic determinants for a good outcome at birth was the mother's feelings about the pregnancy. A study by Dr Helmut Lukesch has described the mother's relationship with the father as the second most important factor in determining the infant's physical well-being. On the basis of a survey of 1,300 children, Dr Dennis Stott found that a woman trapped in a troubled marriage has a 237 per cent higher risk of bearing a physically or emotionally damaged child than a woman in a relationship that is not severely disturbed.

Some research suggests that a father's feelings about his wife and her pregnancy are also crucial factors in determining how well the birth will go. In an E-poll carried out in *The Times* newspaper in London in 2001, British men emerged as 'true heroes of childbirth': 50 per cent, it was claimed, helped with the housework, while 57 per cent had become more kind and considerate to their wives before the birth. These reactions were highly praised by their wives and partners, who found them more supportive and helpful to their well-being than any assistance provided by the professional maternity services. Men's tenderness toward their wives or partners can clearly help to foster healthy pregnancies, while there is evidence to show that a bad relationship can be more dangerous to the pregnancy than other risk factors, including smoking, physical ill-health, and hard manual labour.

According to Lukesch, the father's attention may affect the developing baby directly as well: a baby seems to establish connections with others from within the womb. The fetus seems to react strongly to hearing its father's voice while *in utero*. Babies whose fathers spoke to them *in utero* using brief, calming sounds were able to identify their father's voices within the first few hours of life. Yet despite all this, caring for women's psychological well-being during pregnancy merited hardly a flicker of attention in the obstetrical side of my prenatal care or in many of the pregnancy books I sought out. Our OB-GYNs and birth class teachers told us to eat green leafy vegetables and breathe. They did not tell our close and extended families, let alone advocate to society at large, that women carrying babies must be nurtured and supported intensively. How much more revolutionary and transformative it would be for guides and gatekeepers to pregnancy to tell fathers-to-be, and grandparents-to-be, policy-makers and employers, and the culture as a whole that it is as important to nurture and value pregnant women and new mothers as it is to ensure that they are properly fed, weighed, and medicated.

In other words, we should seek to raise the status of what women do in journeying to become mothers, and crown new mothers with laurels upon having completed the arduous task, not only for moral reasons, but for medical ones as well.

# Eighth Month
# Powerlessness

'Before I was born out of my mother, generations guided me . . .'
Walt Whitman

As my pregnancy advanced, the world seemed far more dangerous to me. I felt increasingly vulnerable.

A veil seemed to have fallen over my mind – a biochemical one, made of estrogen. This estrogen gauze was disturbing because it seemed to verify so many stereotypes about what 'women are like'. In the final months of pregnancy, a woman's estrogen level rises, making her more 'female' than she ever has been before, or will be again, until another pregnancy. The ways in which the hormones of pregnancy affected me called into question my entire belief system about 'the social construction of gender'. I was now a reporter on my own voyage through the Galapagos of this change, and I had to note: The signs were adding up.

The estrogen made me more physically 'girly'. The fur on my shins and the down on my face was lighter. My voice, when I heard it on the tape of our answering machine, sounded, to my dismay, measurably higher. The physical change wrought by the hormonal upheaval of pregnancy is astonishing. The pregnancy-specific endocrine system tries to make the pregnancy strong and last the proper length of time. Four main hormones are produced by the placenta: human chorionic gonadotropin, human placental lactogen (HPL), progesterone and estrogens.

These hormones cause a number of changes. High levels of estrogen and progesterone change the shape and weight of the breasts (human placental lactogen, or HPL, also stimulates the growth of the breasts). Estrogen and progesterone cause the unique skin pigmentations of pregnancy, including the appearance of the *linea nigra* on the stomach, as well as the characteristic darkened areolae to the breasts. The pregnant body is a powerhouse of female substances. The sheer amount of estrogens that pregnancy infuses into the female body is vast: estrone and estradiol, two types of estrogen, increase by a hundredfold; estriol, a third type, increases about a thousand times. It is estrogen that leads to the lustrous hair growth in pregnancy.

Given this factory of femaleness, it is not surprising that emotional changes follow as well. The estrogen seemed to alter my emotional priorities, and those of other women with whom I spoke. The kind of sap that fills women's magazines – 'Sometimes I am perfectly fulfilled just cuddling' – was now comprehensible to me, for the old priorities had shifted: intimacy was now the red meat; all else was expendable.

My temperament was being altered, too, I noticed. Something I did not understand fully from the books I read was that my brain was actually changing.

In their book *Women's Moods*, Deborah Sichel and Jeanne Driscoll describe how women's emotions are affected by their hormones. Estrogen, they explain, helps regulate the neurotransmitters in the brain which are involved with aspects of moods. These neurotransmitters travel along certain pathways in the brain; if these pathways become blocked or altered, the woman's mood is affected.

During pregnancy, estrogen levels rise rapidly. 'Pregnancy is a time of enormous hormonal shifts, during which your body and brain are challenged as at no other point in your life,' Sichel and Driscoll write. By the sixth week, they are three times greater than at the highest point of the menstrual cycle. Estrogen contributes to mood stability. But, also according to Sichel and Driscoll, if the neurotransmitter pathways have been altered at any time previous to the pregnancy – by stress or depression, for instance – they remember it and respond negatively to the steep rise in estrogen. 'When a woman describes how her mood deteriorates in the early weeks of pregnancy, this may be why it worsens rapidly.'

Other hormones also affect a woman's mood. Prolactin, the hormone responsible for milk production, rises consistently throughout pregnancy. Sichel and Driscoll point out that elevated levels of prolactin in non-pregnant women are linked with irritability and anger. (Women in rural Filipino communities studied in the anthropological survey *Southeast Asian Birth Customs* matter-of-factly described a mood in early pregnancy that translated as a 'feeling of meanness' – something that would be socially unacceptable for pregnant women to describe so casually in Western cultures.) Levels of progesterone and cortisol also rise during pregnancy. Progesterone – which has been linked with depression, as have any rapid changes in hormone levels – rises rapidly during the first weeks, and cortisol, the stress hormone, increases greatly by the third trimester, contributing further to depression. This increase in prolactin, progesterone and cortisol could explain the weepiness, clinginess and crankiness that are common experiences in pregnancy – including my own.

The pregnant woman's brain eventually accommodates the rapid increase in hormones, and the pathways settle down. Women often feel better around the second trimester, possibly basking in the luxury of all the extra (antidepressant) estrogen circulating in the blood. I remembered feeling at peace with the world, blissfully connected, around this time; these high levels of estrogen may even contribute to the sense of euphoria that many pregnant women experience.

At the end of my pregnancy, I was aware that I was nesting, cuddly, and more traditionally 'feminine' in my responses. I felt more maternal toward helpless dependent beings, but especially toward babies and children. This could be seen as part of 'women's eternal nature', the excuse given for various anti-woman decisions. Or it could be the result of this temporary brainbath. From 34 weeks on, hormonal changes take place to prepare the uterus for labour. Estrogen stimulates the rise of oxytocin, the 'love hormone' that promotes labour contractions and stimulates the 'let-down' reflex in breast-feeding mothers. Estrogen helps the oxytocin receptors to function properly to encourage maternal bonding to the infant. 'From rodents to primates,' writes anthropologist Sarah Blaffer Hrdy, author of *Mother Nature*, 'oxytocin promotes affiliative feelings. A monkey mother whose brain receptors to these natural opiates are blocked makes few overtures toward her infants, is less likely to put her face near the baby's and reassuringly smack her lips.' Hrdy calls oxytocin a 'natural opiate' that guarantees mothers greet their new offspring in a 'broody, mellow mood'.

As Christiane Northrup's medical manual, *Women's Bodies, Women's Wisdom*, puts it, 'Hormones are . . . messenger molecules for emotions and thoughts.' I am convinced that oxytocin changed me temporarily. I would suddenly weep at long-distance telephone call commercials. I could no longer bear even to scan reports of abused children in the newspaper. I had never cared much for small animals. Now random house pets had to flee from my embraces. Journalist and writer Isabel Fonseca describes a similar experience in an article written for the London *Guardian* entitled 'Mothers Superior' in which, disputing the findings of an American discovery that pregnancy 'may make women smarter', she catalogues a list of symptoms of pregnancy-related 'ditziness'. As soon as she fell pregnant, she says, '(I) immediately began to misplace my keys no less than 12 times a day, to shed hot opalescent tears at the appearance of any baby on television or even in print . . . Ditto for dogs – and I don't even like dogs.'

I became more private, more quiescent. Indeed, the hard energy that used to sustain me in situations that called for debate simply sputtered out. I no longer felt any desire to enter the political fray; it was just too tiring. Even the back-and-forth debate of challenging conversations, which I had once relished, seemed distasteful to me now.

I felt myself becoming stupidly domestic. I didn't want to go outside. My preferred state was to sit cross-legged on a couch, scarcely moving, eating soft, sweet, bland foods at four-hour intervals. In *Cold Comfort Farm*, there are two cows, named Aimless and Feckless. I identified with Aimless.

I grew more physically timid as well. When I walked through an even slightly dangerous neighbourhood, I felt my partner's presence at my side as a physical necessity in a primal way. It was a feeling of dependency I had never felt before. It wasn't something I could like or dislike – I couldn't *theorize* about this aspect of female experience; it was just there, a new condition of my life. The simple, stubborn fact was that I just couldn't run as fast. 'A woman without a man is like a fish without a bicycle,' activist Fanny Lou Hamer has famously said; but I could feel myself quietly lowering that flag of independence as I made my way, belly forward, through dark streets or beside fast traffic, grateful for a mate who was unencumbered. Even danger meant something different to me now. For any danger to me was now a threat not just to me but to the child I was carrying. Was this new temperament of withdrawal and caution brought about in me, I wondered, because I was meant to keep my slow, lumbering self and the baby from danger?

Oh God, I thought as I took my husband's arm to cross a busy street – a street that the single-girl icons I grew up admiring would have waltzed or skipped or strode across, hair flying – did Nature mandate this temporary dependency? Is my lifetime of conviction about women's ability to go it merrily alone a complete evolutionary howler in the face of pregnancy? But the fact was: I was vulnerable, he wasn't, and I welcomed his help. At seven months, the ligaments in my hips had loosened to accommodate the baby, my centre of gravity had pitched forward, and even walking was precarious and slow. The cars whizzed by on the narrow embankment. In that moment, my world view and my sense of self, developed and shaped over three decades, collapsed a bit at the foundations.

This need to lean on one's mate, and this feeling of being so fragile, is a common experience of pregnancy. Dianne, the woman who would tell me about her disappointing birth experience, said, 'My husband travels. During pregnancy, I had fears of a plane crash, a car crash. I had fears of my husband dying. I'd cry sometimes after he'd leave for a trip. I asked that he call me at each destination.'

Greta, another narrator of her pregnancy journey, said, 'I was more adamant about needing things from [my husband] than I had been before I got pregnant. He thought I was being irrational, and he felt he needed to humour me. Typically, I'm a low-need woman. Not during pregnancy.'

Another woman, Pam, would say plaintively to me, 'It turns out you really need one when you're pregnant – a husband. Or at least,' she said with heartfelt surprise, 'you really need a *pal*.'

Perhaps that experience of dependency is part of the reason so many women support the notion of a social safety net. Could that be part of the reason many women vote with compassion for the disabled, the elderly, those who just can't keep up in the race alone – because women who bear children, unlike most men, experience something like the fragility of old age, the challenges of disability, in their prime? Do they remember those few months of having gone from the strength and stability of youth to the relative fraity of pregnancy – needing a few more minutes to get off the bus, an arm to hold on to in the face of hurtling traffic? Could pregnancy give so many women a lasting wisdom about the nature of the race we run? Maybe theirs is the clearer understanding that there is no real distinction between the hale and the frail, but only a moment's grace.

Gradually I began to see things differently than I had before. I noticed in a different way the pointlessness of the traditional male model of performance and autonomy at all costs. I came to feel that it was brutal to be content with a feminism that was compelled to fit into this traditionally masculine definition of accomplishment. True revolution, it slowly seemed clear to me, would come about only when we demanded that the world conform to our needs as women, and that it deal fairly with the fact that we are weakened as well as strengthened by childbirth. Society must restructure itself radically to support babies and new parents, too. Stopping short of that meant that no revolution deep enough had been achieved.

As a society we are a long way from the kind of fairness that can treat weakness in childbirth as a strength, so the vulnerabilities of pregnancy hit home in many ways.

As my pregnancy advanced, I felt a substance was being pumped into my blood that created an almost unquenchable thirst for love; not for more passion or excitement, but for more love in the primal way we experienced love as children: for the love of a parent tucking a child into bed. In short: love as safety and protection. I found the sophisticated adult appetite for new sensations, for ever more refined graduations of nuance and feeling, completely abated: and in its place I experienced this childlike surge of need for repetitive, utterly simple affirmations that I was – that we, the baby and I, were – not going to be abandoned.

When I was small, my mother, who could not cook in the ordinary sense of the word, would make peanut butter balls as a treat. Their greasy, powdery surfaces were indented with my mother's fingerprints; so to me, peanut butter, sugar and flour were the essential flavour of safety. I remember, as a five-year-old, lying on a big pillow, watching television comedies, eating these peanut butter treats, my blanket around me, ready to fall asleep in the familial nest.

I now found myself trying to re-create that nest. I became clingy and dependent in ways I thought I had decades before outgrown, along with other childhood preoccupations. I felt the way children with an earache feel when they reach their arms up to seize the necks of their parents.

My new sense of dependency – which I did not understand was in part the result of a temporary biochemical transformation of my very brain – was scary. Many of my tough-minded women friends voiced the same fears of dependency. '[P]regnancy can be a very needy time,' Louden states in *The Pregnant Woman's Comfort Book*, which had joined the books that I thought of as the 'annoying but reassuring pregnancy genre'. Among the needs the book lists are: 'the need for reassurance that my mate is going to stay with me during delivery and after the birth' and 'the need to know that my husband loves me and still finds me attractive'. Even as I became such a woman of many needs, I thought, 'How *pathetic*.'

Many of the new mothers I talked to began their account of becoming a mother with the words 'I always thought . . .' as in 'I always thought I would put the baby in a backpack and take it to the office two days after giving birth'; or 'I always thought I would rock the baby with my foot while pounding out the Great American Novel'; or 'I always thought I would just have a baby somehow at thirty whether or not I was in a stable relationship.'

Then they would go on to say, 'I never thought I'd be one of those women who, after having a baby . . .' and they would fill in 'became clingy in a relationship', 'gave up work', 'turned into my mother', 'couldn't shower for days', or simply 'unravelled'.

They would conclude, with wry humour and some wonder, 'And of course I became one of those women.'

One of Gloria Steinem's most famous aphorisms about the women of the second wave of feminism states: 'We are becoming the men our mothers wanted us to marry.' In contrast, I, along with other ambitious women of my generation, felt myself gradually becoming one of those women with whom I had always refused to identify.

My self-sufficiency and independence, two qualities I admired most in others, shut down in me like the lights of a business that had lost its clientele.

\*

I was not alone in this new willingness to yield where previously I would have held my ground. At a gathering in the Washington suburbs, the tension among several middle-class professional couples we knew grew palpable when the subject of what last name to give their baby came up. Each couple seemed to have its own necessary mythology: 'Well, you liked Anthrax much better than Smith, didn't you, darling?' said Mr Anthrax with serenity to his wife, Jane Smith. 'Yes, it was an aesthetic decision,' confirmed Jane Smith-Anthrax on cue, holding little Max Anthrax.

Many women told us that they had been surprised by how much more importance the father attached to the choice of surname for the baby than they did.

The men in these partnerships – these apparently pro-feminist, sensitive men – clamped down hard when the time came to decide whether the baby should take the father's surname or the mother's; or at the very least they snatched the olive branch when their wives tentatively offered to concede the matter. The temptation on the part of the women not to fight too hard about this was clearly strong. Giving the baby one's husband's last name alone is not a big deal for many women, I know, but I also knew well that, before their babies had been born, the naming issue had been a big deal to some of these women. I understood what they were conceding, and why – and even why they were rewriting their personal history to make the decision square with their own ideals after the fact.

Thomas Verny found that mothers cross-culturally tend to exaggerate to others their infant's resemblance to the fathers. And psychologists Martin Daly and Margo Wilson report that mothers in hospital delivery rooms regularly insist upon the new baby's resemblance to the father. It seemed to me that this kind of sub-conscious make-the-man-stay behaviour was exactly what my friends and I were engaging in. For was there not some slight anxiety beneath the surface of these dinner table conversations about the decision of what name to give the baby: a fear of carrying our insistence on our rights and belief in equality a shade too far for our babies' well-being? If our children do not have their father's name, if women don't inch slowly toward doing the bulk of the care-giving, if we make too big a deal out of our egalitarian dreams once the baby is born, can we be sure the family will survive? How else, other than pleasing your mate and signing over the identity of the family, can you ensure that you will have a male to help you raise the brood? With a baby, too much depends on stability – and on the father's presence – for that casual young-woman's testing of the limits we used to so enjoy. As new mothers and mothers-to-be, our feminism was undergoing a kind of triage; whatever was inessential got hauled overboard so as not to rock the fragile, all-important little boat of the new family.

It was fascinating to see a group of women who believe fervently in women's equality unconsciously revert to some of the basic tenets of a patriarchy they had all their lives rebelled against – for love.

I felt that pressure myself, on a primal level. I was still a feminist. But I understood, at this point in my life, that it could be dangerous to be one.

# Ninth Month
# Waiting

'Many [cross-cultural] practices are designed to coax the fetus out, based on the belief that the fetus itself determines the time of birth.'

Margarita Artschwanger, *Anthropology of Human Birth*

My night life was taken over by dreams. Each night was peopled with more vivid characters and wilder scenes than I had ever dreamed in my nonpregnant life. 'Pregnant mind' had a subconscious out of the Grand Guignol. Tiny babies appeared with the faces of little men, demanding care. Other dream-babies were lost or abandoned; a tiny baby had fallen behind the headboard or been forgotten in a locked car. They were dreams of overwhelming anxiety and strangeness.

Dreams seem to prepare the pregnant woman for motherhood. Researchers Sered and Abramovitch have shown that pregnant women's dreams are their own unique genre, preparing the mother for the vast responsibilities of parenthood. Many women would tell me that, while pregnant, they too dreamed about a tiny baby whom they had somehow inadvertently misplaced or harmed: 'One of the dreams I often had when I was pregnant,' Greta would tell me, 'was that my baby was a tiny creature who lived in a windup watch with a lid that closed. She was half an inch long. I could change her tiny diaper. One day in my dream I was rushing around doing too many things, and I accidentally closed the watch before she was in it all the way. I felt horrible guilt.'

My friend Sarah told me: 'I had dreams of neglecting the baby. I dreamed we spent a day taking care of errands and we forgot to feed her. A dream where we left her and went back and couldn't find her.'

'I had dreams,' Dianne told me, 'that the baby was in a trash can, and I could not find the trash can. Or I would dream that I was in a supermarket; I pushed the cart aside to run and get something, then came back and couldn't find the cart with her in it.'

Three weeks before my due date, my dreams became extreme. It was almost as if there were a doubled consciousness – the nearly due baby's and my own – and our signals were getting scrambled.

The minds of birthing women and new mothers are intensely focused, more so than usual. In a 1993 study of the short-term memory of women who had just given birth, it turned out that they had poorer memory in comparison to fathers and mothers of older children. (Midwives call this short-term vagueness 'placenta brain.') But, according to Israeli researcher Marcia Kaitz, in a new study, when the researchers asked new mothers to remember baby-related data, their memory improved. A new mother's memory was shown to be selectively skilful with baby-specific information. As one midwife put it, 'It's not stupidity, it is focus.'

Late one night, a crashing operatic lightning storm wreaked havoc in the urban forest behind our apartment. In the midst of a restless sleep – I couldn't lie on my back, was uncomfortable on my side, and felt shooting pains in my hips – my dreams were lit up like the lighting of a 1930s Frankenstein film.

The baby was crashing around inside me as well, a little navigator on turbulent seas. I'd never felt my baby so agitated. With each clap of thunder, the unknown being leapt within me as if flinging itself against my body, desperate to escape. Was it the noise? More likely, I felt in my unreasoning state, it was a reaction to the electro-magnetism, the galvanic quality in the air. Did the lightning's vital force, which filmmakers imagine shocked Mary Shelley's creature into life, trouble this little entity as well, travelling through air and flesh and interior waters?

I had three weeks left until my due date. I was looking forward to the end of my nausea, which had been severe for months. Otherwise, I felt myself shutting down in a kind of terror in the face of what lay ahead.

'How will I ever go through this again?' I asked my brother one day over the telephone.

'Nature will give you a kind of amnesia,' Aaron said. Of course, that was easy for him to say. Although he had been a soldier in a commando division in the Israeli army, and had experienced three-day marches in brutal conditions, what he saw when his wife, Ariela, went through labour, 'put us all to shame. Compared to that,' he said cheerily as my heart rate shot up, 'the IDF are weenies.'

The notion of a kind of natural amnesia in the aftermath of birth came up again and again, as if it were some kind of consolation. It made me wonder, Why are we engineered so poorly that the oblivion kicks in only after the pain and discomfort are over, rather than before? Is mother love a kind of cosmic PCP?

I had trouble thinking about what lay ahead – not only labour but new motherhood; I knew it was going to be momentous. I shakily turned on the 'new motherhood' video handed out in our birthing class. The slickly produced video about how to care for a newborn was narrated by women wearing yoke-collar dresses in bright solid colours, who seemed to be inhabitants of some wholesome American cult, 'Motherland'. The video was like The Stepford Wife Meets Julia Child. The 'mothers' – who were actually nurses, they explained – handled the babies expertly before the cameras exactly as someone on a cooking programme would demonstrate trussing a turkey. They cooed at the 'test babies' ('Hello, Handsome!') as they bathed and diapered them, wreathing themselves in euphemisms: 'If you've got a little boy, you'll want to drape a washcloth down here because accidents can and do happen!' They referred to all babies as 'he' and to all baby caretakers as 'Mom'. The women spoke of the importance of 'letting Father help' even if it means that Baby ends up 'wearing purple socks!'

Their tone, in everything from the correct position of the nipple for breast-feeding, to the treatment of the terrifying, charred-looking stump of the umbilicus that must be swabbed with alcohol every day, was that cloying, infantilizing sweetness that suffused most public discussions of pregnancy, childbirth, and new mothering. The women cooed in their ultrahigh voices at alarmed-looking infants, and at me.

Was this my future? Would I be reduced to sentences of five words, of one or two syllables, simply by dint of having given birth?

What was meant to reassure me made me afraid. The cutesy-pie, baby-love, spring-scented haven of maternity culture seemed insistently to cloak the strangeness of it all: the rodlike lactating nipple engorged with all the force of nature, jetting into the oscillating mouth: the broken-off umbilical stump ('I found it in the futon,' said Yasmin. 'It had come off during the night'); the small, needy infants themselves with their night-soaked eyes.

Nothing around me accounted for the profound un-cuteness of labour and delivery – the fact that pregnant women are not fluffy sheep or cosy cows in pastel-papered nurseries, but blood- and milk-stained avatars, out of all normal bounds.

There was nothing 'cute' about it.

The baby was so big that I could feel, through my very skin, a firm little buttock under my right rib. The line of the baby's back curved down along my right side; I could press into it all the way down. And the skull was lodged directly above my pubic bone, the eeriest feeling of all. When my fingers traced the roundness of that head, which felt something like an ostrich's egg, the baby jerked away, and I could feel it swimming in the tepid ocean that was the rest of me.

My baby was so big at that point that I was in almost ceaseless discomfort. I had a continual burning at the base of my œsophagus. Two new blue veins had etched themselves on the underside of my right leg, and when I stood after sitting for very long, the right leg dragged heavily because of the extra blood that pooled there. My heart sometimes pounded with the effort of pumping all the extra blood, which produced a sinking, swooning sensation.

In preparation for birth, my pelvic ligaments had loosened. This hurt, causing me to sleep badly. If you are able-bodied, you feel a kind of bodily integrity that you assume will last until your final dissolution. But with this loosening of my joints, I felt a weird, disquieting sense of becoming prematurely undone, like a mandolin whose strings have loosened just before a big concert. My body, which I had always felt to be synonymous with life, was, I discovered, in fact provisional and could be done up and undone like a temperamental instrument.

My weight, too, made me feel freighted with gravity in a new way. Twenty, thirty, forty pounds: I felt there was no limit to what I would end up carrying around. As I made my way through the world, a leviathan in a faded black jumpsuit, which was all I could fit into at that point, I felt the weight of the world bear down on me in an intolerable new way. When I tried to lie on my back, the baby pinned me, crowding my lungs, like a heavy little sumo wrestler inside my very skin. It felt as if it would take a crane to lift me.

When the phone rang, I'd flail, hands and feet waving, then roll over to lumber through the house at the pace of a small pachyderm, guarding my stomach around the edges of bookcases, muttering to the caller, who I feared would hang up, 'Damn it, give me a chance.'

I had good days, when I was filled with peace and a kind of quiet excitement. I almost understood – briefly – when women who had already had babies said, 'Try to remember it forever. At the time you feel like a blob. But looking back, you – and the whole thing – are so amazing and beautiful.'

But I also started noticing how much hostility underlay the joking of couples with new babies. One couple called their newborn 'vampire girl'. Another, both of whom are foreign correspondents, called theirs 'Hamas'.

I recalled a story some friends told us about their delivery. The wife had just given birth to a little boy, who had been given a Croatian name, Ivo, to honour his father's heritage. The woman had laboured for over a day, with little help from the staff of the hospital. She was exhausted ('I just wanted to die,' she told me later. 'I kept saying, God, just take me now.') Long after the labouring woman had been calling her, a nurse finally walked in.

'What are you going to name him?' she asked brightly.

'Ivo,' said the exhausted woman.

'*Evil?*' shrieked the nurse.

'No,' the furious, drug-disinhibited mother said, rolling over away from the staffer who had been nowhere in sight when the mother-to-be had wanted her support. 'We're going to name him *Satan*.'

With a week to go, my fear over the impending birth was acute. It intensified at watching Yasmin sit on her dark green couch day after day after day, feeding Amos each hour and a half. The image that I was about to become someone's addiction, a cow to be trotted out of the stable, a lifeline, an oxygen tank, grew in me. 'Once nursing begins, bondage is a perfectly good description for the ensuing chain of events . . . From that point on, a mother (especially one without a breast pump) lies on a mammary leash,' writes Sarah Blaffer Hrdy, anthropologist and mother. I had turned down chances to travel for work that I would have leapt at before, and a sense of claustrophobia arose in me as I began to realize just what my decision to nurse would mean. Because I wanted to be able to travel sometimes, I asked Yasmin questions about breast pumping and milk storage. But my fear of what pumping might do to my state of mind was as intense as my concerns about the fact that nursing would mean I would be unable to leave the baby for longer than a three- or four-hour stretch. Would I have the patience to pump, which can take 40 minutes, breast by breast? I was also aware of a resentful desire to protect my breasts. A pregravid woman's breasts are treated like Fabergé eggs; suddenly, with the birth of a baby, they are flannel-covered hot-water bottles.

Two weeks after the baby's due date, my husband was scheduled to start a new job. I wondered what would become of my own mind. Would I lose my faculties, sitting on our couch all day, nursing or pumping, staring at its khaki-coloured velvet? I feared I would be chained forever to our bilious green couch, sucked on all day by a hungry newborn, like Prometheus chained to a rock.

Alternating with this sense of dread was a calm that was equally deep. I would lie in bed, on my side, with my hands on the baby, and feel drawn into a field of unbearable sweetness. It was like a magnetic field that one can scarcely resist. Without my being able to see her or speak to her, while she was still so weirdly inside my skin, the baby was somehow pulling me into an inexorable relationship to her, like someone, over the steady pressure of months, and with no chance of taking 'no' for an answer, insisting politely, unswervingly, that we must fall in love.

Yasmin, my Exhibit A, was good-humoured about my anxious need to see how she was doing and to see what the baby meant in her life. 'Step up to the bar,' said Yasmin to her son, who indeed had a Damon Runyonesque quality, as she invited him to nurse. And he did, just like a little man leaning against a counter, lining them up.

'There are days,' said Yasmin, after I confided my terror to her, on a day when terror was on the agenda, 'when, after I finally get up and move around, I see that I've made a completely flat place in the foam of the sofa cushions.'

'How are you holding up?' I asked.

'I'm tired,' she said, and exhaustion slipped over her face, a shadow. But then she stretched out one little baby leg in its purple stretch-terry jumper, and then the other, and gazed into her baby's lolling, brown, milk-drunk face with delight.

'Fatty!' she exclaimed. 'Look at the fatty.'

And I wondered: What *is* that love?

The baby now began to *whomp* inside me like someone cleaning out a closet before a move. When I walked, there were stabbing pains in strange new places where I had never felt sensation before. I felt the baby could come at any moment, but also that the baby would never come, that I would be pregnant forever. All I wanted to do was hold still until it happened.

*Part II*
Birth

# Giving Birth

'To give birth a woman needs to release a certain cocktail of hormones . . . the crucial thing is to realize they all originate in the same gland – the brain.'

Michel Odent, *The Scientification of Love*

When I finally gave birth, nothing happened the way I had imagined.

Having arrived at the beautiful, oddly empty Alternative Birthing Center, determined to be brave, I was checked in by an irritable young nurse. It was three in the morning. She sent me away from the comfort of my husband and the big warm delivery bed, alone into a sterile bathroom, telling me, somewhat angrily, to close the bathroom door for what nurses call 'nipple stim', to encourage stronger contractions.

Already in pain, I did what she requested, which only made the pains stronger; but the loneliness and strangeness of being exiled into the bathroom for this activity, which seemed to annoy and embarrass her, made the pain literally unendurable.

Was she mad at me because I wasn't dilated enough?

I thought at the time that the nurse felt that what she'd asked me to do was so shameful that I had to do it alone, as if it were a sexual aberration or a form of incontinence so mortifying as to require isolation, rather than a routine midwifery technique that helps women dilate. My mixed feelings of isolation, embarrassment, and sensitivity to *her* embarrassment made me somehow seize up.

When she checked me again, she was unsatisfied. I had not dilated enough, and the baby's heartbeat – which she listened to for a moment – was, she said, irregular. With an efficiency that seemed positively startling, she rushed me down to the terrifying delivery rooms I had so hoped to avoid, because, she said, the baby was in distress.

Once in the delivery room, the seemingly inevitable high-tech intervention took place. What might have been normal birth became an emergency. I was hooked up to a fetal monitor. (I would learn only later that I could have requested telemetry, a monitor that still lets the woman in labour move around.) The monitor kept me flat on my side and immobilized.

I was told by my entire team that, given my present 'inadequate' degree of dilation, and given that my waters had broken, they wanted to give me Pitocin, in a drip, to increase dilation. (I would learn only later that several influential studies show it can be safe to allow women longer labour after membranes rupture.) But since the Pitocin would make for stronger contractions, they advised me that, in their opinion, the pain would be too intense to bear. They wanted to give me an epidural.

I had now been flat on my side, scared, for an hour or so, without 'making progress', as they put it. (They kept saying the words, 'no progress', or 'failure to progress', and 'fetal distress', a terrifying combination. No medical staffer that I can remember said, 'You can do this.' I learned later the powerful physical effect words can have on labouring women.) I was also starting to feel uncertain about my abilities to labour well, and of course we were worried about the baby. I hadn't been given a chance to dilate naturally, to acclimatize to the pain gradually. The stronger contractions from the 'Pit drip' made me feel as if someone were plunging a sword into the ganglia of my spine. I readily accepted the epidural.

My husband was forbidden to hold me, yet the anesthetist warned me that if I flinched while the needle was going in I could be paralysed. He then bent me over and placed a six-inch needle in a part of my spine. It felt extraordinarily wrong and invasive. Holding still under those circumstances was terrifying.

I was given an IV drip and became a prisoner of the delivery bed. Once the epidural entered my system, I could not feel my legs. There was no longer any question of my walking around to encourage dilation or use gravity.

The fetal monitor, which was strapped around my belly, became the centre of activity in the birthing room. My well-meaning mid-wives were primarily focused on monitoring the continual readout from the machine at my side. The baby and I seemed less real in that room than the machine. At that point the birthing process was so technologized that the notion that 'I' was there to give 'birth' seemed like sort of a virtual aside.

I had imagined a team of birth supporters rooting for me. Instead of such hands-on support, I followed my midwives watching the printout as if I were a commodity on the New York Stock Exchange.

In my delivery, I was an adjunct; I had almost no role. There was nothing I could do to contribute to the birthing process if I wanted to, which I badly did before the epidural essentially neutered my faculties and will. From what we had been told about the monitor's reading, my husband and I understood that the baby's life was at stake. No parent would risk the health of his or her child by questioning the procedures the medical establishment had decreed were necessary. I did not dare risk doing anything other than what the doctors and nurses told us I must do. I lay passively on the birthing bed, letting them tie and tether me down, and anesthetize me.

I still could not feel my legs.

I was told I would have 24 hours to deliver before they would have to perform surgery. That sword over my head, and the ticking clock, marking the moment my doctors would decide to wield it, filled me with fear. The technology, the medical staff, and the social shame that swirled around me continued, threateningly, to keep me from using my body in a way that could support the birth.

My labour 'arrested' completely.

What was left of me as a physical presence felt like a trapped, cornered animal. I did not know then that mammals' systems shut down in labour when they sense danger: cats go away to a safe, dark place to give birth; horses and cattle seize up in labour when stress or danger is present. We women are mammals, too. I did not yet understand how this happened: yet that is what I experienced when they issued me the deadline.

I did not feel safe in the hospital. I did not feel safe. In spite of my best intentions, I could not labour.

*

*After twenty-four hours, I am wheeled into the surgery room. I am anesthetized and strapped down as if on a crucifix. My husband is seated at my head.*

*As the surgeon makes his incision, I say, 'I can feel you lifting my skin up.'*

*There is a rustle of panic in the room, but no one speaks to me.*

*I feel a violent but numb tugging, like someone ripping soft dough. I start to retch. Someone holds a plastic bowl to my mouth.*

*There is a cry. I do not recognize it.*

*'That's your baby! Do you hear that?' Dr Yemeni says heartily. The tension in the room has suddenly broken. In its place there is relief and celebration among the staff crowded together near my head. Everyone has finished his or her job except me. I want only to be closed up again and rescued from this cold, bone-hard place.*

*I begin to shiver. The shivering turns into a rattly, rhythmic quaking. 'I'm so cold,' I say. 'I'm freezing to death.'*

*Why does no one warm me? Or cover me? Why aren't they moving to turn up the heat in the room? My teeth chatter so loudly I can hardly speak. I start to vomit.*

*'Can you stop that?' says the surgeon, irritable or alarmed, I can't tell which. 'I need to get this small intestine back in.'*

*I believe I am dying.*

*'Here she is, a gorgeous baby girl,' calls someone, caught up in festivities far away. My husband turns in joy while my body remains half-submerged in cold, like the cold of a newly turned grave. Far away, I see his face light up.*

*Into my field of vision come a pair of green-sleeved arms. Held up in them, her head high, is a small creature out of a dream. I see my daughter in profile, and she is regal as she passes me by: her eyes are huge and luminous, her nose too aquiline to be a baby's. There is a golden sheen on her skin, and, as she is handed from the doctors to my husband, she seems to be surrounded by a bubble of a lighter, more vibrant air than the air we breathe here.*

*She looks with huge attention at everything, perfectly calm.*

*'Her eyes are wide open,' says my husband. He takes her in his arms and brings her down to show to me, but I am frightened. With my abdomen still split open, I want only not to die. I thought we were going to have a baby: this queenlike, glowing creature is unlike anyone or anything I've ever seen.*

*Things move quickly. The drugs in my system seem to go bad. Fear spills over from the IV into my head. All the tension and uncertainty of the last nine months swirl inside me, a drugged panic. With all this danger around us and all the unknowns we've lived through, it cannot be that she is all right.*

*I begin to toss and shout, just as my mother, in her own drugged state, had done when she delivered me. 'Is she all right?' I ask. 'Is she okay?'*

*'She's perfect,' my husband says. 'Everything's perfect.'*

*My daughter's head is perfectly conical, elongated like the skulls of aristocrats in Egyptian hieroglyphics. 'Her head,' I cry again. 'Have we hurt her?'*

*'No. No. That's normal. Her skull bones have moulded as she tried to crown through the birth canal.'*

*'Did that squeeze her brain?' I am beginning to understand that the medical staff in the room think I am delirious.*

*'No, No. Please listen. She's fine.' Nothing consoles me, and the drugs urge me into a chant of anxiety. 'Please, ask Brenda if she's okay. Is Brenda here? Ask Marcia if she's okay. Ask Dr Yemeni if she's okay. Ask the anesthetist —' The chemical paranoia convinces me that I have to do a survey of them all, that I cannot believe any one of them.*

*'Hush, hush, relax. Now the doctor is closing you up. Look,' says Marcia. 'Her Apgar is eight – that's wonderful. It will be better yet when her hands and feet pink up.'*

*I subside. Whoever designed the room and its procedures did not know or did not care that I can see beyond the curtain that screens my face from my body. I can see, in the reflection of the operating scene that appears in the glass-fronted doors opposite my face, what they are doing. I look past the loving presence at my head, past the thin scrim blocking my gaze at chest level, and into the glass behind everyone, and I see what is real, what I am not meant to see.*

*Seven men and women, in plastic goggles and pale green cotton suits, are working. Their gloves are bathed up to the elbow, and their busy instruments are messy, with streaks of bright red. The locus of their full attention is down where my stomach should be. No one notices that I see what their hands are dipped in: my centre, an open cauldron of blood.*

Drugged and pinned, that is what I remember of the birth.

The first night, I lay alone in my recovery room, sick and dizzy, feeling as if I were still underwater. My daughter was brought to me, and I was afraid: the drugs were still rollicking through my system. (Studies in 2000 and 2001 have found that drugs given in analgesia can delay your bonding with the baby, and the baby's successful nursing.) The morphine you may be given following a Caesarean can delay bonding further and can inhibit behaviour your body is otherwise primed to perform – to nuzzle and stroke the baby – counteracting the oxytocin that promotes bonding. Biochemically, this tiny being was the spark ready to ignite my love and initiate our bonding; yet the drugs and surgery had turned me, biochemically, into damp wood.

When, I wondered woozily, as the tiny child was laid upon my breast, will her mother come for her?

By the second night, I felt humiliation at having to lie for so long, so painfully, in a pool of body fluids, changed irregularly by resentful, overworked nurses. My humiliation was underscored by the fact that people down the hall seemed to have been partying all night; on the other hand, with the drugs I was on, I could not tell how much of that was real and how much was hallucination.

Nurses wheeled my daughter into the room in a clear plastic box. No longer was she a mysterious queen, but the tiniest, most naked human imaginable. They put her on my stomach. A knitted skullcap covered her head to keep her warm. She arched her head back to look, not at me, but at the light.

As I looked at her, my drugged-out emotions distant and uncertain, she began her preordained journey and, hand after tiny foot, crawled up my chest, just as in my dream. By the time she had found my breast, and clung to me like a shipwrecked traveller, I was entirely hers. Though I did not yet recognize that she was mine, neither did I want anyone ever, ever, to take her away.

Several days later we took our baby home. The first week home with her, my mood began to crash. My husband was in love. For what seemed like hours he could sing to her.

She and I had come further together, yet we were shyer.

It occurred to me that I would never be alone with my husband again in the same way we had been before.

My breasts hurt. My scars hurt. Exhaustion set in, and panic at 3 a.m. My post-operative fatigue was too great to permit me to walk a block easily; the nursing drained me.

And yet. The faces she made, in the midst of all this discomfort, were like a new medium we'd discovered. There was her samurai face; her Edith Sitwell face; her Yitzhak Shamir face: her Grand Vizier disdaining a delicacy face; her St Theresa face; her trickster plotting mischief face.

She seemed always to be looking at, or listening to, something else, something other – light and bells – with her little bow-mouth open.

We had entered a new place in the world: the land of parents. Every other routine encounter turned into something startling to us: some stranger, upon learning we had a new baby, would share his furious love of his children. It was, we realized, like being part of a secret cult. A shocking gentleness engulfed us where we least expected it.

A tough-looking Irish manager in our local grocery store suddenly remarked that we should enjoy every minute. His 'little girl' is twelve, he said. With cardboard boxes piled up behind him, and his tattooed co-workers within earshot, he added,

'They say that when they smile in their sleep, the angels are playing with them.'

As we travelled home in a taxi with some new baby supplies, our reserved-looking Nigerian cabdriver suddenly remarked, out of the blue, as if it were his best summary of the true secret of life, 'Yes. Oh yes. You *love* your children.'

# Behind the Birthing Room

'Nurse-midwives who are aware of the difference between hospital midwifery and the real thing call their profession "cattle-barn obstetrics". The more we go into a for-profit system, we're shortening allowable labour to as short as eight hours. We're drugging women to accelerate labour, then banging out babies, but we're not looking to see how they do.'

Ina May Gaskin

I thought my story was unique. I found that was not true. I heard comparable ordinary traumas among many women I talked to – what I have come to call 'ordinary bad births'.

Dianne, a gregarious woman with an air of competence and an easy laugh, was born in Tacoma, Washington, in a middle-class household. She worked for the government. A year after getting married, Dianne and her husband decided to start a family.

'It was an easy pregnancy. But I had problems with the medical practice I was in.

'The monthly appointments were very important to me. I needed affirmation: that everything was going as it should, that I was doing a good job. Nonetheless, I felt treated like a number by the doctors in the practice. I felt I had to write all my questions down, since God forbid I should take up a minute too much of their time.

'I was overdue a couple of days and very anxious. They suggested that I induce. They broke my water.

'The delivery was what I expected. The hospital makes a big effort to demystify what is about to happen. But nothing really prepares you for the actual experience.

'I felt really uncomfortable, and had a lot of pressure and pain. I had an epidural. During the epidural, doctors were chatting about a baseball game, nurses about "Renee's birthday".

'The baby was not coming out unless I pushed the life of God out of me. My doctor doesn't let a patient push for more than two hours, or she has to get a C-section. I said, "I can do it." He cut off the epidural. After the epidural cut off, I realized the level of pain I was in. It was mostly pressure, a splitting sensation. I thought, "I can handle this." It's the mystery of what the pain is going to be like that is intimidating. Lucy was very big. I pushed for two-and-a-half hours. As smart as I am, I didn't really get until it was actually happening that I would have to push her out!

'Finally, it was a forceps delivery. The doctor could see her head. She was right there, but he could not reach her with his hands. One big push and he got her out.

'From that moment forward, there was a problem. They took her away for the Apgar. She had a high fever, I had a high fever. They were worried. I saw her for a second: "It's a girl," they said, and then vanished with her. I saw people's backs. Thirty minutes went by before I even touched the baby.

'I couldn't move. I was lying there and felt I had no control at all. Once they determine the baby has a fever, a standardized medical procedure takes over that you have no say in. They gave her IV antibiotics, a spinal tap, without asking me. I was freaking out.

'I couldn't even see her. I had just given birth to her and they would not let me touch her. I begged for a room where we could be together and I could touch her, hold her. The hospital insisted on separating us. Even after her fever had gone down, the hospital insisted that the baby had to stay because it takes seventy-two hours for the lab results to come back. But they don't let you near your baby.

'So I was put in a space like a bus station, with four other women. My baby was on another floor in an incubator. I had to nurse the baby alone because they make the husbands leave after ten. They kicked me out of the hospital after thirty hours.

'When I asked my doctor, "Can I stay here with the baby?" he said, "It's not a hotel."

'I slept alone in the lounge for three days in a folding chair that smelled. My husband was back at work.

'I have never felt so alone or out of control. Meanwhile she was in the incubator, because of the hospital protocol, hooked up to an open IV for three days, though she had no fever. I didn't even know when she was crying.

'Not only was my doctor not an advocate for me, he was totally irrelevant when it came to trying to stand up against the hospital's protocol. I am not a shrinking violet, but I felt I had absolutely no idea how to speak up effectively to change anything.

'Nothing happened according to what we had wanted or planned. And we had absolutely no say; the institution just took over.'

Despite what I'd heard to the contrary, some experiences in Britain were no better. Teresa, a woman in her early thirties who worked in the media, told me about her delivery in a British NHS hospital.

'My pregnancy seemed to be going very well, but unfortunately at around week twenty, the scan showed that my placenta was too low (so called placenta previa). Apparently, in around seventy per cent of cases the womb stretches and the placenta somehow finds itself in the right position. If it fails to move up the consequences can be quite serious; the baby and the placenta compete for space during delivery and if the placenta is delivered first the baby is starved of oxygen.

'The next scan, at around week thirty, showed that the placenta was still too low, but only mildly so. I felt well, was working and going on tours with authors and generally looked forward to having the baby. The next scan was meant to be decisive. So when I got to week thirty-five or thirty-six, and the scan showed no change I was summoned to see the consultant, who swiftly announced that I should come to the hospital the following Monday, stay on the ward for two weeks, when I would be given a Caesarean.

'All my attempts to ask for more information, some statistics on placenta previa and delivery were met with the man looking at me in a benign and patronizing way and saying, "You wouldn't want to jeopardize the baby's life, would you?" My argument about work was dismissed by "You should be resting now anyway, and preparing yourself for the arrival of your baby." It never occurred to him that my family might need my – a *woman's* – salary. Suddenly I was scheduled to come to the hospital with my bag full of baby things on Monday and stay on a communal ward for three weeks. Then I would have a Caesarean.

'The next few days were pretty frantic – trying to finish everything at work, buying a pram, etc., and trying to get more information about the real risks. I had a very sympathetic midwife who put me in touch with an organization called AIMS (Association for Improvements in the Maternity Services), and they gave me the information I needed. They told me that if I started bleeding and was within a sensible distance to the hospital, there was no need for me to lie in bed and be in the hospital at all. If anything, the stress and anxiety would be a contributory factor in things going wrong. One midwife told me that my consultant was the most conservative one in the hospital, and the most likely to do interventions, and that the other consultants wouldn't have made me stay there. I looked at a few more research papers on the Internet, spoke to more midwives and arrived at the hospital on Monday, without my bag, but armed with more information.

'When I announced to the hospital that I had decided not to come to the hospital, he stopped speaking to me, clearly astonished that his opinion could be questioned by a patient. (I was in his eyes, by now, a hysterical woman.) He started shouting at my husband about the great threat to the baby and told us he refused to look after me. We had a long list of questions prepared. I tried to be calm and assertive, but there was no point at which he listened to what we were saying. We left feeling really angry and confused. But I decided to take the risk. My midwife supported my decision, as did the women from AIMS, so I stayed at home. And guess what . . . Three weeks later, in my next scan, it turned out that the placenta had moved and the baby's head was low enough to have a safe normal delivery. And I did. I always felt very angry about the way I was treated . . .'

Amanda, a soft-spoken woman from a working-class suburban American upbringing, who held her baby as she narrated her tale, with great tenderness, told me another story of 'ordinary crisis'.

'At thirty-two I got pregnant. Pregnancy was really easy. I wanted to give birth to my baby vaginally,' Amanda said. 'She was breech. They did external version – that is, they tried to turn the baby into the correct position by manipulating her with hands on my belly. As a result of the external version, the baby moved from being butt-down, to being feet-down. A midwife there told me, "I could deliver your baby vaginally, I know how to – but it's illegal."

'I was terrified of having a Caesarean-section. I had never had surgery before. I was naked from the waist down, shaved, there was iodine solution on me. I had no idea I would be splayed or spread-eagled on my side. The IV hose was in my nose.

'They brought in Bernie. I was scared because I knew the procedure was about to happen.

'The doctor was supportive to Bernie: "If you'd like to look, now is a good time," the doctor told him. Bernie says it was the most surreal experience of his life – a neat slit in an abdomen with the bottom half of the baby sticking out.

'I heard things: the suctioning, the crying. Then suddenly the doctor said: "Who's the one with the cleft chin? Who has red hair?"

'Afterward, it took an hour for them to sew me up.

'There is not enough support for women having Caesarean-sections. The practice I was in tried hard to support me. But right up until the birth, I never felt reconciled.'

These are three random stories: one mother separated from her baby because of hospital protocols that have to do with medicine but also with litigation and real estate; another treated with contempt by a consultant because she dared to defy a member of the medical profession; and a third with a Caesarean because doctors today are no longer taught the hands-on skills that obstetricians in the recent past possessed, and independent midwives still possess, as a matter of course. But these 'ordinary bad births' have much at work behind the scenes that the new mothers cannot be aware of.

When something doesn't make sense, when what someone is being told just doesn't jibe with what he or she experiences, it is psychologically 'crazy-making'. A number of women who had given birth described a moment at which they felt the medical institution simply took over, oblivious to the mother's wishes, experience, or concerns; many new mothers dissociated from their birth experience because it was so distressing.

This is not surprising, given the realities of hospital birth in many countries today. From preparing women inadequately to manage the physical pain of birth, and advising them poorly about the cavalcade of interventions that not uncommonly turn an ordinary birth into something like an emergency, to failing to warn a woman going home with a new baby, and possibly the after-effects of a

Caesarean to cope with, that the stress of child care and recovery is almost a recipe for postpartum depression – much of the typical birth experience *is* crazy-making. Yet if women are surprised to experience more difficulty than they were prepared for, it is because they are given the wrong expectations.

## TWO DOORS

When women start on the journey toward childbirth, most can see only two totally distinct doors available to them: the 'conventional' door and the 'natural' door.

The first could be described as the modern, high-tech hospital delivery. I call medical personnel who ascribe to such care 'the technicians'. The technicians are the administrators and doctors who run the hospitals and the OB-GYN practices and often employ the certified nurse-midwives. Critics argue that for the technicians, birth is not a natural, healthy process, but a medical problem to be solved, and the high-tech medical intervention they offer is seen as the best solution. It is the technicians who determine the care of the vast majority of women who give birth in hospitals.

There is in America only a small movement of birth professionals who have a far different and less interventionist approach to birth from that of the technicians – one that is medically more successful. These are the midwives, who in Australia, the United Kingdom – and many other European countries – participate in a *major* role in most hospital deliveries, as well as offering support to the mother before and after birth. Midwives not only bring to bear time-tested knowledge about successful birthing practices, but in virtually every aspect of labour, their approach is medically less intrusive, far more supportive of the women giving birth, and, under the right circumstances, safer. In Britain the midwife's crucial role was enshrined in a 1993 government report, 'Changing Childbirth'.

Nonetheless, in America, midwives, with their treasure trove of experience and strong record of experienced outcomes, have little power to influence what happens to delivering mothers in hospitals, officiating at only 10 per cent of hospital births – and even then only in a subordinate role, although women's interest in their methods and services is growing apace. (Lay midwives, who operate outside the medical system, attend only 1 per cent to 2 per cent of births.) Unlike their British counterparts in UK hospitals – who are answerable only to more senior midwives, and are duty-bound to challenge an obstetrician when they think he is wrong – in America, certified nurse-midwives must yield to the judgement of obstetricians and hospital boards. The only ones who can genuinely offer the best of both worlds – midwifery pacing and support with high-tech backup – are the tiny fraction of nurse-midwives who serve in freestanding birth centres aligned with hospitals.

Midwifery is a millennia-old tradition; indeed, the role of today's 'obstetrician' is only about two to three centuries old. Until the nineteenth century midwives used to deliver virtually all babies. Then male physicians aggressively began to take over this lucrative and respected role, as they sought to standardize delivery and medical interventions. They thus relegated midwives to the margins of society, where they were left to attend women of colour, immigrants, and the poor.

Midwives today passionately believe that birth has become too pathologized, and that obstetricians justify a high degree of medical interventions in part because they see almost all circumstances of birth as pathological. Midwives object to classifying all births as 'low risk' or 'high risk', for example – a categorizing system that does little to help women, no matter how healthy, think of birth as 'part of their wellness cycle', as midwives like to say, and something that they can manage with confidence. Midwives argue that birth is best treated as a normal and healthy process – that women, as a rule, are capable of giving birth without undue intervention. Many midwives believe that the way doctors have medicalized normal births leaves women less able to call up the confidence and courage they need to get themselves through birth without drastic intervention.

The ways the American medical establishment has limited what midwives are allowed to do has dampened their effectiveness in many ways. Unless they have been properly trained under strict guidelines they are allowed to perform only vaginal deliveries. Many licensed midwives lack rights as basic as the right to admit patients to the hospitals where they work. In Holland and Denmark, in contrast, midwives operate independently of medical institutions. One in three children in these countries is born at home, under a midwife's care. Yet these nations have the highest percentage of normal childbirths and the lowest percentages of infant and maternal deaths of all the industrialized countries. High-tech, doctor-assisted delivery in America, in contrast, ranks, depending on the study consulted, from ninth to *eighteenth* among these same nations in terms of outcome for mother and baby.

Midwives working on their own terms do not try to guide births along a path determined by unnecessary medical interventions. Rather, they wait, encourage, and prepare the way, successfully keeping medical intervention to a minimum.

How did we develop this expectation that ordinary deliveries routinely require high-tech medical assistance? Some critics argue that once male doctors ousted the traditional female midwife from the centre of the birth experience, they had to offer something that midwives did not to justify the higher fees they charged; and they had to look busy. Midwives assisted pregnant women to give birth by waiting for nature to take its course; high-paid male doctors saw the time in the birthing room differently.

'The doctor could not appear to be indifferent or inattentive or useless. He had to establish his identity by doing something . . .', as one history of childbirth, *Lying-In*, puts it. As a result, over time childbirth became defined as a series of interventions that involved routine anesthesia, early forceps delivery, continuous fetal monitoring, frequent Caesarean-sections, routine episiotomies, and time pressure overall. These interventions proliferated as the technology advanced, not because childbirth ordinarily demanded them medically, but, rather, because they justified the medical institutions that increasingly sprang up around them.

So the interventions begot interventions. As *Lying-In* describes the cascade effect, 'Anesthesia was counteracted by [administering] oxytocin; episiotomy required local anesthesia; forceps required anesthesia and episiotomy; the lithotomy position required episiotomy . . .'

Thus, our modern birth experience was born.

Machine birth accelerated with the machine age. Before 1920, episiotomies – cutting the perineum to ease the baby's passage out of the birth canal – and forceps deliveries were rare. After that era, doctors believed that 'Routine interventions should be made during every labour and delivery in order to prevent trouble.'

As the twentieth century advanced, doctors had practical as well as medical reasons for insisting on hospital birth and interventions. One was convenience – for doctors. The most important thing midwives do, besides simply waiting empathically for the baby, is to care for, support and encourage the birthing woman – a practice that is enormously effective medically. But this activity was increasingly seen as boring, labour-intensive 'women's work' as the male-dominated obstetrical profession developed. Highly paid male doctors did not see this arduous, low-yield emotional work as being their professional responsibility.

This new way of approaching birth set the stage for how birth practices developed in many developed countries. The obstetrical culture trains doctors not to wait and nurture, but rather to act. Each of the landmarks of intervention – even the culture of the typical hospital birthing room – has a profound downside that is rarely revealed to the couple involved. These interventions create a domino effect that can actually increase the odds of medical complications and result in the less than fulfilling, even soulless birth experiences that so many women I heard from described.

What are the typical misconceptions women encounter on the birth journey? Let's look at them one by one:

### The Hospital Approach is the Safest Way to Assist Women in Childbirth

Women are told that hospital is the safest place to give birth and that the way in which hospitals deliver their babies is the safest way. That is profoundly untrue. *What to Expect When You're Expecting* warns strongly about the dangers of home births and does not support back-up independent midwifery as a reasonable option, though it concedes: '*sometimes* [italics mine] such a birth is very successful'. In his book, *Pursuing the Birth Machine*, Dr Marsden Wagner, consultant to the World Health Organisation (WHO), states that the United States, where the majority of women give birth in a high-tech hospital setting, is twenty-first in the world in terms of infant survival.

In contrast, he asserts that the Northern European countries that rely on midwifery and home births actually have the *best* rates for infant survival. In the United Kingdom, it is every woman's right to have a home birth if she so wishes, and organizations such as AIMS (Association for Improvements in the Maternity Services) and the National Childbirth Trust (NCT) are there to support women in this position who have doctors that are unsympathetic to their wishes. At 3 to 4 per cent, the home birth rate is still low, but since this represents a rise of 1 to 2 per cent, there are signs that it is slowly but steadily rising.

Research carried out in the UK by Marjorie Tew and published in the *Journal of the Royal College of General Practitioners* found that home birth was, in general, safer than hospital births, in terms of outcome for mother and baby, and in the United States, where home birth is also uncommon, there have been similar findings. In a 1994 study reported in *Birth* magazine, researchers compared outcomes of births attended out of hospital by licensed midwives in Washington State to those aided by nurse-midwives out of hospital. The authors concluded that the practice of licensed midwives at home is as safe as that of physicians in hospital.

It is important to know about the safety of home births because this knowledge can give us the confidence to question routine interventions in the hospital, which are often presented as a hospital's inescapable standard of care.

There is, even in America, an alternative to the extremes of home birth or high-tech hospital that is safe, but relatively unknown: free-standing birth centres – homelike facilities with a programme of care designed in the 'wellness' model of pregnancy and birth. (This alternative intrigued Jessica Mitford over a decade ago.) The safety of birth centres has been well documented. The *New England Journal of Medicine* published results of the landmark National Birth Center Study. Researchers for this studied 11,814 women who used 84 different free-standing birth centres across America. The study concluded that outcomes for infants born in birth centres were as good as that for similar groups of infants born in hospitals. But with one difference: the Caesarean rate for low-risk women in hospitals was almost twice as high. Studies increasingly show that hospitals are good at providing high-tech care to high-risk patients. But they are also good at seeing every woman as a 'high-risk' patient, and proceeding accordingly.

One factor that should encourage us to challenge birthing myths is the prevalence of hospitals' under-reporting of poor outcomes data that have, according to experts, 'been plagued with uncertainties'. Sydney Wolfe, in a presentation given to the US Public Citizen Health Research Group in 1996, asserted that the 'evidence indicates that there is substantial under-reporting' of mother and baby deaths in hospitals. Wolfe noted that two factors in the data suggest a pattern of under-reporting by hospitals: the difference between projected patient deaths and reported patient deaths was inexplicably wide, and there was a variation of occurrence from state to state that was suspiciously broad.

American hospitals appear to have a pattern of under-reporting the deaths of non-white babies, whose mortality rates are higher than those of white babies. Researchers D.O. Farley and T. Richards found that hospital-reported infant mortality rates based on death certificates underestimated infant mortality especially for babies of colour. As Public Health Reports in 1997 put it, 'obstetrical care in the United States is burdened by soaring costs and the inability to bring rates of infant mortality in line with those of other developed countries . . . a greater reliance on the use of certified nurse-midwives could help solve these problems.'

In other words, we are on medically safe ground to challenge the standard practices, and call for reform of the disclosure methods, of obstetrics practiced within hospital settings.

*You Will Be Hooked Up to a Fetal Monitor, Which Will Help Protect Your Baby*
*What to Expect When You're Expecting* offers this supportive endorsement of monitors: 'It is because there is an element of risk in this successful journey [through the birth canal] – not to promote fetal discomfort or unnecessary cesareans – that fetal monitors have come into such common use.'

Electronic fetal monitors (EFMs) were first promoted intensively at OB-GYN conferences and marketed to hospitals, not only in the US but also in the UK and elsewhere, in the 1970s. Within a decade, every labour room in America had one, as did many maternity units in the UK. Yet they have *never been proven to be definitely effective*, even though every American woman I interviewed had been strapped to a monitor continuously during her birth experience. In *What to Expect When You're Expecting*, the authors soothingly write, 'A fetal monitor gauges the response of the baby's heartbeat to the contractions of the uterus . . . (t)he monitor is able to accurately signal the beginning and end of each contraction.' What a powerful image, a machine hooked up directly to your tiny baby's heart to signal any 'distress'. However, the monitor gauges many stimuli, making the readout not a scientific summary of data but an ambiguous image subject to interpretation. Several studies, in fact, have proved that external monitoring is *inaccurate* up to 40–60 per cent of the time.

The latest research shows that continuous fetal monitoring provides no benefit: 'The results of fetal monitor studies done over the past two decades are now clear: electronic fetal monitoring has no significant value when used on normal, healthy women. It also has no significant value when used on women who are considered "at high risk" for developing problems in birth.' Four rigorous studies, conducted to evaluate fetal monitors' ability to detect real distress, concluded that 'there was no improvement in perinatal outcome' for those babies delivered by Caesarean sections following an irregular pattern on the monitor versus the unmonitored babies. The principal difference between the women on monitors and the women who gave birth unmonitored was that the electrically monitored women turned out to have up to three times higher rates of Caesareans than did the unmonitored control group. The reason for all the Caesareans, according to the authors? 'Attending physicians' impatience and nervousness' upon seeing an irregular printout.

A much larger study of 34,995 American women in 1990 found *no* significant difference between women who were monitored and those who were not, except that, again, low-risk women hooked up to the monitor were more likely to be given Caesareans. Even the high-risk unmonitored women did just as well with only periodic manual monitoring. As H. Goer says in her book *The Thinking Woman's Guide to Better Birth*, 'A bedrock of truth of EFM is that if the monitor says the baby is fine, the baby is almost certainly fine, but if the monitor says the baby is not fine – that is, that she has non-reassuring heart rate patterns – the baby is also probably fine.'

A trial conducted on 13,000 patients in Dublin also found that electronic fetal monitors offered no benefits while increasing the use of forceps and Caesareans. From 71 per cent to 95 per cent of babies delivered by Caesarean section for presumed fetal distress as shown on the monitor show no distress at birth, which would seem to indicate that the Caesarean was not necessary. One 1997 study showed that certified nurse-midwives were less likely than physicians to use EFMs continuously, had lower rates of labour induction or augmentation than the physicians did, and had almost half the Caesarean-section rate that family physicians did.

EFMs have not correctly predicted brain damage in babies. Even that benchmark of the obstetrical profession, the *American Journal of Obstetrics and Gynecology*, has published research – 'more data may not enable us to predict or prevent infant neurologic morbidity' – demonstrating that it was difficult to tell with an EFM any special heart pattern in the baby that accurately predicted the baby's well-being.

EFMs are proven to be effective in one particular way: they do reliably promote an increased rate of Caesarean-section (which, coincidentally, is also more convenient for doctors and hospitals than are long, slow vaginal births). There is much more likelihood that if you are hooked up to the monitor you will have an 'instrumental' delivery – that is, a baby delivered by forceps or a vacuum extractor, or a Caesarean section.

Fetal monitors also guarantee that the centre of attention in the room will be the machine – a situation that drains away the birth attendants' focus and compassion, which is the elixir of successful births.

Yet hospital staffs, including the staff at the hospital we had chosen – even the midwives – seem addicted to EFMs. Why do they hold such a pivotal place in today's standard of care?

The machines are extremely serviceable, I discovered long after I needed the information, litigation prophylactics. In other words, although continuous monitoring can be harmful to the mother in terms of the interventions they encourage, they are a great defensive benefit to the hospital and its bottom line: they produce a visual record that can be used to bolster a hospital's legal position in the event of a lawsuit. As Dr Christiane Northrup recalls about her training: 'If I didn't have a monitor strip for documentation and there was a bad outcome, I knew that I would be in trouble with my attending physicians.'

It has been thought that a hospital or obstetrical practice is in a stronger legal position, and can defend itself against even higher premiums if it can show a court a record of irregular printouts, even if they are 'false positives', and even though the cost is countless unnecessary Caesarean sections.

This is trivial concern on the part of obstetricians: according to T.H. Strong in *Expecting Trouble: The Myth of Prenatal Care in America*, the median net income for American obstetricians was

$200,000 a year. But medical malpractice premium expenses – $30,000 to $80,000 on average – easily pushed the overhead for even a small obstetrician's practice well above $100,000 a year, and a lost legal case drives the numbers even higher.

Women are not generally told that they may go against the hospital's insistence that they be strapped to the EFM, nor are they usually told about the downsides of agreeing to use it continuously. I wasn't. The American College of Obstetricians and Gynecologists (ACOG) has recommended that routine monitoring be dropped from the standard of care. Does that mean that a woman entering a hospital today is any safer from their effect on her and her baby? Not necessarily. According to *Lying-In* by Dorothy C. Wertz and Richard W. Wertz, most doctors acknowledge that they will continue to monitor their patients for fear of lawsuits.

So although continuous fetal monitoring does not necessarily predict a baby's outcome, and although it causes more operative deliveries, and drains attention from the birthing woman, it is still seen as useful to hospitals' legal protection and bottom lines. In 1996, 85 per cent of labouring women in America were monitored continuously in spite of ACOG's own endorsement of intermittent listening to low-risk women. Nonetheless, according to the 1999 *Stanford Law Review*, 'OB's believe that they should use EFM because its status as the standard of care will protect them from liability.' And so the EFMs regulate and determine our births.

### The Normal Birth Position in Hospitals is Conducive to Labour and Delivery

Vicky, a real estate broker, told me she had hired an independent birth coach, who instructed her on truly effective preparation for moving, vocalizing, squatting and tugging. But when Vicky arrived at the hospital, the lessons were ludicrously unusable: 'I squatted at the edge of the high-platformed bed and nearly fell off. I got on all fours on a hard linoleum floor and found myself staring at an oxygen reserve. I asked my husband to stand and let me pull on his shoulders and we nearly crashed into a bank of instruments and the EFM machine. I tried to sit down on the floor, but the obstetrician warned me that the hospital disapproved because the nursing staff were not willing to do the extra work of creating a sterile field in the room. I mean, it was basically set up like a dentist's office for your vagina.

The lessons were simply not workable in that setting.' After her labour arrested at four centimetres, Vicky ended up with a Caesarean.

In many hospitals, architecture dictates behaviour as much as materials do. Birthing areas in American hospitals are typically equipped with a narrow bed and a linoleum floor. Even if you wanted to labour in more effective positions, and even if you were able to brave the social pressure of such 'odd behaviour' in America, in most hospitals there would still be nowhere physically to do so.

In the United Kingdom, the childbirth classes and material distributed through the NHS encourage the woman in labour to walk around for a long time, letting gravity do its work. But here too architecture and lack of space mean the reality may be different. Fetal monitors and IVs are less common and the woman is generally allowed to adopt whichever birth position she prefers. Standard manuals portray the prospective mother in labour squatting, grunting, rocking back and forth on all fours, and using the husband or boyfriend as an easy chair. Perhaps as a result, British interventions and Caesarean rates are lower than in the USA (the Caesarean rate is typically around 20 per cent, and the episiotomy rate is 15 per cent, though both, worryingly, are rising), but UK outcomes for mother and baby are just as good. In America such activities that work to bring forth the baby without episiotomy, forceps, or emergency surgery are frowned upon, and interventions that make 'failure to progress' in labour more likely are the norm, thus increasing the likelihood of interventions 'to save the baby'.

What do women in other countries do in labour? The 'natural position of women in labour', according to many anthropologists looking at hunter-gatherer societies to gather clues to our evolutionary history, as well as according to independent midwives who coach women through successful low-intervention births today, is motion. Most women, left to do what eases pain and helps the baby be born, will squat, sit, or pull on something resistant. Cultural anthropologist Robbie Pfeuffer Kahn and others confirm that, cross-culturally, in pre-industrial societies, most women give birth in such positions.

A nineteenth-century guide to pregnancy practices in different societies shows that women's need to walk around and assume different positions in labour used to be taken generally for granted:

'[T]he recumbent position in labour is rarely assumed . . .' In France and the Philippines in the last century, women mostly delivered standing; in Italy they most often delivered semi-recumbently, seated upon the lap of a husband or midwife. In Peru (ancient and modern), the Andaman Islands and the frontier United States 150 years ago, women generally also gave birth seated on the husband's lap. In Germany a century ago, women gave birth seated in a sling; in Syria, in a rocking chair; in Wakamba, Africa, women delivered standing. In Persia they crawled on all fours. In Venezuela they delivered leaning back in a hammock.

Ancient Egyptian monuments show women delivering squatting, seated cross-legged; pre-Colombian artefacts also show delivery accomplished in a squatting position. Nineteenth-century Irish immigrants to this country squatted to give birth, as did Pawnee and Tonkawa Native American women, writes George Engelmann, MD, in the 1982 classic, *Labor Among Primitive Peoples*.

In the broad array of anthropological literature I consulted, there seems to be no description of birth, outside a modern obstetrical setting, in which a woman in any culture will willingly lie down on her back or side to suffer the pains of labour and try to give birth. There is a reason women in non-obstetrical cultures don't lie down for most of labour: a 1997 British study showed that women who adopted an upright posture for delivery felt less pain, had less trauma to the perineum, and needed fewer episiotomies than did women who remain lying down.

Three other studies found that women who used a birthing bed (which can hold women upright) were less likely to have perineal trauma than did women labouring flat on the delivery table, that women sitting up were able to exert more 'bearing-down' pressure to get the baby safely out, and had a significantly shorter second stage of labour as a result; and that labouring upright made contractions more effective, with no additional discomfort.

The flat-on-your-back, feet-in-stirrups lithotomy position (initiated by Louis XIV, a voyeur who wished to observe his mistress in labour), which is generally used in American hospital birthing rooms today, is convenient for obstetricians, who can sit still, observing and technically managing the birth, at some clinical remove from the intense emotional and physical support that a woman moving about in labour requires. But it is far less convenient for the baby, who is forced, with its mother lying immobilized in this position, to enter the world fighting gravity, trying to make its way *up* the birth canal, and it is far from ideal for the mother.

### The Friedman Curve Determines a Safe Window for Labour

'If we consider mammals in general it is an advantage for the survival of the species that labour cannot establish itself as long as the female feels threatened (so she is ready to fight or run away from a predator if necessary),' says Michel Odent in *The Scientification of Love*. During labour, I was presented with a deadline regarding dilation: if I did not dilate more effectively on an hourly schedule, and produce a baby within 24 hours, I would have to have a Caesarean section. As a result of that pressure, I experienced 'arrested delivery' and the downward medical spiral it set in motion. I would later discover that my story of 'arrested labour' may have been the result of the intersection of politics, money, institutional convention, and, once more, legal interests.

My hospital used the 'Friedman curve' as a timeline for labour. Dr Emmanuel Friedman claimed that women having their first baby should expect to dilate 1.2 cm for every hour of active labour. In the late 1970s, US hospitals began to incorporate Dr Friedman's curve into standard birthing practices. Subsequent research, though, has shown that at least 20 per cent of low-risk women do not progress at that rate. There is a wide range of 'normal' responses to labour. Labour varies so much from woman to woman that a normal birth can last three hours for one woman, and three days for another. But putting women on the Friedman curve allows hospitals to be run as efficient factories, producing the goods on a schedule that suits doctors' convenience and saves the hospital money. Women who do not dilate quickly enough, according to 'the curve', are often brought on with Pitocin or delivered by Caesarean. Midwives report that they are often asked by nurses, who are themselves under pressure to clear the delivery rooms, 'Is your patient still here?'

In our childbirth classes, as I recall, the educator dutifully explained the necessity of birth at our hospital being paced according to the Friedman curve. What she did not explain was the possible effect of that time pressure on labouring women. The mind–body connection in childbirth may, according to increasing numbers of studies, be so strong that this demand that a woman dilate within a certain amount of time, can actually become 'iatrogenic' – i.e. harmful as a result of treatment; in this instance, the pressure can help to *stop* a woman's contractions, thus causing the very 'condition' that surgery or other interventions are then called upon to 'cure'.

'Arrested labour?' hooted independent midwife Ina May Gaskin when I interviewed her. 'There is no such thing. Midwives know that labour starts and stops. You take a walk, you eat something, you take a nap, your labour will start again. But if you have the clock hanging over you and a C-section on the horizon if you don't produce the baby, and impatient doctors checking and hovering, that practically guarantees that your labour will shut down. Besides, when a strange man enters your room,' she said, 'e.g., your doctor – strange in the sense that you're not really comfortable showing him your crotch – labour often stops. It's the same reason pandas don't get pregnant in zoos – there are all these people watching. If you took cows and put them in an unnatural setting, surrounding them with strange people watching them, and did to them what women routinely go through – for we obey the same laws that animals do, we just don't realize it – the same thing happens. We set up an unnatural setting for birth and then we're surprised when women don't perform well in it.'

According to hospital protocol and obstetric practice, if labour starts and stops and starts again, it is no longer medically 'normal', and the situation may call for intervention. A nurse-midwife working at a birthing centre or at home, however, can call that hour or so, after full dilation but before the mother-to-be starts pushing, not a case of 'arrested second stage', which calls for forceps or a C-section, but rather 'time for a nap'.

## Your Doctor and Hospital Staff Will Offer You Adequate Emotional Support

Many women I interviewed felt less than fully supported by their obstetricians. Even the video we watched in class showed women labouring physically alone, untouched except for the anxious ministrations of their 'coaching' husbands, who were likely to become exhausted themselves as the primary, and only half-informed, source of emotional support for a loved one in long labour. Nurses and doctors in hospitals are unlikely to stroke or massage the labouring woman, nor would it probably seem socially appropriate if they did so within the sterile setting of a hospital today.

Midwives working outside hospitals know how important such care is for a good outcome. It turns out that the hands-off style of attending to the woman in labour preferred by hospitals is detrimental to a good delivery: a series of studies by researchers Marshall Klaus and John Kennell discovered that hands-on 'doulas' and birth attendants can significantly affect the length and complications of labour, for the better. So much data has accumulated about the health benefits of having a team of hands-on supporters helping a woman through labour that even the American College of Obstetricians and Gynecologists, in an attempt to lower Caesarean delivery rates, has acknowledged, 'the continuous presence of nurses or other trained individuals who provide comfort and support to women in labour may lead to lower rates.'

Emotional support actually leads to better contractions and less likelihood of intervention. In fact, if you are anxious in your second stage of labour, your contractions may well be weaker because of the stress hormone epinephrine. A 1997 Swedish study found that intense psychological support for women with fear of delivery resulted in a 50 per cent reduction in the need for Caesarean sections. Indeed, another study in 1999 found that women's oxytocin levels respond to social stimuli – they are elevated after massage, for instance, and decreased with sadness. Since the release of oxytocin is crucial to good labour, it stands to reason that hostile interactions with hospital staff or inadequate support from medical personnel and family members, would inhibit labour.

Ina May Gaskin's secret to the remarkable record of successful low-tech births that her cooperative, the Farm, boasts is, she says, to leave the labouring women alone to kiss and cuddle with their partners as labour begins. This releases oxytocin, the natural version of the chemical Pitocin, which the hospital administers via IV in a 'pit drip', to achieve the same result – stronger contractions – but excruciatingly. The release of oxytocin, however, loosens up the birth canal naturally. Midwives at the Farm ask the couple privately to stimulate the labouring woman's nipples and vulva in preparation for stronger labour. 'Arousal opens the cervix and the birth canal,' Gaskin asserts matter-of-factly. 'The same sexy energy that got the baby in there is the best energy to get it out,' she is famous among midwives for saying. The Farm midwives also encourage labouring women to moan, groan, vocalize, and move at will. The release of natural hormones to take the place of the painful and abrupt work of Pitocin is well documented. But this widely proven technique to enhance and ease the pain of contractions – stimulation and arousal of the woman in labour – can hardly be managed in the cold and clinical setting of a typical hospital.

Gaskin attests to the medical importance of women's emotions in labour: 'We've been centring everything on the baby and ignoring the moms . . . without realizing what happens to the mom is integral to the baby,' she says.

In a low-tech house in the woods, scarcely more than a shanty on the outside and a simple little cottage on the inside, Ina May Gaskin has for three decades been producing a record of results that would be the envy of any high-tech obstetrical practice. She believes that the secret to this success is the intense physical and emotional support she and her fellow midwives, alongside the women's partners, give to women in labour.

In a hospital, underpaid and harried nurses and other staff (likely to include, if you are a low-income woman of colour in America, doctors in training, using your case to gain experience) come in and out of the labour room at will, check you, change shifts, leave and are replaced by others. The Farm midwives, in contrast, assign three female supporters to each labouring woman. These additional mid-wives and helpers stay for the entire experience; they tune in to each woman's unique emotional state and requirements, and give atten-tion to whatever support or guidance the husband or partner needs in order to give his utmost to the woman in labour; they stroke, comfort and hold the woman hour upon hour, as she requires it, or back off as she requests, while she sits in the lap of her husband or partner or on a low bed, on pillows on the floor or in a rocker. They set their pace to hers.

Gaskin claims a woman's state of mind can completely transform the progress of labour. One woman's labour went on and on, she says.

'She was labouring and not progressing. I said, "Pamela, is there anything bothering you?"

'Her husband had avoided exchanging a full set of marriage vows with her; he thought vows were square. She was feeling insecure. She needed to feel safe.

'[My husband] Steven, who is a minister, conducted the marriage ceremony – right there on the bed between contractions.

'When it was done,' Gaskin went on, 'her labour became very effective – after two days of waiting. Imagine how deep the lesson was. That birth underlined how important commitment was. I found out those words, arranged the way they are in marriage vows, covering all the bases – "in sickness and in health, for richer, for poorer, *until death do us part* . . ." (that was the part Pamela's partner objected to) – are so powerful that they let the baby be born when the parents spoke them.'

Several European countries, whose health care systems, as I have noted, are not profit-driven, make use of the massive data showing the correlation between emotional support and healthy mothers and babies in determining the country's standard of care: many British mothers, for instance, are visited at home daily for 10 to 28 days after the birth by a midwife or Health Visitor (another trained professional), who helps the new mother with her initial baby care, offers psychological support, and carries out medical follow-ups, in the reassuring surroundings of the new mother's own home.

Why the difference in approach? Money. Since pre- and postnatal care and childbearing expenses are paid for by the British government, the NHS stresses adequately supported approaches to childbearing because it is in policy-makers' interest to conserve money by avoiding the expense of costly interventions, a policy which also happens to best serve mothers and babies. (A 1 per cent rise in Caesareans in England is reckoned to cost £5m.) The American system, too, is driven by money, but unfortunately in the opposite direction: American women, who lack a national health service, are most likely to have birth experiences influenced by the high profit margin of C-sections and tight hospital and OB-GYN scheduling, as well as by the hospital's need to create a defensive legal record.

*Epidurals Are Necessary*
All the women I spoke to said that they had been both physically and psychologically unprepared to deal with and manage the pain of labour – and that they were not offered the range of non-epidural

pain-management techniques that midwives know can work. Women should certainly have access to epidurals, which deaden sensation, if they want them. Women should *not* be expected to endure great pain just to live up to a 'natural' ideal, an expectation that some zealots on the 'naturalist' end of the spectrum sometimes impose upon them. But they should also know the real facts about their choice. Most women who give birth in hospitals are presented with the epidural option in a way that makes choosing it a 'no-brainer': *Gee, do you want birth with agonizing pain, or the same birth without?* But it is not that simple.

What most women don't know is that the sooner you are given an epidural in labour, the more likely it is you will have further interventions. These interventions can seem routine, such as needing to have an IV, needing to have the fetal heart rate continuously monitored, needing a catheter put in to empty your bladder.

But the risks linked with epidurals can also be more serious: twice as many severe perineal lacerations, a higher likelihood of a vacuum-assisted or forceps delivery, and higher rates of Caesarean sections. Another complication that's been linked with epidurals is a maternal fever in labour – between 11.8 and 28 per cent of women with epidurals developed fever, a rate that rises with every additional hour on the medication, versus 0.2 per cent for women without. Maternal fever can mean a 'sepsis work-up' on the baby, which keeps the baby separated from the parents after birth. Another study also found epidurals were 'strongly associated' with maternal fever – 14.5 per cent of women who received epidurals vs. 1 per cent of those who did not. The babies of women with epidurals are also 400 per cent more likely to be treated with antibiotics. (This is what happened to Dianne, a woman who suffered overtly from the separation that this can lead to.)

These are risks that women need to know before they are in the throes of labour pain, so that they can make an informed choice about whether to have an epidural. 'He was like a pusher,' said Yasmin of the hospital staffer who kept proposing anesthesia to her. 'I overheard him saying to a resident, like I was crazy, "She won't take the drugs."' According to Henci Goer, 'Epidural charges range from $500 to $2,500 . . . hospitals have to maintain staff anesthetists around the clock to handle obstetric emergencies. In order for these doctors to make what they consider an adequate income, the hospital has to maintain something like an 80 per cent epidural rate.'

A conversation on the subject of epidurals with Catherine Moore, a licensed nurse-midwife who advised me on these issues, raised two kinds of reasons for women to get all the pain support they possibly can as alternatives to early epidurals: 'An epidural is not just pain medication along the normal route to birth. It is, rather, a *highly* technological intervention that totally changes the way birth proceeds,' points out Ms Moore: 'It involves serious narcotics, administered by an anesthetist, to achieve the proper anesthesia, and also requiring IV, fetal monitor, often a straight or Foley catheter. When you request an epidural you are not just cutting off pain; you are really taking a sharp detour into a completely different birth experience. Most women are really not fully informed about this as they consider their choices.

'In our experience, epidurals do not allow a woman to be physically *or* mentally present at the birth of her child. Epidurals don't just give women birth without pain: they also give women birth without *feeling*, which a lot of women would consider seriously if this were really made clear to them.

'They also help women carry on as if they are not really engaged in something incredibly difficult, disruptive and important – which is the same social expectation they will face as new mothers. The labouring woman on an epidural can be counted on not to make noise or to ask for much from the staff. The partner of the labouring woman on an epidural can go for coffee, watch TV, read the paper – really a minimal expectation of support versus the kind of involvement that a birth supporter for a nonmedicated birth must offer. This kind of birth definitely does not hurt, but it also does not really give mothers the sense that they were there for or involved with the birth. That is more than just a pain management choice; it is a big difference that women should be made aware of as they decide.'

### An Episiotomy Should Be Part of Your Standard of Care

Fifty to 80 per cent of women who give birth for the first time in America receive an episiotomy (as compared with a UK average of 15 per cent of all births), a 'routine' cut in the perineum that widens the birth outlet. 'The baby was almost out and the doctor picked up these big shears and, though I was shouting at him to wait, he just started cutting,' as one dismayed father put it. Though *What to Expect When You're Expecting* covers both sides of the debate over what it describes, with great understatement in my view, as a 'minor surgical procedure', the authors' preference for 'traditional medical wisdom' in favour of episiotomy seems clear. They note that women who give birth in birthing centres can tear badly enough to need repair, which indeed sounds awful.

But that caution is misleading – as was my obstetrician's terrifying and graphic description of the risk of a 'ragged tear to the anus' if I even thought of resisting an episiotomy. What the standard guidebooks and doctors do not tell you is that a tear, when it occurs, generally takes place in the superficial tissue and is usually easily repaired, whereas an episiotomy is deep-tissue surgery that weakens the entire perineum. (One midwife, to make her point, pulled hard on both edges of an uncut piece of paper to show how strong it was – it did not rip; then she cut a straight nick into it, and of course it ripped in two.) What anxious women are not usually advised is that an episiotomy is a serious cut right into the muscle; many women remember it as the most painful and traumatic part of a medicated hospital birth. Nor are women generally informed that, since their sexual responsiveness derives largely from the rich network of nerves and blood vessels in just that area, an episiotomy can cause pain during sex and loss of sexual responsiveness for up to seven years.

Nor are women advised by *What to Expect* of the behind-the-scenes pressure on the hospital to opt for an episiotomy: if you are delivering a great many babies with a time-dictated bottom line at stake, you can get them out *faster* with a cut; a straight cut, even if deep, is also quicker and easier for a rushed obstetrician to suture than is an irregular tear, even if it is shallow. Another reason for the popularity of episiotomy is a lack of skill on the part of obstetricians. Obstetricians are not typically taught in medical school the basic skill of mending the more ragged edge of a shallow tear; they prefer to cut straight and deep instead.

I discovered that independent midwives and birthing-centre midwives know many ways to protect women from routine episiotomies, as well as from bad tears. One key is patience. According to British childbirth expert Sheila Kitzinger, when a woman can give birth at her own pace, injury to the perineum, and to the muscles, ligaments, and nerve endings deep inside it, is far less of a risk.

Are routine episiotomies genuinely medically called for? In countries that typically supply women with midwives, new mothers emerge from birth much less likely to be cut than they do in the USA. Fewer than one new mother in ten will have to have an episiotomy in Holland. Fewer than one in five British women who give birth attended by midwives have episiotomies – though when British obstetricians attend even straightforward vaginal births, that rate can soar to 90 per cent. Just as my own intimidating obstetrician warned me, most American first-time mothers will be cut, whether their personal circumstances really warrant it or not.

When I later interviewed midwives at the Elizabeth Seton Birthing Center, I walked in on what looked like a party. Three exhausted but satisfied midwives were drinking tea and eating cookies around a table after having been up all night 'catching' a new baby. The mood was congratulatory. The reason? 'An eleven-pound, four-ounce baby girl delivered over an intact perineum!' said the birthing centre director with pride, sounding like a female version of a football stadium announcer calling a new record.

According to Dr Marsden Wagner, the obstetrician who advises the WHO, and who is critical of interventions, episiotomy is the most common surgical procedure in birth care after the cutting and tying of the umbilical cord. The arguments that obstetricians give for performing an episiotomy are: to prevent severe tears in the perineum that extend to the anus and/or rectum; to prevent long-term damage to the pelvic floor; and to protect the baby from the adverse consequences of an extended second stage of labour.

But the risks are these: blood loss, infection, pain, painful sexual intercourse after episiotomy, and emotional trauma.

Do the reasons obstetricians give hold up under the latest research? Six studies examined the effects of 'restrictive', or much less frequent, use of episiotomy compared with the routine episiotomy during vaginal birth that is now part of the ordinary standard of American care. With restrictive, as opposed to routine, episiotomy women suffered *less* posterior perineal trauma, *less* suturing, and *fewer* complications.

Is it worth it to prescribe perineal massage and utilize patience in the birthing room in order to protect the pelvic floor, as some midwives do in Europe? Is risk of damage to the perineum through either tearing or cutting really such a minor matter, as *What to Expect*

*When You're Expecting* seems to suggest? A 1994 study showed that women with an intact perineum had less perineal pain immediately post-partum, required less pain medication, had greater pelvic-floor muscle strength three months post-partum, resumed sexual relations earlier, had less pain during sexual intercourse and were more satisfied sexually than were women who had episiotomies. Another study in 2000 found that poor perineal outcomes were not usually a result of labour – but were rather due to the use of episiotomy.

Is episiotomy routinely necessary to speed up delivery of the baby? Studies have shown that women can labour and push longer than most hospital guidelines allow without increased risk.

Is the procedure necessary to protect the baby from 'the perilous journey through the birth canal', as *What to Expect When You're Expecting* alarmingly puts it? As researchers E. Eason and P. Feldman put it, 'There is no evidence that delivery practices that avoid perineal trauma (that is, birth styles that try to avoid episiotomy) are correlated with low Apgar scores, birth trauma, or cerebral palsy.' Nor is there evidence that babies arrive healthier because they emerge faster due to the episiotomy. In a study of 1,000 women, restricted (rather than routine) use of episiotomy made no difference to how well babies did. Three studies did find ways to help women avoid unnecessary cutting; one found that when women delivered kneeling on all fours, and with hands supporting the perineum, it remained intact; another found that often a ten-minute perineal massage from week 34 until delivery made a big difference; and a third found that whirlpool baths in labour resulted in less perineal trauma and fewer Caesarean sections.

Is your episiotomy going to be dictated by your medical condition or by your doctor's attitude? Physicians who viewed episiotomy very unfavourably used the procedure less often than did doctors who liked the procedure; and the patients of doctors who disliked episiotomies had *less* perineal trauma, *less* perineal pain, and higher levels of satisfaction with the birth experience than did patients whose attending physicians viewed the procedure 'favourably' or 'very favourably'. In fact, 'the highest rate of perineal trauma occurs in women delivered by obstetricians in larger urban settings. The lowest rates occur in women attended by midwives in or out of hospitals.'

Finally, the culture of the delivery room, as well as factors such as legal pressures and scheduling pressures, can affect your likelihood of having what should now be understood to be a possibly risky and not necessarily helpful surgical incision in the perineum during your labour: as Eason and Feldman put it, 'Don't just do something, sit there!' – the patience prescription for a midwifery-paced safe, normal birth – 'requires discipline and assurance, which is particularly difficult while watching disconcerting second stage variable decelerations [on the EFM, which we know to provide uncertain data] under the omnipresent cloud of a malpractice suit [which are common]. Doing an episiotomy can also minimize time spent at the bedside, which might be important when facing the conflicting demands of a busy office, operating room, and emergency department.'

### You May Well Require an 'Emergency' Caesarean

'I was never reconciled' to the Caesarean, 'right up until the moment it happened,' Greta told me. This was a reaction I heard often, and felt myself. It is a sentiment that *What to Expect* seems to frown upon.

The hospital had eventually prepared us to accept the strong possibility that I might require an 'emergency' Caesarean. All women I interviewed who had Caesareans had been told that 'something was wrong' as they were rushed into surgery. Yet new research shows that a midwifery-centred pace of delivery might have given many of them different choices.

Until the 1970s, Caesareans made up about 6 – 10 per cent of all births in the USA. In the 1980s the figure rose by 40 per cent. Americans began to believe that Caesareans were a fast, simple and risk-free solution to any medical challenge that birth presented. By the 1990s, one in four of all US births was performed by Caesarean section; in some areas, a third to half of all babies are delivered by surgery. The US Center for Disease Control reported in 2000 that C-section rates were up 4 per cent in a year, the third consecutive increase. Between 1989 and 1996, the rate had risen 50 per cent. During those decades, obstetricians perfected the 'bikini cut', the horizontal incision that replaced the more shocking vertical incision. Medical experts began to assume, in spite of current research to the contrary, that subsequent births by a mother who had had a Caesarean section for her first child would have to be done by Caesarean as well.

Now, at the beginning of the twenty-first century, many women have begun to see Caesarean birth as quite routine. (A Paris obstetrical conference belatedly asks the question: 'Caesarean Section – Mode of Delivery: Should We Have a Strategy to Minimize Caesarean Deliveries?' and then casts routine C-section not as a convenient resource for busy obstetricians and hospitals but as a feminist blow for equality: 'Caesarean Section Upon Request: Women's Right'.) A *Wall Street Journal* article, on 15 June 2001, describes a new trend of obstetricians who recommend C-section in order to enhance their patients' sex-appeal – what the doctors call the prepartum 'honeymoon vagina'.

But in terms of terms of risk and recuperation, a Caesarean is *not* a routine procedure. It is the equivalent of any other major organ surgery. Bruria Husarsky, a critic of hospital births, claims that C-section is more accurately called 'open uterine surgery'. Indeed, most women do not realize that in a Caesarean, their uterus will literally be taken out of their body. In *What to Expect When You're Expecting*, on the other hand, the authors note, 'Today . . . cesareans are nearly as safe as vaginal deliveries for the mother, and in difficult deliveries or where there's fetal distress, they are often the safest delivery mode for the baby. Even though it is technically considered major surgery, a cesarean carries relatively minor risks – much closer to those of a tonsillectomy than of a gall bladder operation, for instance.' However, the authors go on to advise women to learn 'all they can' about C-sections to 'ease [their] fears' – though the book itself shows how difficult it can be to get straight information. Their depiction of the baby's 'perilous journey through the birth canal' is a characterization that does little to reassure women that they can manage a vaginal birth safely. '[C]esarean delivery,' the authors go on to say, 'has become an extremely quick and safe option – and in most instances mothers can be awake to see their babies born.'

Are Caesareans, in fact, 'nearly as safe' as vaginal deliveries? Not in fact. In most pregnancy books and hospital-directed birth classes, Caesarean surgery is presented as having risks – but as a procedure whose benefits far outweigh the risks. And yet in her book *Immaculate Deception II: Myth, Magic and Birth*, researcher Suzanne Arms makes it clear that: 'The risks are the same as those of any major surgery: unexpected adverse reaction to the anesthesia or other drugs used, uncontrollable hemorrhage . . . or infection that does not respond to treatment . . . risk of an injury to other organs such as the bladder . . . The long-term dangers of Cesarean are adhesions in the scar tissue that can cause chronic pain, bowl obstruction, infertility or miscarriage; and placenta acreta (where the placenta grows into or through the wall of the uterus) in the next pregnancy.' Complications in Caesareans are five to ten times higher than in vaginal births, and Caesareans are also two or five times more likely to be fatal to the mother. A Caesarean section is not like a tonsillectomy.

Calling attention to the serious downsides of the surgery is not to suggest that the decision to have the surgery or the decision to avoid it is the 'right' decision. Nor is it to overlook the fact that when Caesareans are truly medically necessary, they are a godsend for mother and baby, rescuing them from situations that might have killed either or both a century ago. I am struck, however, by how little real information is available to women to help them understand the pressure toward Caesarean sections that are not necessarily called for.

In the United States, more than 870,000 babies are delivered by Caesarean sections each year. Yet research shows that in the majority of cases, they may well have been medically unnecessary. A Public Citizen Research Group report estimated that half of the 906,000 Caesarean sections it assessed were unnecessary, causing 142 avoidable maternal deaths. The report called Caesarean section 'the country's number one unnecessary surgery'. Dr Sydney Wolfe, head of the group, states, 'Mothers are not being adequately informed of the risks involved.'

When midwives, rather than obstetricians, deliver babies in American hospitals, Caesarean rates drop to less than half the national rate. This is not surprising given that obstetricians are trained to perform high-tech deliveries and are more likely to see risk when it isn't there. (One very remarkable aspect of watching Ina May Gaskin's midwives at the Farm work close-up is that their hands look so skilled and their gestures so subtle.) These skills are like heirloom roses that are dying out because they are not being propagated. Such hands-on skills were once taught in medical schools, but are no longer. Is your likelihood of having a Caesarean delivery affected by your doctor's gender, I wondered. A recent Yale University study found, indeed, that male physicians were far more likely than female doctors to perform Caesareans.

How does the Caesarean section rate in the USA break down by class? Healthy middle-class women in their thirties and forties in private hospitals have about a 50 per cent Caesarean rate, while healthy women in public hospitals have a Caesarean rate of 1–15 per cent. In other words, women whose health plans can afford to reimburse the hospital for a Caesarean section are more likely to be told they must have one.

The same is true for Australia, where 16 per cent of women who give birth in private hospitals have Caesareans as opposed to 10 per cent of women under the public health system, Medicare.

The American College of Obstetricians and Gynecologists has acknowledged that their members' most likely reason for performing a C-section was fear of lawsuits, though their reasoning was not generally explained to the patient. Though in 1998 Dr Ibrahim I. Bojali acknowledged to the *New York Times* that doctors have an incentive to do C-sections to avoid law suits: 'Doctors have little to gain and a lot to lose by not doing a Cesarean.' 'Dystocia', the condition in which the baby is apparently stuck in the birth canal, is the reason most often given to justify surgery. Yet many midwives and childbirth activists regard the term 'dystocia' along with the terms 'arrested labour' and 'pelvic inadequacy', as cover language for a situation in which the real reason to operate is that 'a woman has spent more time in labour than hospital regulators or doctors are willing to allow . . .' Many births become 'emergency' births to meet the demands of the clock. By redefining 'labour' into a shorter and shorter allowable cycle for financial reasons, medical practitioners virtually guarantee more and more 'emergency' situations.

Another reason for the rise in Caesarean rates is the subtle pressure of money. Though doubtless no obstetrician thinks consciously, 'I will make more money if this birth ends with surgery rather than vaginally,' nonetheless the pressure is there in the background. For private obstetricians do earn far more for performing Caesareans than for attending vaginal births, and hospitals bring in more income that way as well.

According to the exposé *Open Season*, if the 50 per cent of unnecessary Caesareans were avoided, American hospitals would lose *$1.1 billion* in revenue a year. Cutting the Caesarean rate back to 5 per cent of all births – the rate in some European countries today, and just under that in the United States before the boom – would wipe out *$175 million* a year in personal income for obstetricians alone, for whom the Caesarean section boom means shorter hours at increased pay. (Interestingly, Caesarean rates spike upwards just before weekends and holidays – which suggests that doctors may unconsciously interpret the medical situation in a way that is more likely to get them to the gym on Saturday, or home in time for Thanksgiving.)

According to the *Health Insurance Association of America Source Book of Health Insurance Data 1999–2000*, the price of a vaginal birth in Denver is $1,379 – while a Caesarean delivery in the same city costs $2,801. In Houston, a vaginal birth costs $1,334 – while a Caesarean costs $2,760; in Miami, a vaginal birth brings in $2,128 from insurers, whereas a Caesarean will bring in $2,760.

'Discuss the cesarean rate at your hospital with your practitioner,' advises *What to Expect When You're Expecting*. This counsel is well-intentioned but not practical: to women's detriment, hospitals are under no obligation in most states to disclose Caesarean rates, and in the few states that do have disclosure laws, according to medical consumer groups, the requirement is often disregarded. Nor are Caesarean rates carefully regulated. There is no limit to the percentage of women a doctor may section without being subject to challenge or censure. Three countries in Florida, for example, have maintained a Caesarean rate above 50 per cent for years.

What does a Caesarean section really feel like? Suzanne Arms' *Immaculate Deception*, the exposé that is not part of the recommended reading of most hospital birth classes, describes it in the following way: 'The woman's abdomen is shaved and scrubbed. Her arm is taped to a board for the IV and blood pressure . . . A screen is put up to separate the mother's eyes from the operating team. Numerous metal clamps . . . tie off bleeding blood vessels during surgery. A metal retractor holds the incision back to keep the abdominal wall out of the way. Once the baby and placenta have been removed, the uterus is lifted out through the same opening, laid on the mother's abdomen, and sutured.'

In *What to Expect When You're Expecting*, the authors reserve some of their harshest censure, not for the obstetricians who perform Caesareans that are unnecessary, but, rather, for women who are upset by having had a Caesarean section. 'The most likely kind of damage a baby delivered abdominally might suffer is psychological

– not from the delivery itself, but because of the mother's attitude toward it.' Activists at the National Cesarean Prevention Movement's Organization report that women often feel angry and confused 'after a cesarean': these new mothers realize that they are 'supposed' to feel joyful about the safe delivery of their baby and grateful that the doctor saved them both from a potential life-threatening situation, yet they feel powerless to take care of themselves after the surgery. They are expected to go home within a matter of days, nurse, bond, and take the lead in the care of a newborn baby, while themselves recovering from major surgery.

Hospitals often tell patients making enquiries that high Caesarean section estimates are distorted because these hospitals admit a high number of the high-risk births in the area. That is what our hospital told us. Unfortunately, given the lack of disclosure of hospital data, there is no way to prove or disprove this. But pregnant women and their partners deserve to know real numbers. A number of critics of the medical institution claim that doctors should be obliged to make their statistics a matter of public record.

Today, Caesareans are so commonplace in America that obstetricians in New York sometimes schedule surgical births with no medical indication as a matter of convenience to their patients. It seems that many American and indeed British high-profile women – wryly dubbed 'too posh to push' by the British press – have begun to demand them as a convenient, quick and supposedly pain-free method of giving birth, with the procedure defended by well-respected female journalists including Mary Ann Sieghart, who wrote an article in *The Times* controversially applauding the benefits of Caesarean delivery, and describing natural birth as a 'pointless' experience, with 'indescribable' pain. This whole idea of elective Caesareans would seem to be a version of the feminist 'your body, your right' principle – except that some women are not given the whole picture of what is at stake. It also discourages women from seeing labour as something they can handle in the normal course of events.

Although the United Kingdom has fewer Caesareans than the USA, it, too, has seen a rise in levels, which have trebled since 1970. According to Department of Health figures released in 2001, average national rates are quoted as 18–20 per cent (another 2001 survey quotes almost 22 per cent), but with some maternity units having levels as high as 40 per cent – well over WHO recommendations of 10–15 per cent. Despite this increase, however, there are signs that many British hospitals are trying to move away from surgical interventions. Some maternity units – most notably at University College Hospital, London – are beginning to employ acupuncturists who not only help relieve common pregnancy-associated complaints such as tiredness and back pain, but, in some cases, can help breech babies turn, thus avoiding the need for Caesareans in those cases. There is also, clearly, some pressure within hospitals themselves to monitor their rates of intervention. One woman I heard from – still too distressed at the memory of her labour to be attributed – privately admitted that she felt she *should* have had a Caesarean, but hadn't because her hospital was desperately trying to keep its rates down.

The reasons for the sharp rise in Caesarean rates in the UK – described as 'ludicrous' by the National Childbirth Trust (NCT) – remain unclear, although under-resourcing and crowded hospital wards promoting a 'conveyor belt' approach to childbirth have been cited. As in America, fear of litigation, too, undoubtedly plays a significant role – of £386 million paid out in litigation claims by the Department of Health in 1999–2000, £200 million was for obstetrics and gynecology alone. While the debate rages on, a British government watchdog has commissioned a national audit of maternity units in England and Wales from the Royal College of Obstetricians and Gynaecologists, the Royal College of Anaesthetists and the NCT in an attempt to find an explanation for this change in British attitudes.

From all these debates, one clear truth emerges. As women we should have an inalienable right to choose how we wish to give birth. But we can only make that choice when we are empowered with the facts, when we know the full implications, in both emotional, physical and medical terms.

A final thought. Despite the rising numbers of Caesareans in so-called 'emergency' births, in 1998 the *Washington Post* reported that 'Maternal deaths have not gone down in 15 years'. Nor has all this surgery resulted in better rates for perinatal mortality.

## You Will Be Treated According to your Medical Needs, Not Your Race or Class

Clear racist patterns have been noted in the medical treatment of black women and low-income women giving birth in America. In *The Woman in the Body: A Cultural Analysis of Reproduction*, Emily Martin reported that 'the labours of black women are more often induced by Pitocin, a procedure that often leads to "failure to progress" and the need for a Caesarean. The casual links between Pitocin and "failure to progress" can be either that the artificially started or speeded-up labour does not sustain itself or that Pitocin produces such powerful and painful contractions that the woman cannot tolerate them . . .' The disproportionate induction of labour in black women suggests that white medical practitioners are simply not as inclined to hang around and support women of a different race or class background while they go through labour. Diana Scully found that poor black women patients are often 'openly regarded as objects of scorn' by their medical practitioners.

A striking finding of medical racism in two New York City and Baltimore studies revealed that: '. . . (w)hen there are clear clinical indications of fetal or maternal danger (bleeding, high blood pressure, prolapsed cord) more white women get a Cesarean section, but when the labour is long or the rate of progression is slow, more black women get them.' In other words, if you are poor or black and your labour is not speedy enough, your obstetrician more likely, consciously or not, to give you a C-section to move things along – to get you in and out of the expensive labour room. Dr Julius Goepp, an emergency surgeon who attends to low-income black communities, reports that many of his women patients profoundly distrust the white-dominated medical system, and that this distrust complicates doctor–patient communication about prenatal and postnatal care. Given the documented history of other kinds of medical racism in America, and given these patterns of discrimi-nation in the birthing room, those low-income women and those black women who do not trust their practitioners to treat them on a medical rather than a stereotypical basis are probably not being paranoid; they may well be responding with insight to a system that treats them with bias.

Under non-profit-making government-funded health systems, such bias does not, thankfully, exist, but in region-funded systems such as the British NHS, another type of bias may creep in, based not on race or class, but on where you live, a situation which has led to the so-called 'postcode prescribing' that has become prevalent in the United Kingdom. Maternity care is no exception. In just a few areas of the country, for example, women will receive one of the jewels in the crown of NHS natal care, one-to-one midwifery – continuous attention from the same midwife from the point where pregnancy is diagnosed till up to a month after the birth, while in most other places women will have a fractured service, seeing a different person each time, who may then not pick up any problems at an early enough stage. Similarly, the type of antenatal screening available, and number of surgical interventions, will vary wildly from one hospital to another – a random nature of provision that has led to the NHS being described as a lottery. This, combined with generalized underfunding and understaffing, and a crisis in midwife numbers, has led to growing dissatisfaction among British women, too.

In a 2001 survey of 2,000 recent mothers carried out by the motherandbaby.co.uk website based on responses from women who used the site, most women expressed unhappiness at the way they had been treated during pregnancy and childbirth. Three-quarters described feeling anxious during pregnancy and frightened during labour, and half the mothers were dissatisfied with the postnatal care, with 79 per cent complaining of still being in pain two weeks after the birth. Less than 50 per cent of the women would have been prepared to return to the same hospital to give birth.

Many of the women I heard from described a general feeling of disinterest in their wishes from NHS staff – many of whom were kind and considerate, but were simply too overworked to spend quality time with them. One woman described the appalling conditions in her London hospital ward which was 'old and filthy with dirty, sodden floors that were cleaned only once while I was there' and had broken showers. In an equally scathing article published in *The Times*, a man described similar conditions in another hospital, where his wife had had an emergency Caesarean section. The hospital had no soap or towels to wash the baby, and he was forced to go out and buy his own, which were then borrowed by the nurses, who had run out of supplies themselves.

In April 2000 the Commission for Health Improvement (CHI) was set up by the British government, to address both lack of funding and disparity in services. In time, it is hoped, such inequalities will be a thing of the past, but there is still a long way to go.

So your journey into a typical high-tech hospital birth experience is likely to have many hidden agendas operating behind the scenes that will shape your experience. They may or may not be about the best approach for you, about your personal pattern of labour, or even about the best outcome for your baby.

Despite all the downsides of high-tech birth many women are, understandably, frightened even to consider the second door – the 'natural childbirth' door – because it, too, has been presented as so rigid an option with such extreme requirements of courage and faith. It was for that reason that I would not consider it as an option.

Unfortunately, the 'natural childbirth' movement, too, has its own ideological slant. And while midwives themselves have a great practical understanding of birth, the 'naturalist' ideology on the fringes of the midwifery movement can be just as extreme as that of the advocates of high-tech birthing that midwifery challenges. While home birth is now as safe as hospital birth, and in some ways safer, it is not helpful for women who are trying to find a way to a birth they can trust for 'naturalist' writers and critics of 'cattle barn obstetrics' to romanticize the truly difficult aspects of natural childbirth in a way that makes thoughtful women of today sceptical of their otherwise important and accurate claims.

In around 1940, a challenge arose to medicalized birth, in the form of 'natural childbirth'. The movement began with the publication of Grantly Dick-Read's book, *Childbirth Without Fear*. It is the pregnant woman's fear of pain, he argues, that creates the tension that results in the 'unnecessary' pain of childbirth.

In the book, Dick-Read recounts the turning point in his view of childbirth: as a young physician in London, Dick-Read was led to a 'hovel' in which a woman was about to give birth. He paints a stark portrait of the grimy walls, the broken window stuffed with a torn rag to keep out the wind, the dying coal on the grate, the bed of tatters on the floor in which the poor woman lay. Yet the woman in labour barely broke a sweat before producing a fine healthy child. Then she told him, 'It didn't hurt. It wasn't meant to, was it, Doctor?'

This atypical experience became the root of the natural childbirth movement, that, at its extreme, frowns upon women's choice to have medication. One of the unintended consequences of the natural childbirth movement is that it can lead women to feel like failures when they cannot manage birth so effortlessly, and it can also leave them underprepared when faced with the real, drawn-out, painful battle that childbirth can be.

French obstetrician Frederick Leboyer, who wrote the 1974 book *Birth Without Violence*, was another influential figure in the natural birth movement. Many of his insights – that after the ease and serenity of the womb, a newborn baby's responses are hypersensitive, and so low lighting, warm water, close physical bonding between mother and newborn, and silence, make for a less traumatic birth – have influenced midwife-assisted births and enlightened many obstetricians. But like Dick-Read, Leboyer seems to romaticize the rough struggle of childbirth. He, too, believes that the cause of pain in childbirth is women's fear – and that if you can remove the fear, you can remove the pain. 'The bodies of women in labour were nothing more than a mass of spasms, tensions, frantic heavings, locked muscles. Their bodies wanted only to escape, to deny what was taking place – mute testimony to their crazed panic and terror.' 'There is only terror and ignorance,' he writes – with what I would say is less than complete compassion – of women who feel pain while giving birth.

Traditionally trained doctors and nurses often deal with the pain of childbirth by assuming that women can't handle it, and medicating them at the earliest onset. Naturalists on the fringes of the movement, on the other hand, can treat pain in a way that borders on the puritanical.

Ideological naturalists sometimes romanticize the pain by either minimizing how excruciating it can be, or idealizing women who choose to undergo it without resorting to drugs. They use euphemisms such as 'discomfort' and 'intensity' to describe the pain of birth, or 'rushes' and 'surges' to describe what can be agonizing contractions. One otherwise persuasive birth activist argues that contractions should be called 'babyhugs'. 'Other words in my class,' she goes on, 'are angeltaps, cuddlebunnies, pillowfluffs, sunflights, bellybounce'. Such vocabulary can be just as condescending and unhelpful to women facing the rigours of birth as that used by traditional doctors. It is as if these naturalists believe that they must sugar-coat the experience in order to entice women to have the kind of birth these activists believe to be 'best' for them.

Some well-know naturalists, whose arguments are extremely important, unfortunately overreach by insisting on what you could call a 'birthing myth'; an idealized Edenic state of perfect, unmedicated, earth-centred, easy birth among women in tribal or pre-industrial cultures. In this sentimentalized picture, our women ancestors took birth in joyful stride, scarcely interrupted their activities, effortlessly produced healthy babies with no hemorrhage or rupture, gloried in their womanliness and were celebrated by a sisterhood of nurturing women collaborators.

This mystique ignores the historical record. The 'purebirth' advocates scarcely address the fact that when women did give birth at home, without drugs or intervention, and before antiseptics and in a time when women's general overall health was poorer than it is today, bad things happened on a regular basis. Two hundred years ago, when there was no Caesarean industry, women in the West regularly made out their wills before 'lying in'. Women in the nineteenth century who birthed 'naturally' certainly knew pain, in fact, they stormed the ramparts of the medical profession to get their hands on chloroform, or scopolamine, 'twilight sleep', when it was invented. Natural childbirth advocates on the extremes tend to ignore or wilfully overlook the fact that women routinely faced danger in giving birth naturally; it was once, and in many areas still is, 'natural' to lose the baby, and 'natural' to die in childbed. Women in preindustrial countries, as the cross-cultural survey *Birth in Four Cultures* points out, suffered and still suffer rupture and hemorrhage, though supported by the earth and surrounded by their 'sisters'. Women's Health activists such as those at the global 'Plan-It' programme know how common death in childbirth still is for women in developing nations; Save the Children includes as one of their projects' goals the right of every woman to have access to a clinic in which to give birth, a goal that should well attest to the fact that for most women labouring in poor conditions, 'natural childbirth' is no picnic.

Fortunately, the 'naturalist' ideologues are at the far reaches of a movement that is otherwise made up of women – and some men – who quietly and even nobly try hard every day, in often hostile institutional environments, simply, wisely and frequently subversively, to humanize in the USA what should be the normal and, dare we reclaim it?, beautiful experience of giving birth.

**THE PATRON SAINT**

Ina May Gaskin, whom I introduced earlier, is a naturalist who is also a realist. Hers is a stunning record of accomplishment that is an implicit challenge to the medical establishment. She is one of the heroes of this story. While many in the medical establishment see Gaskin as extreme, it is a telling indictment of our system that someone like her, with her exemplary and peer-reviewed record of success in delivering babies, is considered a fringe figure by obstetricians, rather than an admired and emulated teacher to the entire profession. 'Most Obs would not sit down at a table with Ina May,' as my midwife informants put it, yet she has reclaimed and taught to other practitioners skills that are dying out in medical school curricula.

Gaskin, a self-taught lay midwife, brought woman-centred midwifery back into the American birth scene. I went to visit her at the commune she and her husband, activist Stephen Gaskin, founded in 1970 rural Tennessee.

Gaskin is a soft-spoken, quietly strong woman now in her sixties. There is an extremely still quality to her even when she is in motion. Her long trademark braids are the same braids one can see in old film footage of her. Part of Gaskin's house is constructed from the original platform for one of the tents the commune lived in during its wild first winter in 1970, after several hundred young people dropped out of mainstream society and went trekking after charismatic leader Stephen Gaskin to found a new community. In its heyday in the 1970s, the Farm was the biggest commune in America.

Ina May's classic book, *Spiritual Midwifery*, is an account of the Farm, a quasi-matriarchal community structured around natural childbirth. The book includes photos of the backs of old buses, the seats taken out and the floors scattered with pillows, where the first such births took place. It includes scenes from 30 years ago of smiling hippie moms, hugely pregnant young women with long braids, and hippie children playing on the banks of mattresses in the backs of the buses. There are photographs of Ina May as a skinny young woman in a tie-dyed halter top and low-slung jeans, kneeling between the open legs of a birthing woman lying on a paisley cloth on the floor, surrounded by other midwives.

In the video archives of the Farm, these women rub the labouring woman's shoulders in a soothing rhythm. The images of these births are very different from those of the hospital birth videos: the women lying naked on batiked pillows are never abandoned for a moment; they are never without a strong or soothing touch, a pair of energetic arms around them, if that is what they require, a patient attentiveness and stillness if that is what they prefer. The men, wearing shorts to provide their women with the comfort of skin-to-skin contact, are helped with steady, firm guidance from an expert team of women. Because these men are supported themselves, they are able effectively to support the labouring women, and look visibly filled with joy and excitement, in the thick of the action. There are scenes of drama and intensity, and clearly sometimes the women are in pain; but the mood is a warm one of life coming into its own, of ebullient concentration, and of an almost urgent sense of celebration, as a new family is being made – with every family member, including the new baby, fully involved. In contrast, the women in the hospital settings look so desolately alone with their ordeal, lying on their beds, and their 'coaches' so peripheral, so uncertain, and so tired, as a medical process takes place.

What is amazing to me about the Farm births is that the women in labour are clearly working, clearly struggling, but they do not seem frightened; instead, they seem focused on their efforts, labouring in a kind of ecstasy. The women in the photos and film clips at the Farm look present; they look proud and sensual and ready for the battle; they look strong.

Ina May Gaskin has become a patron of saint of the midwifery movement in America, and an evident love of women and reverence for their fertility is at the heart of the kind of midwifery that she has developed and that her admirers practise as well. Her method combines dexterity and skills no longer taught in medical schools with an extraordinary level of support in a peaceful environment. She essentially had to teach herself these skills from nineteenth-century birthing guides.

The Farm is still delivering babies naturally today. The midwives there have a good working partnership with the local medical authorities in case there is a birth that natural methods can't handle. Gaskin's record of success in births over a 30-year period is in some measures about 20 to 30 times better than the national average, and far better than the success rates of the top-ranked hospitals and OB-GYNs to which my friends and I entrusted our births.

In fact, the most impressive part of *Spiritual Midwifery* is not its endearing but dated rhetoric about earth mothers, but the page that tallies the outcomes of births on the Farm – unmedicated births in the cottage in the woods – from 8 October 1970 to 1 December 1994.

Of the 1,917 total births on the Farm, there were only 35 Caesarean sections – or 1.8 per cent of the total. And only 1.8 per cent of the total births called for anesthesia; 60 were successful vaginal breech births. None of those was unsuccessful, or had to be referred to the hospital for Caesarean section. Twelve of the unusual presentations were face or brow presentation. Sixty-seven per cent of the women delivered with intact perineums (whereas 90 per cent of the women in my first obstetrical practice were expected to receive episiotomies). Sixteen out of sixteen vaginal births after previous Caesarean sections were successful.

'Obstetricians have an unnatural fear of birth: they come to think, "Nature didn't design it very well, nature needs a lot of help,"' says Gaskin. 'My experience is when moms are treated right and they are not scared, almost everybody gave birth well herself. We had a random sample of American women and our experience proved it. They weren't self-selected healthy. We had people who used drugs, who had taken crack – if we had them long enough and we could put some weight on the baby, they did well too.'

In her videos, despite the fact that the women are in pain, they are smiling. In one, a woman labouring on flowered sheets, radiant, held and supported by three women and her husband, gave a full smile as the baby's head emerged from between her legs. In general, I found that the women labouring with the support of the Farm midwives looked radiant. Older women, obese women, plain women, young women: they look as lovely as women can be – in striking contrast to the drained, fearful look on the faces of the women in videos of hospital births. Under Gaskin's hands women glow at the height of labour, their cheeks are red, their eyes dilated, youth and energy infuse even the most tired of their features.

In a birth like that, says Ina May, 'your colours come out'.

**A THIRD WAY: FREESTANDING BIRTH CENTRES**

In spite of the accomplishment of Ina May Gaskin and her colleagues at the Farm, I knew that I would not have had the courage or faith to give birth with no access to drugs if I found, after having tried all else, that I needed them, in that freestanding little house in the whispery pine grove down a bumpy dirt road.

Today, a 'gold standard' middle option to the extreme of high-tech and natural births has emerged. Although it is appropriate for the majority of healthy women, only a minority of Americans even know this option exists, let alone have access to it. Some women can choose to give birth at a free-standing birth or birthing centre, a facility affiliated with a hospital, run by licensed midwives, for women who are likely to have low-risk births. This option has been available in the UK for some years, both privately and on the NHS, and is also available under the Australian equivalent of the NHS, Medicare.

Long after my own delivery, I went to the Elizabeth Seton Birthing Center in New York, which is affiliated with St Vincent, a major metropolitan hospital, to see what such a place might provide.

It could not have been more different from the hospital practice my friends and I experienced. I felt I was home.

A sculpture of Elizabeth Ann Seton (1774–1824; wife, mother and Sister of Charity) holding a baby, a child at her skirts, stood in the hall. Ruth Watson started the Birthing Center under the auspices of the Maternity Center Association in 1974 and had the original vision of the freestanding birth centre.

As you enter, you immediately feel the hush of something exciting taking place. You are greeted quietly, since there is a birth in progress down the hall. You feel a warmer, lighter, somehow more tender air. The whole institution is, rather astonishingly, configured around the *babies*; whereas in a hospital setting, one can feel the baby is almost a happy but incidental byproduct in an institution configured around illness and machines. The Center feels oddly like the opposite of even the best hospital obstetrics ward; it was about vitality, not technique; about health, not crisis. It was about life processes, not a series of unhappy conditions; relaxed and cheerful, with no fear.

Here, on the wall, are what seem like hundreds of cards, with photos of new families of all kinds. The inscriptions express such sentiments as, 'We thank God for sending us here.' On one wall are snapshots of that year's 'Summer Babies'. On another are framed photos of the centre's midwives with their own families and babies, posted under their framed diplomas.

Indeed, not only is the presence of babies everywhere, but that of children and families too: bigger kids are welcome to the Center. Toys are scattered about the waiting room. Signs remind adults not to leave kids unattended.

When I went to the orientation, Pat Troy, the executive director, stood welcoming couples individually. There were young African-American white and Latina women, with their mothers, who would occasionally rub their daughters' backs or give their hands a reassuring squeeze. Young fathers looked tense, excited, and pre-occupied. There were preppie white couples, African-American middle-class couples, a lesbian couple, Pakistani couples, and a single Black Moslem woman in a headscarf. The diversity in their population was achieved because, as a matter of philosophy, Elizabeth Seton reached out into the local community, and also because the centre had made the decision to accept Medicaid.

Our orientation took place in a room where a framed cross-section of the female body with baby growing in stages took pride of place. Ms Troy remarked, 'We had two babies this morning. We may not be able to go on tour. When there is anyone in the centre we don't allow anyone back for privacy reasons. If we have a family in labour or postpartum you won't be able to see the facility.' Indeed, the back of the facility, where the birthing rooms were, did appear from a distance to be extraordinarily private and safe; warm, a bit dark, with low lighting; almost sleepy; like a womb. This respect for the labouring woman's privacy was remarkable in contrast with the lack of privacy – junior doctors and swinging doors – that can inhibit labour in the best-appointed hospital settings.

Just as hospital birthing room architecture discounts labouring women's needs, the architecture of Elizabeth Seton supported it: soft built-in foam-covered seating lined the waiting room, in stark contrast with the hard upright plastic chairs all the heavily pregnant women had shifted about upon in all the hospital waiting rooms I had seen before. Ms Troy told us right away where there were mats to rest on, or to sit crosslegged upon on the floor. The whole institution conformed to the pregnant woman's body, and to the newborns.

'It is a freestanding birth centre and a traditional community centre, a group practice of six midwives,' said Ms Troy. 'Whoever is on call is the one who has the honour of sharing [the birth with you.]' Midwives provide complete pregnancy care for women who are having a normal pregnancy.

'In this practice,' she explained, the midwives' Board chose the obstetrician – not the other way around – 'because he treats our clients the same respectful way we do. He is a very compassionate physician.'

To give birth at Elizabeth Seton you need a partner for support. You are also expected to attend childbirth classes because 'we encourage you to become an active participant in prenatal care, labour and delivery.'

Their philosophy could not be more distinct from that of a hospital practice, which categorizes pregnant women by 'risk'. 'More than eighty per cent of women give birth without event,' said Ms Troy. 'Birth is a part of a woman's wellness cycle. Most women do best in homelike settings supported by family and friends in an environment that allows for individual labour patterns. Postpartum we will visit you at home the day after you give birth and a visiting nurse will examine you and your baby wherever you are more comfortable. If you are having trouble breast-feeding, we will send someone to help you.'

A potential client asked, 'How many women decide to transfer out in order to get the epidural?' The answer was that, because of all the alternative methods used to help women with pain, out of 402 women, ten decided to transfer to the hospital in order to receive an epidural. Everyone else found they could handle the pain.

Elizabeth Seton, which admittedly takes only women who do not have a condition that requires unusual medical care, has a 9 per cent Caesarean rate, extremely low for New York and the country as a whole. 'We do not routinely cut episiotomies; only in the event of fetal distress', said Ms Troy. 'Our episiotomy rate is 3.7 per cent. Fifty-four per cent of the rest have superficial tearing. We prefer a slight tear to routine episiotomies because every time you cut an episiotomy you are cutting into the vaginal muscle, and it goes deeply into the muscle. Every time you cut an episiotomy you are severing muscle that is part of the female sexual response system, rich in nerve endings. For this reason, some midwives call episiotomies "cliterotomies".'

Midwife Elissa Marsh said, 'Physicians are supposed to inform women of special requirements such as episiotomy. I have never yet seen a physician show the respect of informing a woman of what is required – "I need to do this procedure"; instead they just cut, often without even telling the woman – sometimes when the baby is just about born; sometimes the husband is shouting for the doctor to stop. Many women find this cut the most traumatic part of the birth. Yet episiotomy is seen in the same light as taking a temperature – it's that routine.'

The midwife is there for clinical care and emotional support. The midwives have varying degrees of knowledge of herbs. They also have alliances with acupuncturists and massage therapists, as well as with 'doulas' for additional emotional support. Women at the Center are expected to give birth at the pace of their own bodies, and guided by the midwife's clinical judgement. 'I can't imagine doing something important that I *like* in twenty-four hours,' said Ms Troy quoting a comedienne, 'let alone something I am in pain for.

'Our clients don't have to stay in bed, they can squat to deliver. It's about being able to relax and push your baby out – not just physical but psychological and emotional. At the end of this,' she went on, 'you're going to have a fabulous baby. Most births here,' said Ms Troy, 'are intimate, candlelit, aromatherapy kinds of events. We have had a church choir. The mother had been in the choir. She sang through her labour. She hit notes you would not believe. She gave birth to her baby, and then the choir came in and sang to her.'

Troy concluded: 'Let me congratulate you all on your pregnancy. It is a wonderful time. Wherever you go, definitely come back and show us your beautiful babies!'

On the tour I was continually amazed and envious: three birth rooms were set up with queen-size beds. But unlike the 'ABC' at my old hospital, there were real places to labour effectively in the set-up: mats were on the floor, and women were encouraged to change positions a lot. Barbara Schofield, one of the communications directors who showed me around on a second visit, demonstrated the various birthing positions one could assume by getting down on her own knees – something that had not been possible in the hospital where I had laboured. There were dimmable lights – again, something you could not control in most hospitals, but that made a tremendous difference in the mood of the room as a place conducive to yielding to a natural process. There was a real birthing rocker: Ms Schofield showed me how a piece can actually be removed from the seat, so that you can rock and give birth at the same time, the better to manage your pain.

'All equipment is hidden,' said Schofield. 'Trays of tools are not staring you in the face. There is no limit to the number of people you can have with you. We encourage you to eat and drink, to keep your strength up – in fact a kitchenette and dining area for the family is next to the birthing room – and births turn into big family feasts here,' she said.

A shower, shower massage, and private jacuzzi, large enough to accommodate two people, was attached to each room. Ninety per cent of the birthing women use water to help them with their labours: 'Hydroptherapy,' said Schofield, 'has been shown to be a very effective analgesic.' (As Pat Troy had put it in her introduction, 'If your baby chooses to be born into water, it's fine. This is not California, we don't let your baby be born underwater, with everyone getting into the tub as a rebirthing experience. This is New York: the baby's head will be gently brought up.')

Even more startlingly, given all I had seen elsewhere, you are asked to take off your shoes before entering the birthing rooms. 'First, for cleanliness,' said Schofield. 'But second, because we really respect the birth room as a sacred space where families begin.'

'The PPD [postpartum depression] group meets here,' said Schofield, gesturing toward a heap of pillows in a comfortable room for postpartum women to recline upon. The centre keeps aroma-therapy among its stores if labouring women request some. 'We wanted,' explained Schofield, 'something to acknowledge the sacred-ness of birth within the centre.'

The lactation room, next on the tour, had an early labour pull-out couch, low lights, violet walls, tufted embroidered footstools, even a framed photo of a newborn in profile with a full breast in its avid mouth and a blissed-out expression on its face. There was a Gauguin print of barebreasted women carrying fruit, and an oval mirror as if in a boudoir. Surfaces were covered in lace. It was like a Victorian lady's seduction dressing room. I was almost embarrassed – but at the same time I felt a shock of recognition, or rather of 'being recognized' as a new mother. This was a site for physical closeness, for letting down one's guard along with one's milk, for animal responsiveness, attachment, connection: the setting acknowledged, actually cosied up to, the connection between femininity and maternity. A seduction scene was appropriate, for you must fall in love with your baby.

In that room I became aware of what is usually left out – the most important elements of the whole business of making babies and mothers. Most delivery and postnatal care settings, I realized in that dimly lit 'boudoir' for babies, do not just leave out the baby – they leave out the woman; or the womanliness in the woman that got her that far, and that the baby–mother relationship will have to depend upon.

After the baby is born, the activities offered by the Center continue: it runs various playgroups and information series, all suggested by the clients themselves.

'Our philosophy,' said Schofield, 'is this: birth centres need to be separate and independent to demonstrate efficacy of midwifery. Hospitals are institutions, and the pressure to adhere to bureaucratic policies is very strong. Our centre is set up very differently. As a free-standing organization we are in a much more empowered position than the standard midwife-OB partnership. Our obstetrician works for the birth centre. We don't work for him.'

I came back later to talk to the midwives one to one. Elissa Marsh and Janette O'Sullivan spoke to me at the table in the back by a kitchenette, surrounded by the birthing rooms, now quiet, as did midwives Esme Howard and Erica Lyon. Barbara Schofield joined us too.

'Midwifery practices save money because they reduce the C-section and complication rate [a fact that would make midwifery's critique of obstetrics appealing to HMOs and to government-funded providers of health care, but not to profit-driven hospitals or obstetricians themselves]. If you have a profit motive you make more money for C-section. If you have a health care motive, midwifery saves money. It is sustainable but it is not going to be the money maker that interventions are for hospitals. But balance it out: you have better infant mortality, morbidity. What is that worth to us as a society?' asked Elissa Marsh.

'Since midwifery is so clearly proven to be a safer approach, why the resistance?' I asked.

'By putting the [midwifery] model of care out there,' responded

Marsh, 'you are asking the obstetrical profession to step back; you are noting that we need obstetricians only for the births that are atypical. We do need them as backup for the ten to twenty per cent of births that are unusual.'

I described my own Caesarean. 'You really can't know if it was necessary or not,' said Elissa Marsh. 'But the main point was that the context in which you gave birth was not a context you could trust. My goal as a midwife is to create a context that you trust.

'Esme would have stepped you through it,' she continued. 'She would have held your hand, wiped your brow, been a sister to you.'

Esme said: 'A lot of times, support pulls you through a difficult labour. Midwives and OBs differ in their training, their caring.'

I heard Pat Troy say, casually but firmly, to a roomful of prospective clients, fathers-to-be and women who were pregnant, many for the first time, filled with excitement and trepidation, just as I had been: 'At no point will your baby be taken from you.'

Though I was wearing my reporter's hat, I found myself startled by hot tears. I could not staunch them. It was as if her declaration touched a terrible place I had been numb to. In spite of my best efforts, for a few moments, in a dark corner of a room full of pregnant women, I was unable to stop myself from silently weeping.

Amazingly, when I was pregnant I had little idea from my reading of what birth actually felt like – except that it would hurt. This story, from a young woman who had an unmedicated birth at the Elizabeth Seton Center is compelling. If women have more of a sense of what might actually be ahead, they could make better-informed choices about whether they can manage, or how they want to handle, the pain – and other emotions of birth.

The story was told me by a young mother, originally from Guyana, who was determined to give birth without medication. She switched to a midwife practice late in her pregnancy.

'My mucus plug broke at five thirty in the morning. I thought it was my water. We called the midwives . . . I was only four centimeters dilated. They said, "Go take a walk."

'So, I'm with my family. The feeling is festive. We get on the train and go downtown, to Bleecker and Sixth. I told them I had to eat Italian: a friend had said spaghetti sauce brings contractions . . . At the restaurant, I was about to tear into my ragu sauce, and these pains started hitting. I went in to the bathroom. I tried not to cry . . . Then I couldn't really take it any more. I said, "Okay, everyone has to eat up right now." I hurried everyone up. The guys are taking a while – Italian tradition, taking their time bringing the bill. I am like, "No, I am serious, can you bring us the check?"

'I went into the centre at four fifteen. They said, "We can't really admit you because your water hasn't broken." They put me in a room. The minute I got into this room and lay on the bed those pains just started coming. The doula kept coming in and telling them how to relax me: telling Matt to rub my back, pressing his hand on my back, showing him how to put the heat of his hand on my back. Then I started throwing up, which is normal for me. I throw up with pain. My water still hadn't broke but I was eight centimeters dilated. I stayed at eight till about ten thirty. I was in pain, starting to feel really weak. I had this bit of honey. Everything kept coming up.

'I spoke to the doula a couple of times about the water not breaking and I didn't want to go into 24 hours of labour. She agreed. We stared doing intense stretches, lunges, in and out of the tub, butt naked. My mother, everyone was in the room, and with Matt's help I am doing these lunges with the contractions. The water still didn't break.

'The midwife started giving me this great, intense lower back massage. It got really painful; I had to say, "Stop." Then they checked again and the water bag had broken at the bottom but not at the top. So I said, "Go prick it." They said, "Once we break it, it won't be long before you start feeling intense pains," I was like, "What the hell is this?"

'I stood up, and a contraction hit me. I was like, "OHHHH!" the water in the jacuzzi felt so good at that point. Matt said that when I got in, my eyes rolled back in my head; it looked like I was going to pass out, both from the pain and from the relief of the water.

'I couldn't have told you what happened to me for ten or fifteen minutes because I was in so much pain. I just told myself, "Marsha, you can do this." It [felt] like someone pulling on one leg, someone else pulling on the other leg, and they were pulling me apart. I was talking to [my daughter]: "Come out nice, baby." I had made arrangements with her: I will be nice to you; you will be nice to me. We were going to make it.

'The doula and I were going tiger growls – "EERRRRR!" I

laboured mostly in the tub, and standing outside the tub doing lunges. When she said, "Tiger," I immediately jumped into character, growling with a low moan. She said, "No, deep in your body. You should feel this growl coming out of your mouth." I started this deeper growling. Then Matt and I did it together. Our mothers just burst out laughing. We growled in the tub for like half an hour.

'Some pain, you get it and you think, "I am going to die." I didn't think I was going to die. It was actually kind of joyful. You have this pain and it's a process and you know something wonderful will come out of it. But I really started begging her at this point: "Please, please, baby – if you want brothers and sisters you have to come out soon because I can't make it . . ."

'I never once laboured on my back on the bed, or on my side. The pain was too much to just lie there and take it. It hurt so much more when you lie on your back. When I tried it for a moment it was torture. I thought, "How the hell do women do this?" You have to move, to keep moving, during the pain.

'All of a sudden, I got this pain and I was like, "Head, head, hey hey—" There was burning. Now that felt like,' at this point, Marsha burst out laughing. 'Someone was slowly taking a scalpel and slitting a new opening next to the one I already had! I felt this little head right there! No one can tell you what your pain is going to be like. I had asked so many questions . . . People had said, "The head and shoulders hurt most." But no one told me it was going to feel like that. That my whole body was going to rip in half . . .

'I had her in about six contractions. I couldn't push because of the position I was in so I squatted. The contraction picked me up out of the water. I was pointing – not able to speak – "Baby – umumumum – Baby – Baby – Oh, Baby!"

'Then Manya came out – boop!' Marsha recounted triumphantly. 'Matt and I both caught her. They said, "It's a girl!" And then they told me to sit back in the water to warm her up. She came out clean.

'We got in the bed, all together, the new family. After about forty-five minutes, they cut the cord. Manya never left my arms till they did. Esme checked her heartbeat in my arms. Matt was holding her, snuggling her, and he cried for an hour. His dad had just passed away and it was profound [for] him to have such a beautiful baby in the same way that his father died – so much pain and then a serene moment after. Matt said he looked at me quite a few times and said I looked like his father right before he died: in a place trying to bear the pain – in a place between here and somewhere else. He said I had scared him because of the peace that was on my face. He had thought I was going to die.

'I was home by two thirty that afternoon. I felt great. I went to the supermarket, Healthy Pleasures, getting food, at two thirty p.m. on the day I gave birth. I felt extremely at peace for having done it naturally. I felt that I had given my child a great gift . . . I was on a high – a huge high.'

### A REAL SYNTHESIS, A REAL CHOICE

In the end, at present, there are for most women only two doors that most of us have access to. Each one – the traditional high-tech hospital route and the natural childbirth approach – has great skills to share with the other. Each needs to be talking with the other in a relationship of equality and respect, collaborating with the other, and creating a birth culture and real choices for women out of the best that each has to offer. Women would be best served if all birthing establishments were shaped by the insights of both camps.

The best care for women would provide the medical back-up of today's hospitals and obstetricians to the labour-intensive close physical and emotional support of the midwifery movement. Each birth could thus make the most of midwifery's insights, its manual skills and its patience, while following best medical standards and keeping the technology in the wings for real emergencies that are medically, not bureaucratically, driven.

Such a birthing revolution would put a midwife's view of birth. It would centre labour around the woman and her baby, not around institutional convenience. It would provide a range of less drastic and intrusive, but still effective, pain management options to fully informed and well-supported women, with epidurals being readily available as a resource of last resort.

Yet today these two schools of thought scarcely communicate in America. 'They don't believe in what we do. We have trouble getting medical backup because OBs are hostile to us. They see us as being part of the Middle Ages. It is one hundred per cent antagonistic,' said a midwife, not for attribution, of her medical colleagues.

Hospitals and obstetricians have little incentive – indeed, they have a financial and status-driven disincentive – to learn from the record and lessons of midwifery in a way that would benefit their clients.

Women deserve a birth culture that unites the best of these worlds without ideologues at the two extremes, who do not take the needs of individual women into account, tampering with the agenda. Women deserve honest brokers and true advocates who will inform them about all risks and options available; who will explore what pain can be and what it might not have to be; who will make a concerted effort to eliminate unnecessary interventions; and who will stop romanticizing either the controlled nature of high-tech mechanized labour or the culture of alternative birth.

When I was having my first baby, I had wanted the comfortable birthing room of the Alternative Birthing Center that I had been shown, with an emotionally supportive staff around me and patient pacing to help me. I had also wanted the latest medical care if I needed it. I had wanted beauty and support and safety, as well as help with pain.

What I had wanted, when I gave birth, I did not find.

# PART III
## New Life

# Joy and 'Blues'

'Even the mother needs a mother.'

Erica Jong

Our baby gave me joy beyond words. She was like a little forest creature, swaddled; loosened from her wrappers, she waved her limbs dreamily, as if swimming in ether. I lay on the floor of the kitchen as she lolled about on her quilts, content to stroke her and gaze at her.

But the joy did not keep me from an undertow of depression. We had named our daughter Rosa – yet, both because of my emerging depression and my drug-slowed sense of understanding her fully as my child, I had a hard time thinking of her by her name. Now I know that is not surprising – and that this drug-affected delayed bonding did not mean I was a 'bad mother'. Two weeks after the baby's birth, my husband was back at work. That first morning, after I had said goodbye with the baby in my arms, my grief surged out of all control and did not go away.

By three weeks after her birth, I had slid into a chronic field of grief. Tears welled up at the least provocation. My incision, my wound, felt in every way as if it would never heal.

My life as a mother had become just what I feared. My delight in our child was absolute. At the same time, I experienced a tightening of the world's circumference; I *was* chained to the couch, nursing; I *was* stunned with fatigue; I *was* a vast primate of flesh – none of the weight gained in pregnancy had 'melted away'. I had become all the things I was most afraid I would be.

Slowly I took to my new rounds. I had become one of the moms joining Yasmin and six-month-old Amos, hanging out in the shade at the local playground, chatting about formula and breast-pumping; one of the moms with the stroller pulling up to Quartermaine's for one blessed cup of coffee and a quick glance at the paper while the baby slept; one of the moms driving, in my case badly, out to that awful indoor play area, located in a far suburb, to keep Cara and Daisy company on a rainy day. With my mind wholly preoccupied with keeping up with the work of baby care, the idea of an idea seemed like an impossible luxury.

After many weeks I started to surface into the outer world. For each venture outdoors I packed as if going on a walkabout: into the hideous diaper bag every day went diapers; wipes; Q-tips; Vaseline; bottle; spare bottle; bottle cap; spare bottle cap; nipple; square nipple; formula (to supplement my milk); water (to make formula); laminated cloth, and God help me if I forgot one item, I soon discovered. A hungry or dirty baby brooks no margin of error.

That laminated changing cloth soon came to symbolize to me just how reduced the status of motherhood I had just entered into was. Contempt for the labour of new motherhood, I found, was built into the very architecture of our communities. Why did we carry the laminated cloth? The laminated cloth, I saw from watching Yasmin, was for when you must get down on your hands and knees with your wriggling, shit-covered baby on the dirty floor of every public bathroom that has no changing table – that is to say, almost every bathroom – as well as for spreading under your wriggling, shit-covered baby on the benches of every park that has neither shelter nor changing table – that is to say, almost every park.

Eventually the playground became the centre of my world. This too was a shock. It seemed to me amazing that at the end of the twentieth century, playgrounds were still built in an open pattern, often with no gate around them, which required mothers and baby-sitters of toddlers to hover continually behind small children to keep them from darting into the street. It seemed obvious to me that no one who had designed a playground in our suburb had ever cared for a child. All around us, the neighbourhood was a cornucopia of consumer comfort. But out on the playground, for women, it was 1947; no shelter from sun or rain, no heated area for cold days, no food, no bathrooms, nowhere to get a cup of coffee or even a box of juice.

The message you receive from your work environment about how valuable your work is affects your psychological well-being. Every day I was getting the message that the work the women I knew and I were doing had little value: the needs of people sitting in bus shelters and municipal lobbies, I saw with amazement as I began to hobble around into the stations of my new life, were more carefully met than were the needs of moms and kids in the places in which we gathered.

Then there were the tasks of taking care of the baby. Tender and intimate, yet also difficult and boring: the burping, spitting, feeding, changing, bathing, sleeping – and waking when I had fallen into a rare moment of sleep.

That was my day now. Immense and pale, hoping I was doing my best, I began gingerly to re-enter adult life.

I went to a party, and found myself chatting with a noted biographer.

'What do you do?' he asked me.

'Well, I'm at home with a newborn, and . . .' Before I had finished the sentence, he had tuned out. With scarcely a murmured excuse, he moved on to more promising social pastures.

As my life slowly resumed, I received one tough lesson after another in my sharp demotion of status. So many new mothers I spoke to felt, as I did, a sense of acute social demotion that came with motherhood. From both men and women, from young baby-sitters to plumbers to cable installers, I noticed a new flippancy in relation to my time: it was newly valueless. People who would never take for granted that my husband should sit around waiting for them seemed to assume that I had nowhere to go, and nothing important to do.

These new lessons in my own life continued day after day, as I struggled to regain the balance in my emotions and in my recovering body. I was asked to be a guest at a feminist organization's dinner and had to decline because the event had no child care – no one to hold the baby for the twenty minutes for which I was asked to speak. No one at the organization seemed to think the lack of child care was a lapse of planning or integrity. Even in the feminist world, it seemed, institutions were not going to adapt to this life change. I was slowly beginning to realize that, in spite of lip service to the contrary, my baby was seen by ideological friends and foes alike as my personal hobby; my awkward, living handbag for which there was no room.

On another day, I became engaged in writing again for the first time in months. It was one of those rare good days when a writer can lose herself in time. Caught up in my excitement, I stayed too long at the office. It meant that I was late for a feeding. By the time I snapped out of my state of concentration and raced out of the building to run the few blocks to cross the street to reach our house, I was very late indeed. Christine, our new care-giver, was standing on the other side of the busy boulevard, holding the baby, on her way over to come get me. The wind was whipping her hair and skirt, and the baby was howling. I tried to lunge across, but with six lanes of traffic roaring between us, I couldn't.

I felt guilty almost to the point of crying at the baby's hunger, but in the midst of my guilt, intertwined with it, was a sheer vexation, almost a childlike anger, at having had to interrupt my work. It wasn't just the one interruption, but the realization that this was a condition: interruption was now my life. I was crying because I could not win. Because, as a worker, I was turning away from my work at exactly the most important moment; yet at the same time, as a mother, I had already stayed too long at the fair.

As the weeks progressed, I slipped deeper into depression. I tried to treat my aching, constant feeling of loss by going on compulsive walks around our neighbourhood in the evenings after we had put the baby to sleep. I walked with Yasmin, who was the one mother I knew who had just sailed through pregnancy and childbirth, and who listened patiently to me, understanding somehow that what looked like a perfectly serene life was in a state of catastrophe. She understood that I felt alone in the suburbs, was a bad driver and so had a difficult time getting around. She understood that I was covered with milk stains and applesauce stains and felt myself to be bovine and teary. Even as I loved my beautiful baby with a crazy love, I was bottomed out on some weird biochemical grief.

Years later I would read that many of these feelings are part of the wide range of 'normal postpartum adjustment':

> I am so irritable.
> I can't sleep.
> I can't think straight . . .
> I am nauseated.

I feel so nervous.
I feel so guilty.
I feel so ugly.
I feel like a failure.
I have no interest in sex or other normal activities.
I cry all the time.
I can't get going.
I feel so worried.
I can't stop eating.
I have scary thoughts.
I feel so alone.
I feel so ashamed.
I feel so tired.
I can't feel anything.

Most of these feelings were shared to some extent, at some time, by me, and by most of the new moms I knew.

I took our baby to visit another neighbour named Robin, who had a ten-month-old girl, Cleo. 'Minnie's in a state of total exhaustion,' she reported. 'Her baby was deceptively calm. You know, she used to lie there and gaze serenely around. Now, Minnie hasn't slept for a week. She's a basket case. She's calling me up in tears several times a day, saying, "I can't stop crying. I've never been so tired. It's a madhouse here: I'm crying, the baby is crying . . ."'

'I'm really surprised,' I told her. I had thought Minnie was doing great.

'When was the last time you saw her?'

'About ten days ago.'

'Things change fast,' she said flatly.

Robin herself looked terrible. I hadn't seen her for about three months. She had gone back to work part-time for a financial marketing organization. Robin's hair had been a lustrous black; now it hung lifelessly in thick sheets on either side of her face. Her ordinarily optimistic demeanour had sagged; the corners of her mouth, the lines that extended down either side of her nose, her eyelids themselves all seemed suddenly to have been weighted down. Whatever energy had animated her ordinarily bright features had vanished. Her skin, always a little raw in the DC winter, had coarsened. She was always thin – 'I'm one of those stupid women who forgets to eat,' she used to say to her girlfriends, apologetically – but her frame now seemed enervated. Her spine bowed at her shoulders; her head hung limply forward. It didn't take long for her to cut to the chase. Talk was medicine for the new mothers in our small group, and we treated it that way. When something was wrong we could scarcely stand chit-chat. Robin was clearly sick and she knew it.

'Well,' she said, brooking no small talk, 'I'm clinically depressed. I'm on Zoloft.'

'What happened?' I asked.

'It's been building up for about a year . . .' Robin said. 'It's, you know, composed of a bit of everything. My job was taking a lot out of me; I'm trying to work part time, but of course I check my e-mail every day and they haven't hired anyone to replace me the days I'm off, so I do the same amount of work in less time and for less money. Cleo has trained herself to cry like a demon at just those moments when I have a client or an important call on the phone. Tom's new job means that his hours are longer and he travels more. So I'm alone a lot with Cleo, who has become really clingy since Tom has been gone so much. Plus, the baby-sitter quit. So Cleo has regressed; now she comes into our bedroom about ten times a night, for reassurance.' She spoke in a kind of quiet, compulsive monotone. 'Are you sure you want to hear all of this?'

It was merely a courtesy question, I knew. It was like asking a rescue crew if it was sure it wanted to throw a lifeline to a shipwrecked survivor. 'Yes, yes, go on,' I nodded.

'Well, I started getting more and more overwhelmed. So I started to, you know, withdraw from Cleo. I was just getting so tired. I couldn't function properly. And Tom tried to help, but his job is more, well, demanding than mine, I guess, so he doesn't really get up with Cleo very much. He can't function at all without sleep, and he's at the office and needs to really be on the ball during the day –'

'Don't you?'

'I can fudge it more. Then, of course, things started to get hard with Tom.'

'What's going on?'

'Well, I had to use all my energy for dealing with Cleo. I have nothing left for Tom. Tom comes home and needs me. And I am just so tired and angry. And I think, all I want is to be held. I just need to be held, you know, and courted a little. I mean, I tell him that flowers would make me really happy, and he feels he's gone out of his way if he gets something at Safeway while he's out getting milk or something. And he hands it over sort of resentfully like, Oh, hi, honey, you're my irrational wife. Have some chrysanthemums.'

Among our group of friends, chrysanthemums had become a red flag. There was such a hunger among the new mothers for pure appreciation from their mates for what they were doing; an offer of chrysanthemums when a new mom hinted at flowers had become code for being taken for granted.

'So then when he wants to, you know, make love, it's like, he wants to just have sex. You know, straight to the point. And I'm like: Get away from me.

'My mom is no help; she gives me advice out of the mists of time. She wants me to greet him at the door with a smile wearing Saran Wrap, you know, and says if I just tried harder things would be fine.

'So now I'm seeing a shrink, who says my sadness is hurting Cleo. That's why she's so fretful and teary and colicky. So she gives me this homework: I have to spend half an hour a day gazing into her face and mirroring her expression. I have to do it even when I just can't stand it. When I just want half an hour to myself, once a day, to just stare out the window or something.'

'Jeez,' I said.

'I feel like Tom's blaming me, though he doesn't come out and say it. I just want things to be the way they were.'

'How long has it been since things were good between you?'

'Oh . . . you know,' she said confessionally, her voice dropping further, 'since Cleo was born. Sometimes, I swear to God, I walk the street wondering what the easiest way is to kill myself.' She laughed uneasily. 'Like, okay, what's most convenient? Least trouble to others? You know? But fortunately the medicine seems to be working. I'm still sad all the time. But not suicidal!' She smiled the saddest smile imaginable. 'Bagel?' she asked brightly, satirically, pushing the platter of bread over to me.

The sun was setting. Bright plastic rings lay scattered across the hardwood floor. Cleo lay asleep in her bouncy chair, flossy hair tousled, her mouth open. My baby was flopped over my shoulder on a cloth diaper, wriggling, as I patted her warm, huffing little back with its ribs like a bird's. I was not ready to confess that I understood her depression first-hand.

I imagined Robin, who was clearly racked with grief, arranging the bagels in their circles on the plate that morning for the guests who would be arriving. I thought about her, sleepless, sitting down every day in the sliding nursing chair, training herself to show appropriate love to her baby. I thought about Cleo, chubby, red-nosed with a cold, asleep and entirely dependent on this emotionally exhausted woman, her medium and protector. I kept quiet, determined to manage my sorrow without naming it, though I knew Robin knew.

Robin and I looked at one another, each of us understanding that the other stood over an abyss, in shadow. In the pain of the moment, knowing there was little more to be said or done, we both burst out laughing.

What had I read or been told about depression when I was pregnant? I recalled one memorable mention in the frightening 'new mommy' video we'd been given in birthing class. 'You might have a mood afterward called "the blues",' the fresh-scrubbed, Peter-Pan-collared nurse with the Elizabeth Dole hair had said in that chipper tone of voice, as if women's 'moods' were just plain *silly*. 'The "blues" are normal, and temporary. But if this mood lingers, do consult your doctor.'

I might have 'a mood' afterward, I thought; that 'lingers'. And that was it.

What I did not know about postpartum depression was that the 'baby blues' affects 50 per cent to 80 per cent of women. 'The "blues" are so common,' one guide to postpartum depression puts it, '. . . that most health professionals pay little attention to the phenomenon'. This is in itself a profound comment about medical complacency in the face of women's suffering.

The 'baby blues' are defined in medical texts as: 'a transient state of tearfulness, anxiety, irritation, and restlessness'. Why do women experience this? After the birth of the baby, the hormones that were elevating mood in pregnancy go into a steep drop (estrogen levels that were as much as 1,000 per cent greater in pregnancy return to normal levels within 24 hours after birth), with mood levels crashing accordingly, usually the worst is over by day ten. Postpartum depression is more intense and lasts longer than the 'blues'. It may start any time during the first year after the birth of the baby. Postpartum depression affects 400,000 mothers per year in the USA. Studies show that postpartum depression is affected by the hormonal changes women endure. This is the data that few practitioners give us when warning us gently about the 'baby blues'. A new mother's main source of postpartum support, her partner, typically returns to work in America, a culture without mandated or paid parental leave, two weeks postpartum – exactly when the new mother's supposed to be feeling the lift from the 'blues'. But the combination of the husband returning to work, the sleepless nights, the lingering effects of hormonal plunge, the aching body, and demand to single-handedly care for a new baby, can send many women into downward spiral.

That biochemical crash happened to me in a profound and dramatic way, and my depression, which I scarcely recognized – partly because I was so reluctant to admit that anything about the baby's arrival could possibly be a cause for anything like unhappiness – did not lift until six months later. Yet this was an entirely foreseeable crisis.

If the new mother has had a Caesarean, her incision will have only begun to knit at the time she is usually left alone with the baby; the wound is six weeks away from healing. Certainly no one expects men recovering from major organ surgery to do *anything* continually strenuous in the weeks that immediately follow, much less provide daily care, mostly alone, for a tiny, demanding infant.

In her book *Life After Birth*, British writer and journalist Kate Figes explains how conditions in hospital postnatal wards can often in themselves contribute to PPD, their noise and lack of privacy often forming a disastrous combination for women who are in pain, 'shaken by the experience of labour and in need of deep sleep'. This is what happened to Jackie, an English editor in her thirties, who suffered PPD after giving birth in an NHS hospital.

'When I had my first baby I couldn't sleep in hospital for three days,' she said. 'I had trouble breast-feeding, which got worse with lack of sleep. The baby couldn't sleep because he wasn't being fed. The call button by my bed didn't work properly, and I felt too tired, disorientated and bewildered to do anything about the situation. I had no sleep for seventy-two hours and I remember that, in spite of my terrible emotional state, the midwife kept shouting at me in the middle of the night, telling me off for not drinking water to help the breast-feeding, but no one had told me before and I'd never breast-fed before.

'This bad start took me about a year to recover from, and I really believe that it was this that brought on my postnatal depression, which I suffered in silence – too scared to admit it to the health visitor in case they took my baby away from me. I hated being a new mother, and felt my life was ruined for ever. I hated my husband for being able to go to work and for not understanding. My baby couldn't be put down without crying, so days went by when I didn't eat anything until my husband came home late in the evening.

'I felt desperate and wanted to have a minor "accident" that might put me in hospital – not so that I would die, but just to get some sleep, and also so that my husband would have to look after the baby. That way, I thought, he could find out what it was really like; find out why I couldn't iron his shirts, cook dinner, wash clothes and clean the house every day. I couldn't wait to return to work.

'It took me almost four years before I could face having another child. The whole experience put me off having more children and almost cost me my marriage.'

Such stories were common among the women I met, yet with forethought and proper government funding for counselling services they could have easily been prevented, or the symptoms improved. A 1989 randomized controlled trial involving home visits by a trained counsellor showed that two-thirds of women suffering PPD had recovered within three months, compared with one-third of women in the control group.

In some European countries, new mothers are routinely screened for PPD, their well-being tracked by an obstetrical psychologist, a profession that does not exist in the United States which has the highest postpartum depression rate in the industralized world. European research shows that it is easy to identify which new mothers are at risk of developing PPD, and that early intervention shows excellent results.

In America, we don't screen new mothers for mood disorders, apart from a few perfunctory questions. 'Even though PPD is very common,' write Karen Kleiman and Valerie Raskin, in their book *Postpartum Depression*, it often 'falls through the cracks in the medical profession'. The authors point out that if a woman turns to her OB-GYN for help, she is likely to hear that she is merely 'going through a period of adjustment'.

Factors that contribute to PPD include: chronic sleep deprivation, colicky hard-to-care-for babies, hormonal fluctuations, and medical complications in either mother or baby. Other factors, which show the powerful effect of social expectations on this medical problem, include the new mother's inclination to be critical of herself, inadequate support from family and friends, and isolation.

In other words: there are good reasons for other cultures to treat new mothers as if they are in a heightened, vulnerable state. They are. And it is not all in the new mother's head, either. As I mentioned earlier, after giving birth there is a severe hormonal drop comparable to, but much more intense than, the depressive symptoms caused by PMS. Among the hormones that drop off postpartum are prolactin, cortisol, and human chorionic gonadotropin (HCG). The placenta has been stimulating the production of endorphins throughout the pregnancy, causing those feelings of euphoria and peace. But with the placenta gone, those natural opiates are no longer in the new mother's bloodstream. She is, in a sense, in a kind of drug withdrawal.

According to postpartum depression experts Ann Dunnewald PhD. and Diane C. Sandford, PhD., most women who experience PPD feel ashamed, and even a little crazy, as if they are abnormal. Little do they realize how very normal they are.

British childbirth expert Sheila Kitzinger believes that one primary cause of the high rate of postpartum grief in our society is social isolation. Though the women I knew in Washington gathered in playgrounds and at the local Starbucks, there was still plenty of time every day when we were alone with our babies in our homes; and during the day, most of the baby work was usually done by two hands – ours. When the baby got fussy at 5:00 – or 6:15 or 6:27, according to his or her own internal clock – that was what we called 'the witching hour,' when nothing we did seemed to help, and the walls seemed to close in.

It is not the depressed new mother who is aberrant; it is her situation that is the aberration. In most other cultures, and in America in the not so distant past, a new mother, at least for the important first 40 days, typically has had many fresh hands to pass the baby to.

In Greece, Guatemala, Burma, China, Japan, Malaysia and Lebanon women who have given birth are expected to take it easy if circumstances permit, being nurtured by the women of their community for some weeks postpartum – a culturally consistent minimum of 40 days – while they bond with their baby and recover from the rigours of birthing. In Malaysia the new mother is supposed to rest for 40 days after childbirth; she is given a ritual bath scented with hot, sweet-smelling leaves and rubbed with ginger, garlic, tamarind and lime to help her circulation. Obviously, not all women in these cultures are so lucky.

Many non-Western cultures believe that the healthiest mother–baby bond depends on the community of women doing everything possible to mother the new mother, so that she can focus on becoming a mother herself to her newborn. New mothers are treated for those days after birth as if they are in a psychologically sensitive state. Pediatrician Donald Winnicott calls this state, which our own culture scarcely allows for, 'primary maternal preoccupation', and notes that it is so intense that in someone who was not a postpartum mother, it would be considered an altered psychological state.

In some places, such as India, Pakistan, Ecuador and Brazil, this special postpartum care even involves feeding the new mother special ritual foods – often chicken- or marrow-based soups – that replenish her lost protein, blood and fluids and build her iron levels. This tradition of older, more experienced women feeding and essentially 'babying' the new mother, so she has the resources to baby her baby, also gives the new mother the nurturing that frees her to grow into her own maternity. It is natural, as a new mother, to regress. But Western cultures, in contrast, operate under the misconception that the woman who has just given birth will automatically know how to be a mother, and will naturally have enough left in her, after the crucible of birth, to give her all without replenishment.

America treats new mothers unusually badly, even compared with other developed countries. In Britain, new mothers receive home visits; Holland arranges for new mothers to receive home help; some of the helpers, paid for by government funds, actually live in; in Japan the new mother has the option of staying in hospital for a week. Of course, these are countries that levy much higher taxes for such services than America does. But given the data on how much better new mothers and babies fare with more intensive postpartum support, and given Americans' willingness to consider extending benefits such as broader medical coverage, it should not be unthinkable for politicians who genuinely support family values to divert some of our tax dollars to American mothers by providing them with guaranteed postpartum home support and intensive care.

Little in my birth experience, or in those of my hardworking women friends, was designed to support us postpartum in the intensive way that other cultures have relied upon. On the contrary, we were supposed to – and we expected *ourselves* to – produce the baby, and get on with it, nearly alone. This is what Mary-Lou found so hard. An Australian systems coordinator in her late thirties, she had her children under a private health scheme in New South Wales, and suffered for two years after the birth of her first child before finally being diagnosed with PPD and receiving the psychiatric help she so badly needed. As she described her painful experience, she expressed astonishment at the fact that no one had warned her about the possibility of being depressed after giving birth and, indeed, about what motherhood as a whole entailed. 'I feel very frustrated at the lack of information offered about mothering and depression,' she said. 'Motherhood didn't come naturally to me. Why should it have done? I really think that, just as midwives and doctors tell you what to do throughout the labour and delivery, antenatal classes should provide info about postnatal depression too. When you leave hospital you feel completely responsible for something you know very little about, and that's scary.'

Only in the developed world and only since the 1950s, with the advent of the socially isolated suburb, the atomization of the extended family and the separation of women and children from the public arena, has there been this expectation that one woman alone in a house, recovering from birth and for months thereafter, must be able to do the primary work of comforting, caring for, and entertaining a restless baby, let alone more than one child, mostly by herself. As anyone who has cared for babies knows, our one-on-one system is an aberration: a single care-giver or mother gets tired; a single care-giver or mother needs a respite. A 'system' such as ours is virtually designed for failure – and for making new moms feel they are not able to live up to expectations. This is a most atypical and unnatural expectation from both a cross-cultural expectation and an evolutionary one: observing a group of Seneca Tonawanda Native Americans at a softball game, one anthropologist noted that a nine-month-old baby was 'passed around' to eleven people – from close to distant relatives and friends – over the course of 50 minutes, giving the mother a welcome break. Anthropologist Sarah Blaffer Hrdy notes that in 'humans and a few species of prosimians that bear multiple young . . . infant survival depends on the mother being assisted by others . . . "alloparents" '. (Edward O. Wilson coined the term: 'allo' from the Greek for 'other than', and 'parent'.)

Sheila Kitzinger is passionate on the subject of the harm social isolation causes. 'Women are isolated,' she writes, 'if there is no good public transport and they do not have the use of a car . . . They are isolated when a partner works outside the home for ten hours a day, or brings work home and settles down to catch up on it with doors closed against children's noise. They are isolated if there is no extended family to give support, and when any relatives they do have live a long way away. They are forced into isolation when there are no local leisure and recreational activities which welcome small children, and when breast-feeding outside the home is thought of as vaguely indecent.' 'Women,' she writes damningly, 'are struggling to be good mothers in any society in which they are kept in virtual solitary confinement with young children for much of the time.' And, of course, for those women compelled to return to work sooner than they are ready – or wishing to return to work but unable to modify their hours – it is not social isolation that is likely to trigger their postpartum sadness, but more complete separation from the baby than they would wish for.

I don't believe most of the risk factors individually would tip so many women over the edge. But add them up: the low status we assign to mothering; the high value Western cultures place on a girlish figure; the isolation of today's nuclear family; the workplace pressure that sends husbands away from home when their partners need them most; the absence of ritual that would allow the new mother to mourn her lost self; the trauma of Caesarean section or high-intervention birth; the lack of adequate follow-up care, and the overall censorious whitewash of the whole experience – the surprise should not be how many new mothers are depressed postpartum in our society, but, rather, how many, in spite of all this, do well.

# Calling It Fair

'The heart of a mother is a deep abyss at the bottom of which you will always discover forgiveness.'

(Honoré de Balzac, *Mothers: A Loving Celebration*)

'The job market holds out an all-or-nothing prospect to new mothers: you can give your body and heart and lose much of your status, your money, your equality in your marriage; or you can keep your identity and your income – only if you abandon your baby all day long and try desperately to switch off the most powerful primal drive the human animal can feel.'

Robbie Pfeufer Kahn

All around me, it seemed, the baby's birth was cleaving couple after couple – once equals in roles and expectations – along the lines of the old traditional gender roles. That was certainly what I experienced when my husband went back to work and I found myself with a tiny baby, staring out the kitchen window into the backyards of the suburbs, living life much as I had read about it in Friedan's *The Feminine Mystique*. The baby's arrival acted as a crack, then a fissure, then an earthquake, that wrenched open the shiny patina of egalitarianism in the marriages of virtually every couple I knew.

I felt this when we started to venture out again as a couple. My husband and I were invited to dinner at Yasmin's apartment with some other thirtyish couples. Yasmin and I had both been with the babies all day, while our partners had been at the office. That evening, both babies had played with their dads until they had both collapsed in sleep on the men's laps. A single woman gushed: 'It's just wonderful, wonderful that we live in a time when fathers can act like this with their children.' Yasmin and I exchanged an amused yet angry glance: no one bothered to mention the fact that we had merely been caring for our children all day long and what a wonder *that* was.

The couples of our generation had long seen things from a similar vantage point. Now, with the baby, and the issue of work, men and women began to see things from completely different perspectives. For instance: in our exhaustion, we women saw the *virtues* of men working flexibly to take more care of the babies; the men, no matter how much they adored their kids, and how hands-on they were in many ways with the babies in the evening, primarily saw the professional and economic *drawbacks* of trying to work flexibly to take more care of the babies.

One guy we all knew took Fridays off to be home with his new baby and his wife. She worked at home every day, trying desperately to telecommute on half salary. She looked wiped out; he, a Gen-Xer with a goatee who helped to manage his family's small business, looked happy and relaxed.

No one else's husband among the couples we knew had been able, or willing, to make any kind of change in their work schedules. The women around me, I noticed, began to treat this young man as a demi-god. 'Dan takes *Fridays* off,' they would say meaningfully to their husbands. To the women, Dan's having taken even such a small step toward sharing responsibilities at home gave him an aura of desirability: he was a winner. To the other husbands, I began to realize, the fact that he could afford to take Fridays off meant his job wasn't that important. To the men – these egalitarian, pro-feminist men – Dan was a loser.

Of course, the men did not say this. But neither did these professional men – who could have afforded the material luxury of trying to work fewer hours – seriously attempt to renegotiate their own schedules. And the women were abandoning the negotiation to get the men to negotiate.

It dawned on me gradually what was happening. When the negotiation had been simply between two individuals, the women had been able to dare to insist on equality. But with the baby's arrival, social and economic pressures conspired with a kind of internal vulnerability to shunt the woman back into the more dependent role. The woman was no longer willing to take risks that involved the baby – risks of abandonment, of loss of love and financial help – that she would have been willing to take when it was her life alone that was at stake.

All around me, no matter how much couples adored the baby and one another, their marriages were in upheaval as these negotiations were overtly or quietly initiated – and broke down or were abandoned. According to psychologists John M. Gottman and Nan Silver's study of 1,400 couples, one of the most likely times for a marriage to fall apart is following the birth of the first baby, when almost 70 per cent of couples they observed reported a decrease in marital happiness.

The couples I saw around me were in good marriages. But the new parents were brittle. Both the men and the women were exhausted and irritable. The women were wiped out from baby care and whatever other work they were doing. They looked at the conflicting expectations of motherhood and the workplace, of their feminism and their marriages, and thought: Nothing I do is enough. The men, too, were tired – they worked all day and came home to have a baby thrust at them. They looked at their father's lives and saw that expectations upon their own lives had doubled, and thought: Nothing I do is enough.

## SOLOMON'S SWORD

Most people remember the story in the Book of Kings, where two women appear before King Solomon with a baby. The baby of one mother has died, and both women claim to be the living baby's mother. King Solomon puts the women to a test of true maternity, saying, 'I will cut this child in half, and give each of you half the child.'

According to the story, one woman agrees; the other woman cries out, 'My Lord, give her the living child, and in no wise slay it.' Thus Solomon knows that the second woman is the real mother.

As I talked with countless new mothers, it seemed that a version of King Solomon's strategy dominates women's choices today. Indeed, I think Solomon's sword overhangs us all in different ways. Women's willingness to sacrifice themselves for the good of their children is something that our society – from individuals to institutions – relies upon. It is useful leverage in pressuring women of all classes into giving in, in different ways, to unequal deals, negotiated hesitantly from the place of weakness that is one's concern for one's child.

Corporate life today relies on Solomon's sword – on what women will accommodate to in order to have jobs and still give time to their children. Solomon's sword hangs over us in the refusal of national government and corporations to support the crucial bond between mother, father and baby that is formed in the first year of life.

The marketplace created its own mystique of new motherhood – what I call 'Machine Mom'. This is the ideal of the superfunctional mother/worker, who is able to work at top capacity up to the due date, takes one to three months off to deliver, nurture and bond, finds top-notch child care, and returns to work, where, if she breast-feeds, she will pump discreetly in the employee ladies' room. Corporate life has thrived on the fruits of this pressure on women to conform to its relentless rhythms.

Tina, a Marketing executive in a highly successful British commercial company, described how she had been made to feel guilty about her 'demands' as a mother. 'I was able to negotiate a four-day week', she said, 'but this was a concession made only in terms of hours and pay not really reflected in workload. Whenever I raise the issue I'm usually made to feel (both by colleagues and managers) that my four-day week is a privilege and if I have a problem with it I should just work a five-day week like everyone else. It's also been made clear that promotion can't even be considered until I return to "full-time" working. But as I suffer from constant guilt about not seeing enough of my daughters during the week as things are, that's not an option I'm prepared to concede yet.'

Tina's story is a typical example of women's fear of the repercussions of demanding the time they need to birth and nurse and bond becoming cost-effective, playing into the hands of this corporate culture.

Workplaces emboldened by the egalitarian language of second wave feminism that often insisted women could do the job just like men (1970s feminism, for instance, objected to employee benefit guidelines that gave women reduced hours for pregnancy, categorizing the condition as 'a disability') have covertly coerced working women to delegate the details of pregnancy, birth and early motherhood to some offstage setting – as if all this were some messy, slightly alarming private hobby, like taxidermy or beekeeping, to be dealt with strictly in one's off hours and kept politely out of the field of vision of clients and co-workers.

But the fact is that a heavily pregnant woman, a woman who has just given birth, and a new or nursing mother – all are 'disabled' in a sense. They *do* need 'more' from their employers and families than men do. Post-feminist women's own guilt at needing special treatment has helped to ensure that women are slow to ask, let alone demand, their right to more at such times.

As Cara said, 'We need a feminism that says it's okay to take a break.'

Women themselves have been slow to lobby for their rights as expectant or new mothers in the workplace because they know corporate culture prefers unfettered working women, unstained by milk and unencumbered by demands. It is also very hard to lobby for better pay and conditions in order to do the work of motherhood *if good motherhood is itself emotionally defined as sacrifice*. In other words, if you say, I need to get paid for this – or put any other demand out on to the social table of negotiation – you hear the echo: Why isn't love enough for you? and the subtext *Bad Mother*.

If you looked only at its no-win policies, it's easy to conclude that society, particularly American society that claims to revere new mothers and newborn babies, does not bear out rhetoric with the real help that mothers and babies need.

The guidebooks on my shelf tended to treat the work–family dilemma as a private problem, offering little help. Some suggested daily grieving sessions; others encouraged mothers to feel their sadness and move through it. But deep breathing exercises could scarcely help us new mothers cope with our responsibilities in the only industrialized country without national maternity benefits, paid leave, or a coherent day care policy.

According to the 1993 Family and Medical Leave Act, American working mothers with newborn children get 12 weeks off without pay. But there are a few catches. First, women earn no income when they take leave – thus helping to bring about just the kind of dependent role that the mothers I spoke to were finding themselves in. In Australia, unpaid parental leave is available to all workers for 12 months, but only 17 per cent of female workers receive paid maternity leave from their employers. In contrast, most countries in

Europe pay home-based care-giving parents a benefit, stipend or salary – for from six months to up to *two years* after the birth of a baby. In the United Kingdom, the statutory maximum is now 18 weeks *paid* leave, although 35 of the top British companies pay far more. These rates, while much higher than American counterparts, nevertheless lag well behind those of other European countries, though improvements are planned. A group of female MPs are even pressing Prime Minister Tony Blair to guarantee a woman's postpartum job at flexible hours if she chooses that option. Of course, these countries provide such benefits through a level of taxation that Americans might resist, unless Americans were to come to see the birthing and early development of our future generations as being as valuable to society as public education or Social Security.

There's another catch. If women do decide to stay home, as Ann Crittenden has pointed out in her definitive book, *The Price of Motherhood*, they are punished economically for that choice: not only do they earn no salary for their important work, but the work of stay-at-home motherhood is not even calculated in Social Security benefits, leaving stay-at-home moms significantly impoverished, compared to working moms (and the husbands of stay-at-home moms), when those women retire.

Various states have sought to tap reserves of unemployment benefits so new mothers or fathers staying home with a baby can earn an income; however, the business community sees this money as its money. Local Chambers of Commerce have resisted this effort vociferously, and politicians, reliant on big business for campaign contributions, have neither motivation nor courage to take up the fight on behalf of mothers, who lack a powerful lobby.

It was not always thus in America: for one brief instructive moment, corporate and government leaders united to make things easier for mothers, rather than uniting forces to deal them out. The National Building Museum in Washington, DC, in its 1995 exhibit, *World War II and the American Dream*, showcased some of women's lost history that demonstrates just how achievable a real support system for working or stay-at-home mothers could be if there were a serious government/corporate push behind the effort.

During World War Two, the US government and corporate America desperately needed the mothers of the country to work in the munitions factories to supply weapons for the war effort, since the men who had once done those jobs were at the front. The Maritime Commission, working in tandem with manufacturers such as Kaiser, which was building shipyards, developed and deployed a massive strategic programme, reimbursed from government appropriations, to make it possible to free up women with small children for full-time or part-time shift work. Regional planners advised that women's burden be lightened 'by providing services – from shopping to laundry, cleaning facilities, a catering kitchen, and child care centres – in each neighbourhood clustered as close together as possible and supplemented by family health and recreation facilities.' In ten months' time, this private–public partnership established clean, bright, well-staffed 24-hour neighbourhood-based child care centres for children aged six months to six years, which raised women's productivity far above comparable factories without such child care. These attractive community child care centres, based in the women's own neighbourhoods, where teachers would dress and feed a hot breakfast to a sleepy child whose mom had to work the early shift, allowed women to feel secure about leaving their kids with familiar care-givers, even at irregular hours. Nurses monitored kids' health with preventive care and immunizations; the centres were seen as a community resource, with staff willing to take in children when parents had to shop or attend a meeting. Staff also welcomed older siblings to join their brothers and sisters on sleeping shifts. There was even a mending service for the kids' torn clothing on hand; and, 'most revolutionary' of all, as Donald Albrecht's book, *World War II and the American Dream*, about the programme describes it, on the way home, the tired mother could even pick up a nourishing hot meal, prepared and packed for her at the centre, to bring back home along with her children!

After the war, the men needed their jobs back, as Betty Friedan documented in *The Feminine Mystique*, and this elaborate, smoothly operating and highly successful solution to the work–family problem was simply shut down. Not even a memory remained in most history books to give women a blueprint with which to agitate for a comparable solution, let alone show naysayers that such a thing could be done.

Now, at the dawn of the twenty-first century, there is no such supporting structure for us as mothers – not even a trace of it – and politicians and corporate leaders rely on the fact that what can scarcely be imagined can rarely be lobbied for.

## MARRIAGES

The men in women's lives, too, it seemed, were sometimes touched by the shadow of Solomon's sword as they refashioned the new family's arrangements in directions that best suited them.

When the women I heard from described the rebalanced economy of the family's time and work after the birth of a baby, they had developed a strategy of denial to protect themselves and their marriages from the resentment that these unbalanced arrangements caused. Nonetheless, the resentment was there, expressing itself more often than not in quiet ways – 'bitchiness', depression, sexual withdrawal, even in possessiveness of the child's affections.

I found this same quiet, stubborn knot of resentment about the division of labour after birth among many of the mothers I interviewed. I was reminded of an interview in Arlie Russell Hochschild's book *The Second Shift*, about how women who work outside the home also do the lion's share of work within it. She describes how one woman repeatedly tried to get her husband to share the work; finally, in an act of capitulation, or of emotional survival, she decided to simply call it fair: she kept the upstairs clean, she reported, referring to the house, and he was responsible for downstairs. What was 'downstairs'? The garage.

The men in our group of friends and acquaintances believed expressly in women's equality. Yet according to Gottman and Silver's landmark research, men who hold such beliefs commit only four more *minutes* of domestic labour daily to the household than traditional men do. What was happening was that gradually many of the new moms were finding they had less of a say in their family lives than they had expected. Money, politics, commerce and a quiet but forceful ambience of male privilege in our culture all helped to shift their place in their relationships toward the 'less equal' side of what had been, before the baby's arrival, elegantly balanced.

Our talented, hardworking friend Gina was among the first of our acquaintances to discover how little say she had in balancing the couple's arrangements after their baby was born. She wanted badly to stay home for a while with her baby, Hannah. Her husband, Joe, wanted her to keep working at her highly paid job as a manager, which she loathed, since her high salary let him stay at his low-paid, but interesting and career-building, job in the non-profit world. If she stayed home, it would mean he'd have to get a job like the one she had now: a less intriguing but better-compensated one in the private sector. Though both were working full-time, and though he would play with Hannah and read her stories, he did a fraction of the housework and seldom changed a diaper. Yet he saw himself as a hands-on father and equitable mate.

Gina had given up arguing with him about how much she wanted him to take his turn now in the private sector so she could do something she wanted and stay home for a while. Yet when my husband and I visited for dinner, she slammed down the lasagne she'd prepared on to the table; after dinner, when Joe wandered into the living-room, where a pleasant fire was lit, and she was left to clean up as well, she whacked the Wedgwood plates, a gift from her in-laws, into the dishwasher angrily, declining our offers of help with an edge in her voice that was clearly not aimed in our direction.

When she sat down with us all on the couch at last, she welcomed the extra-tight hugs of what had become *her* small daughter, whom she cared for daily, the extra-hard tail-wagging of what was now *her* schnauzer puppy, whom it was her responsibility to walk and feed. To them, she was the goddess of breast, bottle, and Milk-Bones. Her body language voiced her feelings eloquently. It said clearly, *They love me best.*

Gina confided to me later that Hannah's closer attachment to her made it 'worth it' for her, and made her feel at times less resentful. It made her feel, at that moment, that the stacks of dishes waiting for her, from the dinner she had prepared for both of them after a full day at the office, were a small price to pay; or even that they were somehow part of the sweet natural order of things. This was the 'deal' that had clearly evolved. Joe's extra half-hour of sleep under the warm duvet while Gina wiped off the baby's bottom was compensated for by the moments when he would apparently helplessly turn over the crying child to his wife, like a parcel with her name on it, and Gina would feel the deep peace that came from the fact that she alone was able to silence her baby's cries.

But I couldn't help wondering, while watching the scene: Who wins here? Was there not some part of Joe that felt the lasagne weigh a little heavily in his stomach as he gossiped pleasantly with us, the sounds of Wedgwood crashing into the dishwasher in the kitchen behind him like the bombing of a small village? Was there no part of him that might like to find out whether he himself had the tender power to dry his child's tears?

But no – I was projecting. Joe was fine. He drank his micro-brewery beer, leaning against the white brick mantel, pleased with the good dinner and the company, apparently unaware of the unspoken melodrama that was making my husband and me prac-tically flinch as the dinner dishes went flying. It was an almost deliberate obliviousness I was starting to notice a lot in men in similar situations: an unconsciousness that was also deeply useful. I noticed a kind of 'default mode' that many of the supposedly 'new men' we knew fell into. With the arrival of the baby, in spite of their best intentions, perhaps, they were slipping back into the cultural roles with which they had grown up.

Dianne Paulson, the woman whose baby was kept from her in the hospital, described the slow shift in the balance of her marriage after the baby was born:

'I didn't realize how it would be all me, all the time. From bathing to feeding, I was shouldering the whole thing by myself. It was like another task to pull him into the process. And I could only handle so many tasks. I totally set this environment where I was the primary person and he was secondary. But he let me. And I resented it.

'I would say, "Would you give her a bath?" But he wouldn't realize she needed a bath and give her one if I didn't ask.

'When I cook, he does the dishes. A perfect example of an egalitarian relationship. But because it's such a pain, it's like Groundhog Day, to wash the same bottles over and over, he will wash an entire sink filled with dirty dishes, and leave the baby's dishes.

'So after the twentieth time, I said, "Do you somehow think that the baby's dishes are my responsibility?" He got very defensive. He doesn't really have an answer. I don't think he was conscious of it. And this is the most reasonable man I know.

'We had a couple of really big fights. I acknowledged that I was in over my head. His feeling was, he was working and stressed out. He felt all he did was not enough. He came home and had nothing left, and I expected more. But the bottom line was, he would not agree to do more.

'I was angry, but I expressed it in a passive-aggressive way. If we were going on a trip with the baby, I would say, "Why don't *I* go pack the baby's bag? Because it will be me." The fact is, I didn't trust him to pack what she needed. He would pack her bag and leave out her *diapers*.

'The packing is a metaphor for the myriad other things that go into caring for a child. Aside from his playing with her, everything else is me. Toys, food, books, doctor . . .'

I asked Dianne: 'He's a smart man and a high achiever at work. How hard would it be to pack what she needed?'

'How hard would it be, indeed? It requires a day-to-day knowledge of what she needs.'

'But,' I pressed, 'it's a limited set of items. What if you made a list?'

She erupted at me. 'A *list!*' she cried. 'Why should I make a *list*! That's more work for me! *Why should I make a list!*'

'You consciously think you have a modern marriage,' she said after a moment, more calmly. 'You are equals. You have this expectation there will be more parity in terms of responsibilities. But subconsciously it's a battle for both of you.'

Much depends, it seems, upon women's ability to find some way to 'call it fair'. Greta and her husband Bernie are both software designers. Her employers agreed to let Greta work three days a week, but they were giving her her usual workload, which she was accomplishing at reduced pay. She was also caring for the baby many more hours than her husband. As a result, she was staying up until one o'clock every morning to get it all done. And when there was a moment of downtime, her husband got it. When I talked with her, she began, as many women did, by expressing complete satisfaction with her domestic arrangements. But before long she was observing, 'Over the first nine months we've become farther and farther apart.' As she spoke more about the 'subtle' imbalances in her workload and her mate's, she sighed deeply.

'This division of labour is an issue we have had,' she said, 'since we brought the baby home. Before, we both had personal freedom. Now, when he says, "I want to play on the computer on Saturday," or go to the gym, or go out with friends, it comes out of my time; really, out of me.

'I said he couldn't hit me with a double whammy: he couldn't stay out so late that I have to both stay home alone with her at night *and* be expected to take care of her alone in the morning so he can sleep in.'

'How much of that conversation did it take to change the situation? Or did you have to adjust your expectations?' I asked.

'I adjusted,' she said. 'Plus, I know what his kind of creative work takes.'

'But – you do the same creative work he does,' I said. 'Do you get time for the things you like to do too?'

Greta did not respond immediately. 'When we talk about Ben's career, there is this small bite I feel – a twinge of chagrin. We talk about, "What if he's at the top?" But I never entertain that possibility any longer for myself.'

The baby's toys were scattered on the floor. Greta's workspace was set up in a corner, with spreadsheets posted on the wall.

'Are you tired?' I asked.

'I am tired,' she said.

'What time does the baby get up?'

'About six.'

'You work till one a.m. – you've been going on five hours' sleep,' I said.

'Yep,' she said shortly.

'You give your husband time to do the things he cares about on weekends,' I said again. 'When do you get a chance to do the things you care about?'

'If I asked him, he'd say I don't ask him to do enough,' she said somewhat sadly. 'I'm one of those women who compares myself to women on a farm with twelve children. I'm kind of a stoic. I never felt I was entitled to ask for more.'

I thought of how many women told me dispiritedly about how their husbands waited for them to ask – or to make a list – and how demoralizing that was for them. I could not help thinking that there was some element of passive aggression in this recurrent theme of nice men, good playful dads, full of initiative and motivation at work, who 'waited to be asked' to do the more tedious baby-related work at home, until the asking was finally scaled back or stopped.

Then Greta told a story, startling to me in the context of the interview, about how, some time before, because she had felt that things were so unbalanced between herself and her husband, she had gone so far as to consider being unfaithful with a man at work who had treated her with great consideration. She had pulled back through force of will and was justifiably proud of the work she and her husband had since done on their marriage.

But the rumblings could still be heard, faintly, in the distance: 'My almost having that affair that time was a result of my adapting too much,' she said.

'Am I making myself unhappy again?' she asked herself, looking out with an expression of sheer fatigue into the middle distance. 'I don't think so. But that is my tendency.'

Sarah, head of the Marketing department of a major hotel-supply company, told me about 'the deal' she had struck several years before with her husband, a hotel consultant, before she had her first baby, in order to have that baby. Sarah's situation was particularly intriguing because, while it was much the same as that of many other women I heard from, in this case she and her husband had spelled out and negotiated the inequality – 'the deal' – in advance, whereas the other women and their mates talked about the expectations as equitable, but then the women found that they were not able to negotiate the agreements they had expected, and so felt obliged eventually to 'call it fair'.

'We don't talk about the deal anymore,' she said. 'The deal is implicit and unstated.'

'And what is "the deal"?' I asked.

'I am responsible for the kids,' she replied.

'The deal', she explained, was this: 'Ed and I wanted to get married. He had already had three kids, as many as he'd wanted. It wasn't conceivable to me that I wouldn't have kids. We were dying to be together. We both recognized that we were made to be together. So his way of squaring this circle was to say, "Okay, we will have kids – but you will be responsible for them."

'Unfortunately, I didn't know enough at the time to say to him, "What exactly does that mean?" I was predisposed out of the ignorance that all people have before having kids to underestimate what a *big thing*, an overwhelming responsibility, it is.

'Ed warned me, many times, "It's easy for you to accept the idea of being solely responsible in the absence of actual children." I said, "No, I know what I am talking about." I didn't have a clue.

'Until the child came along.

'I can remember reading in all those books, how some mothers in the first six weeks never get dressed, and forget to eat. I thought, What kind of women are these? How could anyone forget to eat, not find the time to take a shower or get dressed? It sounded as if these were some slovenly, preposterous women. And of course, I had my child and was completely overwhelmed by it, and didn't find the time to eat or take a shower or get dressed.

'I was solely responsible for everything, from making sure we had enough diapers, to actual feedings and every bath. Every aspect of child care was solely my responsibility. After our second child was born, this changed somewhat.

'But I was still bathing both kids by myself nightly. They were at an age where it was impossible for them to share me; they were both clamouring out of the tub at the same time. A point came where I said, "I can't do this alone; you have to help me get these kids to bed at night." And he did. Happily, by the way.

'Still, I basically came to understand that he was never going to initiate anything to get the child-related work done, but that he would respond to instruction, if I could bring myself to give instruction. But I didn't want that role. I really hate issuing instructions. It makes me feel like a general. I don't like how it makes me feel about myself: that I am bossy, a control freak. But more than anything, it makes me feel responsible for everything. That feels burdensome. Lonely. Pulled in fifteen different directions. I resisted it. My natural tendency is to do everything I can myself.

'This is Ed's idea of packing or even going somewhere: He puts on his coat; he puts on his shoes; and he says, "I'm ready." And it is totally up to me to get the kids rounded up, get them shod, put the coats on, when they were infants to pack diapers, diaper wipes, formula, a change of clothes and all the things you carry around with you when they are little.

'When Nico was about nine months old, I was on the floor with him playing the way you do with a nine-month baby – sorting cubes. We were doing this for what seemed to me to be a really long period of time. Ed came in, saw this scene and said, "Oh you're just entranced." And I said, "Are you out of your mind? I am bored silly."

And he was stunned – he had no idea.

'Sometimes, I hate to say, I go on a business trip just to get away from all the demands. I sometimes feel I am getting pecked to death by ducks.

'Other mothers say that I have one advantage: The deal is overt. I am liberated from the arguments they have. They have arguments because there isn't any clarity; there is this fictional ideal the women are hoping for that is constantly in tension with the reality. My friends say that their husbands don't take equal responsibility for the kids, but they claim equal say in decisions about the kids. And let's face it, there are all kinds of different ways you can disagree with your husband about how the kids should be raised. For me it is different: No representation without taxation! Because I take all the responsibility, I have all the power.

'But that is small compensation. I was feeling overwhelmed by the experience of being a mother. But we still haven't really changed the expectations of the deal.'

'Why haven't you renegotiated the deal if you are finding it overwhelming?' I asked.

'I am loath to push the negotiation any further. I am loath to experience the disappointment, which I don't think I can bear. I feel I can best preserve Ed as my friend by not pushing these issues. To push him in these other ways infringes on our friendship, which has always been a healthy part of our great romance. To push him puts us into a struggle. Part of me says, "Just accept his limitations." Also, I have an almost impossible time asking for help. I am reluctant to admit to myself, "I can't."

'Occasionally I'll revolt. I'll sit down in the car and buckle up my seatbelt and fold my arms. And he'll pause and wait for me to buckle the kids up – and eventually he'll turn around and do it. Or occasionally, if it is he who is driving and wants to be somewhere on time, I will put my coat and shoes on and say "I'm ready." And leave him there to corral the children. Once he gets it, he will take charge. But at the same time, he'll see how hard it is, being the organizing principle of the family.

'There was this magnificent moment, once. Ed came home, and when he walked in the door, Becky started talking to him, Nico started in, I tried to get a word in, the sitter started, we all just descended on him – and you could see that he was absolutely spinning. I so enjoyed the moment because it is what I face every day when I come home.

'It does help that he understands how hard it is on me, keeping all the balls in the air. Both of us try to deal with the tensions around "the deal" with humour – as much as possible.

'The other day, I was taking a nap and Becky asked her father, "Daddy, when Momma is sleeping, who is in charge?" And you know what he said? "Momma."

'Finally, to tell the truth, even though I made this deal, I thought he would change. I thought gradually it would be different, and in fact, as the kids get older and he gets more interested in them, he does get more involved. But I am still the one with the main responsibility. Part of me does not want to try to change the terms directly because I keep hoping he'll do it on his own.

'That part of me is a place of hope. It is a little burning ember.'

As many other women were describing it, the part of them that hoped their mates would shoulder responsibilities more equally at home was a hopeful place, and it was also a romantic place. The men involved did not really seem to understand the connection between the amount of domestic labour they were willing to do and their wives' enthusiasm, or lack of it, about their intimate life. (Greta had said right after describing her resentment about the division of labour, 'There is a lot less sex – half to a quarter as much.') It was not a conscious 'boycott' on the part of the wives; but a subtle connection often seemed to be there. What the men were saving in child care and housework after the baby was born was also costing them, erotically and romantically.

Indeed, Gottman and Silver's data shows that there is a common connection between sex and housework among the majority of couples (in addition, his research team at the University of Washington found that men's willingness to do the housework and child care that their wives thought fair was one of seven main factors that predicted whether the couple's marriage would thrive, or whether they would eventually divorce). Gottman discovered that women find men who are willing to do their share of the housework erotic.

Women's voices seemed to confirm the direct connection: 'I have never withheld sex consciously,' said Barbara, a part-time data processor and mother of three, 'but I know from my own experience that there is a direct correlation between your partner's helpfulness and your sex life. My friend and her boyfriend were visiting, and Steven is great with the kids. Putting my kids to bed is a thirty-minute ritual and it drives me crazy. Steven emerged from the back of the house and said, "The kids are in bed." I didn't have to lift a finger. Somebody had handed me this enormous present. And . . . I wanted to have sex with him! I never had that feeling about him before and believe me, I haven't had it since.

'Certainly on days when my husband has been really helping, I have wanted to be romantic. But when he is assuming I will be able to handle everything by myself, then when he approaches me, I can't respond.'

Cara and Yasmin and I were with our babies at the playground. The ground was frozen, and the wooden benches uncomfortable for the long stretches of time we spent waiting and chatting while kids slept.

Cara, a sweet-tempered, statuesque woman with a buttery Southern accent, told us that her marriage had begun to founder after the baby's birth.

'From the start,' Cara said, as she rocked the Peg Perego stroller gently with her foot, 'I was willing to do the lion's share of the care-giving. I just wanted true love in return.

'When I met Sam, he made me feel safe. We were inseparable.'

After they married, Cara kept working doing architectural drawings. When she became pregnant, they moved to a development in DC. 'Sam was now a manager in the union, and better paid than I was. Both of us had decided, together, that it would make sense for me to take an extended leave from work.

'Sam loved the move. But I was missing the office, and I hated it. I was very pregnant when the movers finished unpacking and closed the front door behind them, and I just remember looking at this sea of boxes and at the cars parked outside, there was no one there but women and small children, and I remember feeling frightened of eventually being alone there with a baby. I did not know where to begin.'

Daisy was born – Caesarean section, eight pounds, six ounces – and Cara's marriage started to suffer. Cara had not wanted sex for a while after the birth, and Sam felt rejected. In addition, Cara said that Sam, overwhelmed by the baby's demands, and by Cara's lack of availability to him as she cared for the baby, began to withdraw. The more Sam ignored her, the more heavily her baby's demands weighed upon Cara. And there it was.

According to Cara, after the baby she and Sam had become different people from who they had been before the baby was born.

Sam would come home and scarcely pat Cara on the shoulder. He would make a beeline for Daisy, pick her up, and rock her, stroking her hair, and sparking one elaborate word game after the next. He would take Daisy out to look at the stars, and take her in to give her a bath, making a duck family interact in complex ways in the bubbles.

Cara, in contrast, said she felt she was treated increasingly like a junior staffperson in the family firm. 'Okay,' he would say to her by way of conversation, 'you need to submit our insurance form for the car. And you need to make an appointment with the lawn guys to aerate the lawn, before it gets too cold.'

Sometimes, she confided, after a morning when Sam would give Daisy a nose kiss, and hold her in the air until she squealed, Cara, holding her coffee, would feel her eyes fill with tears that, since there was no point in crying, would never quite spill. Then after he left for work she would sit with her baby in the dining bay of the nice little apartment, dressed in the robe that Sam had bought her as a wedding present, now tatty with Daisy's accumulated stains. She used to feel cute and cuddly in that robe, she said. Now she felt dingy and old.

As time went on, these small demotions became the texture of her life. 'My self-image was changing,' said Cara. 'I used to think of myself as an attractive woman. But now I feel . . . like a drudge. Sexless.

'I have zero sex drive,' she said. 'I mean, I know I'm still breast-feeding, but I don't think that's the reason. And that's not like me – no joy about that part of living.'

At length, Cara said, she felt increasingly alone in her marriage. At the tough moments, she said she thought about divorce: I could support myself, she thought. Why not go away with Daisy?

But then, each morning when she looked at Daisy gurgling at her daddy, full of glee, she would think to herself, I can't do that to my child. It will get better. And she also thought: If I had to work all day to support my child, who would be with her? She saw Daisy in a one-bedroom flat on a foldout bed, with some careless sitter who didn't read to her or play with her or love her. And Cara would think: My happiness is not as important as her well-being. I have to stay.

Cara tried hard to be all things to Daisy. When Daisy wept, Cara rushed to comfort her; when she howled, Cara tried to still the inner demon that occasionally said to her, 'Let her cry!' or: 'Tell the little brat to shut up!' But some days were just too hard.

Getting Daisy dressed was nearly impossible. Daisy had figured out that if she made her feet rigid, her mother couldn't get her socks to go on; and if she screamed loudly enough, her mother would yield for a while to soften her daughter's howls. So Daisy, when she felt like it, would scream directly in her mother's ears; the stress made Cara's stomach knot up.

There were times she had to walk right away from her shrieking Daisy, go into her bedroom, close the door, and pray, just to keep from harming herself or her daughter.

And Cara is a good mother.

The fact is, she would never have dreamed of raising a hand to Daisy. Cara did all the things good mothers are supposed to do. But the demon voice inside her, filling her with anger and despair, would not be stilled. Yet Cara was not permitted to acknowledge even to herself these feelings of impatience, let alone of jealousy.

After all, this was a baby – her precious daughter – causing her to feel such anguish. So she felt ugly on the outside, and monstrous on the inside. What sort of mother could be jealous of her own child? And how could those emotions co-exist with her passionate love for her child? She was caught in a love triangle, and like all love triangles, it interspersed bliss with unhappiness.

After my baby was born, I joined a support group of new mothers who met at the local YMCA. This group became Cara's primary relationship. We could be regaled for half an hour with the saga of her trying to exchange a pair of shoes while Daisy whacked at store displays. We consoled Cara when she was sad, and were tactful when she didn't feel like talking; we noticed Cara's hair when she got a new haircut, and applauded her creativity when she made squishy paste out of flour and water for Daisy to play with. We cooed over Daisy's new teeth and sounds. But we also listened to Cara's opinions about politics and the news, and told her our own. The new mothers' group became not just a group of colleagues, people who understood and appreciated how challenging mothering could be, but also a source of the emotional support she was not getting at home.

Still, although she could talk to us individually or within the group about diaper rash and nursing problems, there were things she knew she could not say. Even to us as a group, as responsive and accepting as we were, she couldn't admit what she told me and Yasmin privately: 'Sometimes,' she said, 'I feel my child has destroyed my marriage. Sometimes I want my child to disappear so I can have my husband back.'

An image often stayed at the forefront of her thoughts, of a teapot, tilted over, with the proverbial last drop hanging from its lip: 'Tip me over and pour me out,' the motto beneath it might read. At other times she imagined herself to be a little generator with another tiny appliance plugged into her, sucking energy. And yet her own power source had been disconnected. They were powerful, and disturbing, images. To my mind, Cara was a good mother who was not getting enough love and support. She was burning out.

She had begun to think about going back to work. In broaching the back-to-work issue with Sam, she found her husband would start to add up the costs: 'There is transportation. Dry cleaning. Child care,' and point out that it was not 'worth it' economically. In fact, it would be slightly more expensive to the family than Cara's staying home. But his calculation was a particular kind of addition: he would take the child care out of Cara's projected income, rather than counting it as a family expense. (This assumption – that her own salary, even in the short term, must somehow cover child care and a reasonable profit or else 'it doesn't make sense' for her to go back to work – was reasoning I would hear from women whose partners wanted them home, just as I would hear 'We need your salary to cover expenses' from husbands who were reluctant to scale down their standard of living in spite of their wives' longing to stay home.) The trouble with the discussions was that by now, with Sam as the breadwinner, the balance of power in decision-making had tilted away from Cara. She could not convince him that it was worth the initial expense to invest in her career, and certainly could not convince him that if he tried to negotiate coming home earlier a couple of days a week to relieve the sitter, they could easily afford it.

She did not feel able to persuade him. His work schedule was non-negotiable, and anyway, she had lost clout.

'He says "It doesn't make sense objectively,"' Cara told us, referring to Sam's position on her returning to work, 'just because it makes sense to me and not to him. Meanwhile it's I who am getting older, with an ageing résumé. I feel it will be like this indefinitely. Because I sure don't see him adjusting his schedule *ever*: his day just gets longer and longer. But I feel as if he doesn't see that it is my having stayed home that has made his job possible, and that should count for something, too.'

Yasmin said: 'You need to stand up for yourself more. Change your part of the dance. You know, like: "I'm happy to listen to whatever you want, but please respect what I want too and listen to what I have to say. We need to compromise." You guys have to find a solution that works for you both.'

The phrase 'a solution that works for you both' hung in the air. We shifted uneasily on the icy wooden seats. The phrase was a sort of euphemism to salvage our self-respect. For no one's equation included a husband who was going to scale back his work hours, or take flexitime. That option was not on anyone's table.

Cara had stayed home with the baby all day because Sam was not about to stay home with the baby for even part of the day, and Cara believed, along with Sam, that the baby should not be left with no parent around all day. Having made that choice, and having stopped bringing in income, Cara lost negotiating clout. Having lost clout, she was in an even more difficult position because, now that she was ready to go back to some kind of work, child care would be calculated by Sam out of her earnings. If Sam refused to be flexible with his hours, she was forced to be flexible with hers, if one parent was to be with the baby part of the time. But then she might *never* have a job that paid more than child care, let alone a career she cared about.

Solomon's sword hung over Cara.

Sam knew how unhappy Cara was, and understood her sense of loss of control over her own path. He loved her. Yet, rather than renegotiate his work life and 'take a hit' professionally – something they could reasonably afford to risk – he was willing to tolerate her distress at having no tolerable way to resume her career and still ensure that Daisy had a parent around at least part of the time.

Sam wasn't a bad guy. And we did not know what it felt like from his point of view. He was like a lot of the other nice guys in our circle: they believed in fairness. They were men who believed in the values of feminism, and wanted to raise their daughters in a world that would be fair to them. They loved their wives. It was just that the child care sacrifice wasn't going to come out of their professional chits pile.

Cara had been labouring under a misconception. She had fallen in love and married and given birth with the understanding that there was an 'us' underneath it all. But in this negotiation, it seemed Sam was willing to pit a 'his' against a 'hers'.

At that private insight, she said, something in her broke. She was facing the loss of what had made her fall in love with him, as a younger woman: the faith in the 'us'. He had promised to be her best friend, and with this categorical refusal to really negotiate from a position of being willing to sacrifice equally, she felt he had, in a way, tricked her. She said she wondered if he had never really meant what he had said about being her best friend, with its implicit promise that all would be fair between them.

And there it was.

Daisy had woken up. She began to whimper. Cara carefully guided a bottle into her mouth, but the bottle was not yielding apple juice fast enough. The baby took the bottle out of her mouth, and stared at the nipple in helpless outrage. Cara knew that the whimper would shortly escalate into a truly brain-piercing scream. As if on cue, it did.

'I've got to go,' she said to us. 'Midget meltdown.'

Minnie, who was feeling a bit better since Robin had last reported on her distraught condition, talked to me while we sat in her yard about her sense of having 'slipped' in her marriage since the baby was born.

Minnie was the model of a modern woman: organized, competent, amiable, blessed with a calm spirit and unthreatening, healthy, young-motherly looks. First, she had quit the job she loved, working for a ceramics production company in Seattle, because her husband's work took him to Washington. Then, she had their baby. Her husband made plenty of money. Now, she was reluctant to hire a baby-sitter, even for a few hours a week to rest or read a book, because she no longer brought in more than the pin money of interest on her savings. Her husband said she could do it all by herself. She resented it but chose to set aside her resentment or, rather, rename it, calling it fair, because he was 'working all day'.

'But you're working all day too, and starting at six in the morning,' I noted. 'Does he realize how much it would cost to get someone to do the things that you do? You are contributing economically to the household,' I said, about to trot out statistics compiled for decades now by feminists: child care worker, $20,000 a year; cook, $8.50 an hour; chauffeur, $12.00 an hour, etc.

But like Yasmin's comment about 'a solution that works for you both,' those statistics vanished like smoke in the air between us, because the marketplace in which her husband earned his living did not credit them to her as real.

Minnie had two degrees and had once earned $50,000 a year. She had owned a vintage motorcycle. Today it was all gone, along with her Skechers boots and double ear studs. She was now a stay-at-home mother, and she had gladly sold her motorcycle to help put together the down payment on their mortgage. But she had never dreamed that their relationship, her partnership, would become so unbalanced.

Rick, her husband, had been her best friend. They had gone to the same college, gotten equally good grades, shared doing the laundry together in their first apartment, applied for the same kinds of jobs. Usually she had done even a little better than he at school and in the marketplace. As young lovers, she had worn his comfortable T-shirts while she had balanced her ample chequebook as they paid their bills together, her feet tucked under his on the couch.

Now they were living in different social classes. He wore Hugo Boss ties to work and drove a Miata, while she stayed home wearing sweatclothes mottled with formula. He was clean at the end of his work day, and she was dirty. He was working with his mind, and she was doing repetitive manual labour, along with the labour of love that is taking care of a baby. If the baby spat up while Rick was still in his impeccable work clothes, he would hand him over to Minnie; more spit-up would not make a difference to what she was wearing. When they went out with the baby, they took Minnie's old car, because it was already filthy with baby stains.

All that she could take in stride. But when Minnie wanted to visit a friend in her home town, and she had asked for the plane fare from Rick, she faced a struggle. It's not that she didn't get the money eventually; it was the way that she had to petition for it. 'Like Lucy asking for pin money from Desi,' she said. Because he thought of the money he earned as being primarily 'his'.

The change was not a sudden, evil, Jekyll-and-Hyde transmogrification. It was subtle and evolved day by day. Rick thought he was a good father, a good guy. He thought he was being reasonable. 'I bring in the money, Min; I work for it,' he kept trying to explain to his increasingly alienated wife. 'I just think I should have more of a say in allocating how it's spent,' he said. It was an argument that might have been made fifty years ago, as if the women's movement had never happened.

How did she handle how she felt? I asked.

'Well, first of all, no sex. You know?' she said as she wiped her baby's mouth. Like a lot of women I knew, she was turning her day-to-day frustration into a kind of ongoing irritable humour. There was no 'second of all'. We both knew the conversation had hit a wall.

I stood to bounce my baby, who was waking up in her Snuggli and starting to get fussy. Despite our degrees and our assumptions and expectations about equality, I thought with exasperation, our generation of new mothers was a train wreck waiting to happen. Was there much difference between what Minnie and Cara and I were experiencing and what Minnie's grandmother had felt contemplating a load of wash and a wringer by a well, or what Minnie's mother had felt, in Betty Friedan's era, gazing out the back screen door on to an empty clothesline in a cul-de-sac in Levittown?

Women who work in countries offering paid maternity leave, such as the UK, must face a different challenge: after enjoying a special period of closeness and bonding with their newborn often denied to their American counterparts, they must return to work and face a separation from their baby that can seem all the crueller for its postponement. For many women, work can be a welcome release from the day-to-day drudgery of changing diapers, endless washing and cooking, and can give them a new joy in rediscovering their old selves, the selves they were before having their baby. But for others, the mere thought of going back to work on a regular basis can prove intolerable. One such woman, a successful graphic designer in an advertising company, described 'sitting on a bus looking at a picture of my baby and sobbing my heart out'.

But for women like this, a return to the workplace is a matter of economic necessity. In the United Kingdom today, 62 per cent of mothers of pre-school age children are employed on a full- or part-time basis. In a Birth and Motherhood Survey commissioned by BUPA and *Mother and Baby* magazine, 81 per cent of women interviewed said that if money were no object they would rather stay at home with their babies. Only 6 per cent said they enjoyed working full time, while 82 per cent were 'less career-minded following the birth of their baby'. A further 50 per cent claimed that having a baby jeopardized their career prospects.

## BABY-SITTERS AND DAY CARE

The couples who do both work and share child care after work hours also, of course, usually rely on baby-sitters, nurseries and day care centres. This third leg of the footstool brings its own fragility of equilibrium into the young family's life.

Yasmin and I regularly took our babies to the playspace on rainy days. There was literally nowhere else comfortable to go if we wanted to get out of our houses. Now I had a baby daughter sleeping peacefully – or mewling and squirming – in a Snuggli of my own.

When I first saw the population of moms and care-givers at this indoor playground, I was taken back. In my naivety, growing up in a feminist household, I had thought that such spaces would be sexually integrated – even racially integrated – by the time I became a mother.

But the scene before us was as stratified by gender and colour as any place in America could be. The kids were almost all white. Women cared for the children. In our Washington neighbourhood, during the week, there were no men. The women who cared for the white children were brown and black care-givers and white mothers. The brown and black children of the care-givers and the mothers of their communities were nowhere to be seen in that picture.

This was what has come of the women's movement's challenge to the workplace, I realized, as Yasmin and I sat on the cheaply constructed balcony of the playspace, listening to the noise of the kids and the tired admonitions of the black and brown care-givers, the less tired but still often irritable calls of the white women rising up to us. This was ground zero. The women of all colours asked the men to share the home work, but to little avail. The middle-class and upper-middle-class women wanted to go back to work or had to, and the men did not or could not scale back; so the women and men who could afford to had subcontracted childcare – 'and subcontracted the conflict', as Robin would point out – to working-class women, mostly women of colour, who watched their children for money.

We took up our places in this system nonetheless. My husband and I found we were up against his 50-to-60 hours workweek. We were not, as it turned out, living in a commune and growing hemp, or raising llamas, or working five-hour days each in an entirely remade work economy, or whatever it was I had vaguely imagined in my youth would eventually support a man and a woman co-parenting equally. I looked at a local day care centre, an expensive one, and was horrified at the rows of six-month-old babies held in the arms of depressed-looking women immobile in a windowless room. We looked for a baby-sitter.

So many women had said, about becoming a mother, 'I never thought I would become one of those women who . . .' Well, I never thought I would become one of those women who took up a foreordained place in a hierarchy of class and gender. Yet here we were, to my horror and complicity, shaping our new family structure along class and gender lines – daddy at work, mommy and care-giver from two different economic classes sharing the baby work during the day – just as our peers had done.

We had interviewed for a part-time care-giver; the March of Nannies through our living-room began. It was a job description that seemed rigidly segregated by ethnicity: there were women who didn't seem to like children, and women who loved children but it was their own beloved children they missed. There were Bolivian women, Guatemalan women and Ecuadorean women. With each interview I got sadder: for women, wealth seemed to be gauged not only by economic figures, but also by who gets to raise her own children, with what kind of help, and who must raise someone else's as well as her own, with no help.

We found a strong, loving, accomplished care-giver, for which we were grateful. But my feelings were profoundly mixed. I was shocked at how the 'choices' I had blithely believed I could make were in fact, in spite of relative privilege, still in many ways made for me. I had wished I had more choices about how I was to manage this new thing called motherhood.

When I was growing up, I knew exactly how I wanted my life to be 'after the revolution' in gender roles and work expectations that I fully expected would arrive just in time – that is, before I had children. I had wanted to work at a job I cared about and share child-rearing with a man I loved. I had wanted a mother and a father raising children side by side, the man moving into the world of children, the woman into the world of work, in equitable balance, maybe each working flexibly from home, the two making the same world and sharing the same experiences and values. The extra shift, a part-time shift, I had thought dreamily when I was young, would be taken up by some kind of additional, nurturing, community-based care, one that I had – deliberately? – never peered closely enough into the future to try realistically to assess or even really imagine.

'Ha,' as women usually comment at this point in the fantasy.

I thought about this fantasy one evening as our care-giver and I were bathing the baby. What I did not want was what I had now: a stranger, a 'nanny', that condescending word, however competent and kind, to work with me and mother with me in a world peopled, it seemed, only by women, as evening fell in the suburbs outside. What I didn't anticipate was a cavernous suburban house where many of my most tender moments during the workday were shared with a woman my mother's age, whom I admired and respected but who was not my kin, who missed her own family and children and grandchildren while I missed my husband.

When my husband worked late, our care-giver watched the evening news with me, half-hovering, keeping a dignified distance, because even though she was, through the nature of her workday, 'like a part of the family' – a term I heard affluent friends using without awareness of how insulting it was to a professional, let alone someone who has a family of her own – she was also, under the everyday warmth of our work together, an employee after all.

It was not my dream to do it this way, my husband at work, a competent older woman at home with me slaking down my daughter's little feet, me holding a hand cupped under her and turning her soft little arms and curious porcelain hands to the tepid water, the bathwater splashing our wrists and palms as we handled the baby, apparently intimately, as if we were moulding a sculpture of living clay. We then, working carefully together, wrapped the precious baby in a towel with a hood with little ears on top.

I was loving the moment and my baby with all my heart. I did indeed melt with joy in her. Yet in that joy was exhaustion, and frustration, too, about the life I found I was living, that I had both chosen and not chosen.

This scene was not what I had wanted. What I had wanted was a revolution.

Dianne said, when I talked with her, 'When I asked my husband for more help, his pat response was, "We need the baby-sitter to work more hours." That upset me. It was like his shrugging off a responsibility. It wasn't about a third party. It was about what I needed from *him*. I didn't want more of the sitter. I wanted Emma to have more of her parents. I think that the care-giver alleviates the guilt of the husband. There were a lot of moments that I experienced on my own or with the baby-sitter that I wanted to share with him. I'm not married to the sitter,' she said.

'Has your husband worked less since the baby was born?' I asked, knowing that that was an option for this family economically.

'Not one hour less,' Dianne replied, with no hesitation.

Men and women employing care-givers, of course, are the privileged minority. Most women in the workforce, according to Ann Crittenden in *The Price of Motherhood*, must rely upon a patchy, horrendously expensive – $30 billion – 'toddler/industrial complex', what researcher Kathy Modigliani calls the increasingly exploited, degraded and monopolistic system of 'Kentucky Fried Child Care', the private (or sometimes the undersupported home-based) network of day care centres.

Crittenden points out that, according to the Labor Department, only one-third of day-care workers in the USA earn even minimum wages; a third earn the minimum wage. As Crittenden notes: 'These women's poor pay has less to do with their education than with the fact that they are competing with the ultimate cheap labour: mothers and other unpaid female relatives. As sociologist Paul England puts it, 'We're used to getting it for free, so the attitude is, "Why pay for it?"' A third of all child care teachers leave their centres each year. Many centres have turnover rates near 50 per cent annually – a situation that is a disaster for developing children with their need for reliable attachments to nurturing adults. As Crittenden concludes, and every concerned working mother and father knows, 'what some people call turnover, children experience as loss.'

Meanwhile, the children of the army of private and day care care-givers are watched by worse-paid baby-sitters, or by grandmothers, or by relatives in countries far away – in Ecuador and India, in the Caribbean and Central America and the Philippines.

I learned that if I sat in the park with our baby and chatted with an immigrant nanny who was wiping the drool of a white baby, or teaching a white toddler to share, within minutes she would show a photograph of her own children far away, whom she might not have seen for years. And her eyes would fill with tears. The kids far away heard their mothers' voices occasionally, over the telephone.

These women must often cross oceans and leave their children, big kids and small, with relatives. They often live in rooms at the margins of other families, or in rooms alone, giving love and care to other women's children, so that their own kids – whom they cannot touch, hug or teach to share – can have school uniforms and good food, education and a better chance at life.

The situation for American-born care-givers is different but also too often anguished. Almost all the American-born care-givers in our neighbourhood were African American. One of these care-givers, who looked after a five-year-old white child, described to me her worries about her own five-year-old son in substandard care in which the TV is on all day. Another talked about her twelve-year-old daughter, who is a latchkey child, whom she must phone every afternoon from the comfortable home where she keeps someone else's children safe, to try to make certain her own child is safe.

Solomon's sword hangs over these mothers, too.

Care-givers have no union, no minimum wage, are often paid illegally, thus generating few retirement benefits, and usually lack health insurance, just as their employers usually lack accident insurance if they are hurt on the job. As Crittenden notes, 'the combination of lax standards and an illegal labour force makes it much easier for workers to be exploited. Few laws protect even legal household workers . . . Vacation and medical insurance are rarities . . . the IRS reported in 1995 that many employers are still not paying their nannies' social security taxes.'

This situation scarcely gives workers an incentive to provide their best to kids in their charge – yet the majority apparently do. Indeed, though worries about the level of care given by day care workers and household workers are well known, many care-givers have their own critiques of the care that they see working *parents* provide: Sharon, a woman in her fifties who works as a care-giver in Manhattan, told me about the view of modern family life that she formed as she cared for the children of dual-career couples who worked long hours. As a working mother, I found I had to force myself to listen:

'The kids are spoiled,' she told me, 'materially over-indulged. The mother gives them affection when she walks in. What she doesn't give them is time. The kids go home in the afternoon, the sitters are so poorly paid that they have little incentive to turn the TV off. The kids have no imagination, they don't make up stories. The TV has become an emotional substitute.

'These families have bookshelves stuffed with books, but the parents have no time to read to the kids. That's what we see. It's *not* the blue-collar parents who don't read to the child. It's the upper-class homes. The yuppies are too tired.

'The parents who work these long hours are tolerating things they hate. The TV, the no vegetables; they capitulate because the precious time they have at home, they don't want to use fighting.' Sharon pursed her lips: 'If you only knew,' she said. 'Most baby-sitters would not want a family life like yours if you gave us every material thing you have.' And, she said, the care-givers she knew cared well for and even loved many of the children in their charge; but they felt keen resentment, continually expressed to one another but almost never to their employers, about a workplace that the parents tended to treat so casually, so unprofessionally; where, as Sharon put it, 'The kid gives you his measles while you are taking care of him, and the mom and dad won't pay for the days of work you lose when you have to stay home sick.'

Most working families who rely on baby-sitters would resist seeing themselves in Sharon's description. Nonetheless, the economics of the profession that supports the most privileged two-career families, as well as the majority who rely upon child care centres, are grim. In the absence of government and corporate support for raising the pay and status of care-givers, dual-career families rely on one of the lowest paid, least-respected private positions in society to hold their family together during an entire rigid workday. While many parent/care-giver teams work out arrangements of great mutual regard and even a measure of fairness, and while many families adore the day care workers who are their kids' emotional touchstone during the workweek, that is a private stroke of good fortune rather than a national work-family policy that respects the labour of child-rearing, whether a parent is doing it or a professional care-giver. This situation is exploitative of care-givers and often taxing to family life.

The ideals of the women's movement, when it came to child-rearing, were diluted by market forces; when mostly white, affluent women found they could staunch the work-family conflict with the affordable labour of working-class women, mostly women of colour, it 'solved the problem' for one group while draining momentum and pressure that could have been placed upon the marketplace and upon government by a movement to create a systematic solution that worked reasonably well for all.

And for the vast majority of parents in the middle, an inadequate day care system leaves them praying for the best, comforting kids who are distressed at the frequent departures of those tasked with teaching them how to trust and love, and racing against a brutally inflexible pick-up-the-kids clock at 6 p.m., with punitive five-minute overtime costs.

When it came to who would take care of the kids, capitalism happened to the women's movement, and a real gender revolution did not.

This situation is no solution. This is the uneasy truce between the workplace and motherhood; it is the ill-negotiated deal of the women's movement, with kids' well-being still under the shadow of the sword.

We were all strong, progressive women. Yet this conversation about whose career would 'take the hit', as I heard it expressed by one mother, was happening all around us, and always with the same outcome.

Cara was alone in the extreme nature of her situation, but she wasn't alone in feeling that her mate had pulled rank in a subtle way.

Our generation did not think we were marrying breadwinners; we thought we were marrying our best friends. But the husbands were pulling rank in a way that best friends don't do. Simply put, the men were good husbands, loving, faithful and kind; but they had at some level that seemed not very important to them, but very important to women, sent the message, 'I love you, but in some fundamental ways we will live our lives my way.'

And the fact was that most of the men believed themselves to be good, fair husbands. Most of them *were* in fact good husbands. It just wasn't quite fair, and it wasn't going to be quite fair, ever. And that was not something women of my generation had signed on for.

When the subject turned to how to achieve a more equitable arrangement, whether it was whose career would be put on hold, who was making decisions about money, who was supposed to buckle in the children, or who would pick up the socks, I started hearing from women I knew a phrase I had not heard expressed in the courtship and early-wedded stages of what had been equal relationships: 'I decided it's just not worth a fight.'

I could hear in that series of small decisions a bit of what marriage must have been like before the Great Adjustment of 1970s feminism: for the first time, many of the women I talked to were seeing their men's baseline requirements untempered by the values of equal compromise that we had all thought we all believed in.

The things we had believed in as young women – the romance of our egalitarian, or at least reasonably balanced, relationships; the conviction that we would do it oh, so differently from our parents – all that was up for grabs. Our great romance was with the belief in equality itself. Was that, too, not worth the fight?

This generation of women thought it had a new, trustworthy bond with which to replace that archaic deal of pre-feminist marriage: flaming, erotic, friendly, egalitarian love. Many women were finding that that idealistic young woman's love was not as reliable a foundation to support the sweet, heavy weight of a baby in a new family as was the staunch old adhesive our grandmothers knew all about: submissiveness, tolerance, strategy – and a mother's yielding heart.

I saw what mother love was like in relationships in which the pressures of workplace, tradition, and male expectation were slowly making choices seem less and less equal. It made me think of two paving stones set side by side in a jointly built foundation, at first co-equal, perfectly aligned. Then a burden is placed more upon one than the other. It sinks a bit, then adjusts, and pulls away. Mother love is what hangs in there; mother love, and perhaps wifely love in a world not yet changed enough, seemed all around me to decide at last to trade equality for certainty. It was like a root or creeper that reaches out to hold that foundation together; to cover the gap; to refuse at length even to dignify the gap; to make a virtue of imbalance.

That love was, I saw, forging women with babies into mothers. It was strong, tenacious, resourceful, without shame.

Certainly, countless couples do both work, and both share the child care as much as they can, and work hard to find some sort of balance in their lives. It's just that that 'balance' is usually structured around a bottom line that the woman's life is the source of flexibility, and the man's job cannot be touched.

According to British research carried out in 2001, fathers are as important as mothers in shaping children's futures. In his explanation of the findings, one of the co-writers of the study, Charles Lewis, professor of psychology at Lancaster University, said 'Involved fathers can improve the health, emotional well-being and educational achievement of young people,' and stressed the importance of fathers having paternity leave in order to bond properly with their children at an early age.

Indeed, in the United Kingdom – perhaps because of the existence of paternity leave, which has allowed fathers this crucial early bonding – men *have* been more willing to challenge their stereotypes, abandoning the traditional roles as breadwinners, and staying at home to look after the baby, although, admittedly, that too can bring its own tensions. One such couple were Laura and Dan – both working as PR consultants for the same company. In this partnership, Laura was the one with the higher income, and the stronger career prospects, so Dan, who had in any case been contemplating a career change, agreed to stay at home to look after their son, Jack. Laura explained the main difficulties. 'We haven't always agreed on the best way of looking after our son on certain issues, such as, say, diet, and the amount of time spent watching television. I found it impossible to completely delegate this and accept his way of doing things – a situation which probably rarely happens if the roles are more traditional. We did have some rows about this, as Dan felt that I was questioning his ability to look after our child. And I *do* sometimes feel resentful that it wasn't me who was able to take more time with Jack.'

Too many marriages with a newborn child are essentially compelled to go through a period of challenge that is unnecessarily harsh. Good politics is the invisible bedrock of good love. If new mothers could work more easily part-time for a decent wage; if husbands and fathers were not penalized for staying home for a while, if they were granted leave or flexitime without radically setting back their prospects; if men released one *another* to put fatherhood first and eased up on their rigid workplace judgements of themselves and their peers, then surely fatherhood, as well as family life as a whole, would be strengthened.

If, in addition, the new family had ongoing income from a government or corporate benefit coming in to help care for the baby and honour what is usually the woman's work, I doubt that 67 per cent of American families would be strained, as they are reported to be, by the baby's arrival. For all the politicians' lip service in America to soccer moms and waitress moms, women are coming to motherhood in a country that lacks the basic foundation to help support a strong and truly balanced family life.

Several years later, I was walking along the crest of a hill in Oregon with my brother Aaron, in a raw new subdivision where the trees had not yet grown in. We were getting some fresh air, taking a break from the chaotic house into which he and his wife, Ariela, had just moved with their two young children. They had transferred themselves across the country to let Aaron have the professional opportunity of his dreams, the chance of a tenure-track job at the local college. Ariela had wrenched herself away from a happily rooted life, from her graduate studies in a field she cared about, to come with him to a climate she abhorred and a place where she had no friends and could not find a job. My brother Aaron is a feminist. Ariela is a strong, accomplished woman, no shrinking violet, an Israeli immigrant. He and Ariela love each other and have a strong marriage.

We were talking about the fact that Ariela had come with him, grudgingly, to a place so far from her own dreams in order to try to make his dream into hers.

'Here's the secret, Naomi,' he said. 'All the husbands I know are good guys. They honestly want things to be fair in their relationships. They are hands-on dads, and they want their wives to be happy and fulfilled. But when it comes down to it, there is no way they are going to sacrifice a career opportunity.'

I remember pausing in surprise at the rawness of what my brother had just shared with me; the lifting of a curtain. I remember looking out over the quiet suburb, the green plain, stopped in my tracks by this glimpse behind the scenes of so many conversations among the women I knew and later interviewed.

'But how do you all negotiate that if you have equal partnerships? I mean, can't the wives just say no, or ask you to take turns?'

'Bottom line? We know they won't leave us,' he said. 'A: They love us. B: Because of the kids.'

# Making Mothers

'I feel like I have a crush on my child. Like when you're not totally
in control, you want to reign in your emotion to act appropriately,
but you're too smitten, like when you're in high school. You're
supposed to wait for them to call you. But instead you shower
their belly with kisses.'

New mother

The wounds of the birth had begun to heal. I was haltingly
beginning to learn what that waitress I met in my fifth month had
been trying to tell me: For women on this journey, the scar lines
were sometimes the strongest lines.

The field of my grief did not lift all at once, but it did thin, like
rain tapering off into a light fog. My concern over bonding with our
baby was undone with repetition, over time, with the clasp of her
flesh to mine when she nursed.

Even with the rude lessons in how low my status had become,
there was abundant recompense: a love that flayed me with its
tenderness. To put my cheek against hers, to be able to still her cries,
was a joy and a privilege.

In all the paintings of the Madonna, nursing seems like such a
delicate business: in our mind's eye we have dozens of images of her
sitting elegantly upright, child at her breast, both serene and
immaculate, whether painted in the static Byzantine, the cool
northern European, or the lush Italian style. Sometimes the
Madonna will hold a rosy nipple to the child's mouth with long,
clean fingers; sometimes – particularly as engravers of the eighteenth
century began to use lactation as an allegorical motif for abundance

– a sturdy etched nude or a wrought-metal nude in a fountain will send a fine, straight jet spray of milk from her breast. But from all these representations, if you have never actually nursed, you have the sense that it is the most sublime and ethereal merging of mother and child, the most spiritualized form of food delivery imaginable.

Yet when our daughter nursed, it was as rough-and-tumble, as purely animal an experience as a human being can have. Some unfathomable instinct hardwired into her sent her into a rapid panting, her small heart racing, when her face with its buttery skin came near the nipple. Guided – who can say? by the scent of milk, or perhaps by the sight of the darker areola at the outer field of her primitive vision, she would suddenly go into a small frenzy, shaking her head back and forth quickly, desperately searching with her whole face for the nipple brushing against her mouth. When the nipple came in contact with her lips, she would lunge on to it for all the world like a cat pouncing on a mouse. Her concentration – no, let's face it, her savagery – was so acute that she leapt with the force of her whole small body, emitting a soft guttural growl. Her heart-shaped face had the warrior scowl of a samurai. Once she had actually seized her prey – or 'latched on', as the lactation specialists more tactfully put it – the current of connection between her mouth and the longed-for nipple had the kind of electric force that sends lovers searching for one another from half a world away.

If you were to try to dislodge a baby when she is feeding, you would find that you cannot do so without causing harm to the mother's breast: you actually have to insert a finger to break the vacuum created by the force of the suction. As the milk flowed into my baby, I would hear low roars of satisfaction, swallowings and grunts. Her body wriggled with pleasure and her lovely guitarist's hands did a dance of their own, curling and uncurling for sheer joy.

The love bond my baby had formed with this, the centre of her universe, was so profound that she nursed with both arms clasped around the sloping perimeter of the breast. (It was no longer 'my breast', since it had become her possession, so I thought of it as 'the breast'. Really it was 'her breast', though I couldn't quite bring myself to sign it over to her outright.) The milk would act as an opiate, and her eyes would grow more and more heavy-lidded, until, when she was sated, she would fall helplessly down in a swoon, exhausted, her cheek resting against her one true love, all passion spent. In this state, I could lift her arm and drop it, sit her up or lie her down, while she would remain unconscious to the world.

I had never in my life been able to make someone so happy so simply. As Greta put it to me later, 'Now I take off my shirt – and she smiles.'

I was my daughter's drug of choice. I would experience a tremendous feeling of happiness that would come when she was sobbing and I would take her from someone else and she would quiet before I had finished lifting my shirt. I could have been anyone: a brute, a cheat, as cold-hearted as a handgun, but all I would have to do was to give her my breasts and she seemed to experience the distillate of love.

Suddenly I became aware of how many metaphors came from nursing, or from unconscious memories of nursing. We want to return to 'the bosom of Abraham', we seek out the 'milk of human kindness'. Nursing metaphors are natural for bad poetry – 'A tree whose hungry mouth is prest/Against the earth's sweet flowing breast.' Overwrought, we say we are being 'sucked dry' – and indeed, when a woman is nursing heavily, when tired or under stress, she feels depleted, emotionally parched out. When the baby has drunk for an hour and the mother feels trapped by the child's bottomless appetite, she can experience a maddening sense of irritation.

I became aware, too, of how guilty such feelings make a woman feel. I began to notice how the women around me often saw nursing as a metaphor for being a good mother. My sister-in-law had trouble nursing, and went through anguish until she accepted that healthy, loved babies can also thrive on formula.

My own response to breast-feeding varied from hour to hour: some afternoons I would look down into my daughter's face and feel that biological mesmerism: lactation specialists say that nursing mothers feel compelled to fix their gaze on the side of their drinking child's face, thus strengthening the bond. At other times, when I was tired or raw or even just plain bored, I would look through a catalogue or watch the news while the baby nursed, and could feel guilt lurking just below my consciousness. She is so avid for me, I thought, and this act is so meaningful to her; will it harm her if I take a psychic time-out and just let myself be the vending machine that I am?

Dianne said of nursing, 'In spite of all the misery of learning how to do it, the first time I pumped out two ounces of milk, it was so cool – thrilling and humbling at the same time. Like: "I can make food! With my body!"'

The group of neo-natal activists that my friends and I came to call 'the lactation fascists' – La Leche League, which believes in lactation the way some people believe in redemption – sees nursing as a moral imperative. I found such activists to be terribly vexing, partly because it was just not reasonable for most of the women I knew to nurse the way that the Milk Missionaries wanted them to.

Yet, in a world truly of mothers' making, these activists' passion could seem, in many ways, justified. In the United States, only about half of mothers breast-feed their babies at all, and by the time the baby is six months old, the proportion is down to one in five. That pattern was reflected in the nursing decisions of most of the women I knew. Though the American Academy of Pediatrics recommends that babies should ideally be nursed for a year, only 6 per cent of mothers are still breast-feeding by their baby's first birthday.

In countries where many women have to go back to work full-time after three months of unpaid leave, ordinary nursing rhythms are a prohibitive luxury. A Talmudic proverb holds, 'The cow needs to suckle as much as the calf needs to suck.' The anguish many new mothers, who want to nurse and yet must return to work, feel may be as much biological as it is psychological. Babies are biologically designed to nurse, of course, and new mothers are biologically oriented toward wanting to respond.

Mothers and babies who are nursing are like one continually interacting, merged organism. They share the same REM sleep cycles – though mothers don't get the same chances to sleep! Since breast milk itself is a living organism, formula manufacturers cannot replicate it. Breast milk varies in density and nutrient levels according to the needs of each baby, becoming, for instance, one consistency for single babies, and another to better suit twins. Babies who have not been breast-fed face a greater risk of allergies, dental caries, infections that lead to emergency room visits, and chronic conditions such as asthma and heart disease. Study after study has shown that biochemically, babies are primed to need the presence of their mothers and fathers – the voice, the skin-to-skin contact, the holding – in order to thrive and grow, not just emotionally but physically.

Of course, women should have the choice of breast- or bottle-feeding; not all women can nurse, nor will all women see lactation as an important part of their life as mothers. But what interests me is how little our culture adapts to the needs of nursing mothers. In a world of too-rigid work schedules, nursing is one of the first 'luxuries' of motherhood to have to go.

I read new data that showed there were substantial benefits to breast-feeding babies longer than is realistic for most women in our culture. I noticed that every pediatrician I had a chance to ask directly about breast-feeding versus bottle- seemed to downplay the clear benefits of breast-feeding, saying, 'That is a very personal decision.' This is a 'reassuring', and even compassionate response to women who have no choice but to wean and who would feel unnecessarily guilt-ridden if given the facts from their trusted doctors. On the other hand, it is one more case of the medical profession tempering information in order to 'help' women better accommodate themselves to subtle social pressures that make it unrealistic or undesirable for most of them to nurse for any extended period of time.

While I knew that breast-feeding wasn't intended to be a transcendental experience each and every time – in most cultures that preceded our own, babies would be fed while their mothers were pounding maize or weaving bark – I also knew that it was unconscionable for our culture to insist that women 'choose' to leave their suckling babies abruptly at home in order simply to be available for paid work.

A 2000 study shows how pressured and even inadequate many women feel about this issue – the most common reasons women chose bottle-feeding over breast-feeding are: the mother's sense of the *father*'s preference; not feeling confident that she can produce enough milk; and the need to return to work. But what if women had real choices that supported them as much as if they chose to breast-feed as if they chose to bottle-feed? What if a movement put pressure on employers and political leaders to treat a new mother's choice to breast-feed as being as important as her choice to return to an unmediated work schedule? Can government not offer businesses incentives to provide still more supple versions of flexitime – structured, say, around the feedings mothers find most important?

In other words, what if we went further than lip service in support of mothers and babies?

Only because I was self-employed, I had the luxury of unhurried nursing. Thinking of the *New Yorker* map that shows an enormous Manhattan in the foreground and a tiny USA disappearing into the horizon in the background, I imagined how a nursing baby sees its mother: in the foreground, two vast breasts, brimming with milk; in the middle distance, the Midwest, a pair of hands bearing diapers, wet cotton balls and Vaseline, and far, far out on the distant plain, elusive and tiny, a face, a voice, a heartbeat and a scent.

Our baby's father, I was sure, was a person to her who could make her laugh, or startle, or focus; but I was just as certain that to her I was a landscape of ever-replenishing flesh, in which what I thought of as my self came very last.

Cara came over to bring me up-to-date with her life. Things were better. She tried not to dwell on her old self: vibrant, slim, self-sustaining. She told me about the relative peace that she and Sam had managed to engineer once she gave up expecting the things she had hoped for.

That truce had been hard-won, but it kept two elements together. They were no longer best friends, and there would always be an ache when she thought of that, she told me. But they were solidly husband and wife. They were a family.

Cara had found the strength to put her earlier expectations away. Of course, she said, she had found that she could live without what she thought she could not live without. Because there was no other choice for her if she was to be what she was, truly: a good mother. And Cara was a good mother.

Some time later my friend Liza described the following scene. Her daughter Nellie had become very interested in babies. So Liza and Nellie were looking at an anatomy book for kids, *The Human Body*. It had easy-to-understand full-colour illustrations of the various systems of the body: the veins, the brain and nervous system, the reproductive system. Nellie's favourite section was the few pages that traced the growth of the embryo into the fetus, and showed the fetus, tightly curled, enlarging and finally turning upside down within the uterus of a human female. The story's greatest interest lay in the fold-out section that showed the baby's delivery: the big illustration depicted a full-term fetus descending the birth canal – 'the tunnel', as Nellie called it. 'That looks fun!'

she exclaimed at the sight of the round head emerging from the pink, simply drawn birth canal.

On the opposite side, however, was a phase-by-phase scene of a Caesarean section. It showed a schematic image of mommy lying on a gurney, surrounded by doctors and nurses, getting a shot in the belly, showing a shaded area where the belly was meant to go numb: and a close-up of the mother's belly, with layers of fat and muscle being peeled back as the round head emerged.

'What are the doctors doing to the mommy?' asked Nellie.

'They're giving her a shot so it won't hurt.'

Nellie peered at the baby's head emerging from the comic-book envelope of skin.

'That's how you were born, sweetie,' said Liza, who had indeed had a Caesarean. 'The doctors opened up Mommy's belly and gave you to Mommy and Daddy – and you came out with all your hair standing up! And we were so happy to have you.'

Nellie kept staring at the images. 'Didn't it hurt, Mommy?' she asked.

Liza didn't hesitate. 'No, sweetie,' she lied. 'It didn't really hurt.'

For Liza was a good mother.


As for us: We were a new family, with one small magnetic creature and two sleep-deprived adults, drawn to the needs of someone I still thought of as 'the little one', as if under an enchantment. I could not remember when we had last seen a movie, or worn unstained clothing, or slept through the night. I could scarcely recall the self I had been before. But the life of our new family had begun to heal and knit. For almost four weeks, the baby had been an eldritch presence in our home: we would wash and feed and dote on her. Still, we had to take her babyhood on faith, for she was still a half-alien, half-animal being, waving her little limbs, turning her smooth, warm little head, suddenly, inexplicably, as if listening to bulletins, inaudible to anyone else, from home planet.

One night, though – one night: The baby and I were alone. I was sitting on the couch with her; the couch where I had slowly fallen in love with something I did not fathom, something I was imperceptibly part of.

One night I crossed over.

Branches and leaves pressed around the windows of our

apartment. Wind chimes were suspended in the branches outside. The chimes shivered a little. A silver tremor of sound hung in the air.

The little one took her mouth from my nipple, and her head turned toward the sound. Her eyes looked huge. She held perfectly still until the notes subsided. She was listening to music.

She was a human baby, listening.

Her mother held her.

'Do you hear the bells, Rosie?' I whispered. 'Can you hear the bells?'

# Epilogue

Five years later, a healthy baby boy joined our bright-eyed girl.

Because of course, this difficult story that I told you of a first birth did indeed deliver the promised 'happy ending', the joy at the end of the journey, the blessing, the baby. And under her loving insistence and relentless impish demands, the mother – 'the good mother' – in me, was eventually safely born.

But the joy of a new child, of the happy ending, does not do away with the reality of the tough journey we as mothers undertake. We do not so much fall into motherhood as forge ourselves into mothers.

I don't want to forget or downplay, in the face of the joy that our baby brings, the arduousness of the journey mothers undergo. The tough journey and the happy ending are both part of the truth of pregnancy; just as they are part of the truth of motherhood. It is no dilution of our great love for our children to honour the effort that women make.

For our second baby, I found, in the end, a good medical practice. But the path to this practice was not an easy one either.

When we moved to New York I was pregnant with our second child. We made the decision to go with the best obstetrician we could find, one that a friend interested in medical issues had recommended to us: a dashing male doctor who appeared on lists of New York's 'best doctors' every year, and who works out of a nice-looking office in a smart part of Manhattan.

Why on earth, after what I had gone through the first time, would I have taken that traditional route again?

It was a kind of nihilism; my research into the role our medical practices play in childbirth was still in its early stages. All I knew was that the first, 'alternative' birth experience I had had in the hospital in Washington had been brutal and rigid. I felt we might as well just give up, in a sense, on alternative methods; I held out little hope for a more meaningful experience. My intention was to get the best that science could offer and get out of the hospital with the baby as quickly as possible.

Yet my anxiety level began rising as I met this doctor monthly. And as each month passed, I knew, from my research, a little bit more about what was at stake. From his point of view, I was no doubt becoming the patient from hell. I would read about fetal monitors and ask him about their efficacy, and he would look dismayed; I would read about the Friedman curve and ask if we needed to labour under its deadline, and he would look put out. As I learned more about the connection between compassion and a good birth, I began to notice the abrupt way he would begin an exam without a word of preparation, and how he would give me a pat on the knee when it was over, as if I were a child being sent outside to play.

My husband and I would meet with him in his beautifully-appointed office after each prenatal exam and we would try to work out a common idea of what the impending birth could be like. Again and again, he let us know politely, with a bemused expression, that our raising the notion of avoiding unnecessary interventions was, for the most part, pointless. His own practice did not take these concerns to heart, nor did the protocols of the hospital where we would deliver the baby under his care. In my seventh month, exasperated by several such discussions I had raised, he told me, 'Pregnant women often can't see the forest for the trees.' I understood him to mean that, since a healthy baby was the goal, any intervention he routinely performed was appropriate.

The trouble was that by then I knew that this was not necessarily the case. I also did not care much for his assessment of pregnant women's intuitions and needs. Feeling increasingly uneasy with every meeting, I moved into the eighth month of my pregnancy.

It was the final prenatal examination, just weeks before my due date, that brought the doctor–patient relationship to a point of crisis. During the check-up, my obstetrician told me that the baby was not dropping.

'The baby should be dropping by now,' he said sounding disapproving to me. 'If you aren't in labour by forty-two weeks, we will induce. And if you go into labour and can't produce good strong contractions and a baby in seventeen hours, we will section.'

(As a midwife said to me later, 'Would you even talk to your own child that way?')

I had told him repeatedly how traumatic my first birth had been, and of my strong desire to avoid an unnecessary Caesarean. I had made clear that this time around I wanted to be given every safe chance to labour without an arbitrary deadline hanging over my head. The sentence he had just issued caused a feeling of dread in me. The sword was over my head again – I felt it invisible in the air over the examination table. It was a feeling I had never wanted to experience again.

And this time around I knew that what he was ordering for me was not the only safe approach – indeed, that such a timeline could actually inhibit my chances for a successful labour. Moreover, his plans overrode the very spirit in which I had brought him my concerns.

I also knew this time around that, by this point in gestation, only half of all babies had descended into the birth canal. There was nothing wrong my with baby's leisurely pacing.

When I brought that up, trying to sound reasonably persuasive while lying supine, legs akimbo, on the examination table under an awkward paper apron, he ignored the comment. He remarked, 'You had to be sectioned last time. You probably have an unusually narrow birth canal. Maybe your body just is not made to have babies.'

I knew at that moment that on some unconscious level my doctor – a compassionate, highly trained physician – wanted to be right about my being in need of his surgical help more than he wanted to heal. I felt the blade in the room and I knew I did not feel happy about going into labour under his hand.

By now I was in touch with practitioners who held other points of view. Ina Mary Gaskin had taken a keen, supportive interest in my pregnancy. When I told her of my doctor's assessment of my inability to give birth on my own, she asked, 'Did he measure your pelvis before he suggested to you that it was unusually narrow?'

He had not.

'Did he get your EFM tracing so he can see for himself what the problem was supposed to have been last time?'

Though I had asked him to do so for months, he had not.

Other midwives later pointed out to me that when a doctor issues a strong warning against curtailing interventions, and assigns the possible cause of a problem to the patient, it is a way for a doctor to lay groundwork to protecting himself from legal liability. (My new midwife would later note that my pelvic measurement was exactly average.)

The following week I sat in his consulting room once again, trying to explain to him that I wanted to wait to go into labour for the length of time that was normal and safe to do so, and not be cut off by an arbitrary seventeen-hour deadline.

'It is hospital protocol,' he said.

'But can't you advocate for me?' I asked. I suddenly recalled that whenever I had a 10:45 appointment, the receptionist would tell me without a shred of doubt, 'He's at a birth – he'll be back at eleven.' And he would be – as punctually as a teacher for his next class. And of course I wondered, as the months passed and I learned more about time pressure, if he's at a birth, how can he be so sure he'll be back at eleven to see scheduled patients? Now I knew.

'Look,' he said firmly, 'you want a birth that I can't sign on for. If you want to have someone get you through your birth without the standard array of interventions, this is the wrong practice. You can go labour on the floor at home with incense and have candles and whatnot – and you might have a fulfilling experience. But you are taking a terrible risk. I have had patients who wanted to avoid the usual interventions, and I told them I could not help them. They left this practice and their baby was born brain damaged. I tell you, if you take issue with these standards of care, you might think you are doing something wonderful for your birth, but your baby could die.'

He stood up. I stood up. We shook hands, and we both under-stood that I would never go back to him. I left, shaking.

Other midwives later advised me that 'your baby could die' language could also have been a protective legal move. But I was not an attorney or an insurer; simply a very scared mother-to-be.

With great urgency, I looked for the right alternative. My husband and I found SoHo OB-GYN, and I persuaded them to take me. Midwife Maureen Rayson made an exception to their usual cut-off date for taking clients and allowed me in. And I fell into their respectful, skilled and caring practice as if into a pair of comforting arms.

In the end, my second birth was exactly the same in terms of physical upheaval as the first one was. Once again, I underwent a Caesarean section. Yet, though everything was surgically exactly the same, in every other way it was completely different. Despite having to undergo another section, the impact on me emotionally and psychologically was far gentler. I hated the surgery the second time around – it was just as violent and invasive. But this second time I was emboldened by an empowered midwife. One of the first women to bring modern midwifery to New York City, Rayson worked in one of the rare practices in which the midwives had true decision-making power alongside the (disproportionately female) obstetricians of the practice. I was put under and delivered by Dr Deborah Coady, an empathic, wisecracking woman my own age, whose informative treatment of me inspired trust.

I yielded to the Caesarean section in a context of greater confidence, and found upon recovery that my spirit had suffered no incision. I emerged from the surgery with none of the original trauma, and with no depression. Our new baby Joey reaped the benefits of a mother who was whole in spirit. As did I, and our entire family.

Why was it so much easier? I believe it was because of the healing power of compassion, even within a constricted hospital setting. It was also easier because I had better information. More importantly, my practitioners respected my right to it. As a result, I did not feel that I was at the mercy of an institution that was concealing information from me. I understood better what was going on and my husband and I were better able to make decisions accordingly.

I doubt I will ever know for certain whether my two Caesareans were absolutely unavoidable. Even my 'good' Caesarean, brought about by a strong midwife's decision, occurred under the strict protocols of a hospital. On the chance that these surgeries saved our babies, my husband and I can only be grateful.

But the fact that some difficult pregnancies and high-tech births are inevitable does not mean women, and the partners and practitioners who care about them, should not challenge and transform the culture of pregnancy and the experience of birth as a whole.

We need to ask the question: What do mothers deserve if they are to mother well? We need to answer: everything.

Everything that is due to them.

# A Mother's Manifesto

What do we need? The question should be: what do we deserve? And the answer: everything. Pregnant women and new mothers are the frontline warriors for the species.

Here are just some goals for a 'Motherhood Feminism':

We deserve: real flexitime that lets us and the fathers of our babies cycle more easily in and out of the workplace. If the government must compensate the private sector for this interruption, so be it: such a programme is as necessary as Social Security. We need real Family Leave: each parent deserves at least six months off and with the ability to sequence their time off, as UK women MPs are insisting their government provide for. Initiatives that guarantee the care-giving parent his or her job back in flexitime are necessary: so are Canadian-style initiatives that guarantee quality child care for a flat, low fee per day. We need to pressure politicians to boost the minimum wage and offer health care benefits for the part-time work that mothers disproportionately do.

We need tax deductions and benefits to help underwrite the cost of transporting or even housing relatives who are able to come to help care for the new mother and baby.

We need to radically overhaul the birthing industry; to compel hospitals and doctors to disclose their statistics; to ensure that mid-wives, progressive obstetricians, and patient advocates help to influence hospital protocols; and to inform every woman of her right to accept or refuse any medical treatment or procedure after the risk and benefits have been explained to her.

We need on-site daycare and workplace creches so that we can see our children while we are at work – and on-site nurseries so that mothers can nurse in the private sector for as long as they reasonably choose. We need government benefits that new fathers and mothers receive only when they take time off – and tax incentives for businesses to encourage all parents to do so.

How do we accomplish all this? With a new push of 'Motherhood Feminism': a mothers' movement as powerful as the gun lobby in the US to pressure government and workplaces more efficiently than do the lobbies that pressure national leaders to resist taking serious parental programmes seriously.

In the model of Plan-It – the global women's health initiative that unites many disparate non-profit-making organizations – this radical 'Motherhood Movement' could be a coalition of mothers, fathers, and care-givers; women's groups; consumer groups; taxpayer groups; unions; teachers' groups; and existing parents' groups. It could aim to have real clout and to give the needs of mothers, fathers and care-givers a true voice in settling the national agenda.

It could have a powerful consumer arm in which its members could support or boycott products and corporations that are helpful or harmful to the wellbeing of new parents and children.

We need the labour movement to organize on behalf of care-givers. We also need this movement to create new kinds of civic spaces and social structures, bringing children closer to the workplace and the world of adults, and bringing the engagement and world of adult economic activity closer to the hermetically-sealed world of mothers and small children. Women should not have to choose between two such stark exclusive worlds as 'work' and 'home with kids' are now, and children would benefit from the better, happier parenting a bit of change would bring about.

Kids need kids – yet our social life isolates not just mothers but children. Playgrounds today are pockets of isolation in many ways. Let's face it: it's hard for an active, thoughtful mother, father or care-giver to relish four or five hours a day becalmed and uncomfortable at the playground. A consumer/voter movement, spearheaded by the Mothers' Lobby, supported by government grants, could turn them into true community centres where an array of young people could oversee activities, games and art projects.

As any parent knows, other kids' toys are fascinating. A neighbourhood 'toy bank' could collect the current and used toys and games that are gathering dust in the many closets of the homes in a given neighbourhood and keep them at the local 'play centre'. Each community play centre ideally would have a small, heated building to house staff, athletic equipment and art supplies and provide space for dance, theatre and other kinds of activities. But it should also provide for the care-givers of those children: space for reading or political meeting groups, a small library of newspapers; food and coffee, running water and bathrooms. Just as importantly: a facility with internet access and phones, so that during an afternoon of free play, if the kids have an hour of supervised activity, mothers, fathers and care-givers could actually get work done, do household errands online, check mail, or do an hour or so of telecommuting.

Evening activities at the play centre – film screenings, story-telling, adult/child art projects, and potluck dinners – could draw in the working parents of the neighbourhood to meet their stay-at-home fellow parents and their kids. In the many isolated homes in the evening, exhausted parents who often seat kids in front of the television from sheer fatigue, could also, if only once a week, have the option of gathering with them, which can ease the burden of this isolation.

The same principle could spearhead development of a new kind of entrepreneurial space. This would most likely be for-profit ventures that could be given incentives by the government: lofts on floors of office buildings that could rent out cubicles to stay-at-home parents hoping to start small businesses, telecommute, or do other flexible work. In the space at the centre of the cubicles a huge play area for kids and care-givers could be created – again with young or retired people supervising activities, art supplies, shared toys, etc. This arrangement would give kids one another; give care-givers, who are often isolated, a place to convene in all kinds of weather, and give parents the chance to work but also take a break – to paint a picture or have lunch at a picnic table with their kids. Given the explosion of flexible worker opportunities described in Dan Pink's *Free Agent Nation*, this option could give many women (and men) of various backgrounds, who now feel torn between the rigid options of work and home, a chance to be with their kids as well as realize some of their dreams.

These newly-evolved kinds of social and work spaces need not seem Utopian (50 years ago, the idea of a vast consumer base for a commercial space with a lot of exercise machines in it would have seemed a stretch). Such new kinds of work/home spaces, developed by private-public partners, and spurred on by the Mothers' Lobby, would help revolutionize our mothering and fathering arrangements – to the benefit of parents but, more importantly, of children.

But the real transformation is not a matter of overhauling flexitime or medical practices, or shifting our ideas of home, neighbourhood, and workplace. The real transformation is one of the heart.

It will be a revolution when we don't just *say* mothers are important. It will be a revolution when we finally start treating motherhood as if it were important.

# Acknowledgements

This book would not have been possible without the judgement, insight and commitment to it of four remarkable people.

Roger Scholl at Anchor/Doubleday brought the kind of editorial skill and perceptiveness to the drafts of this manuscript that many writers dream of but few are fortunate enough to receive. As an editor he brought intense scrupulousness and clarity of mind to honing the text, but as a family man he also brought heartfelt advocacy to the subject. I deeply appreciate the investment of time, thought and passion he put into this book.

Alison Samuel at Chatto & Windus was an ideal reader for this as she has been for each one of my books, putting the right challenges before me as the drafts evolved, as she has done, to the great benefit of all my books, for a decade.

Without the far-ranging medical research of Catherine Moore, LNM, without her patient explanation of many medical processes to a layperson, and her original insights about the kind of questions to ask of the body of medical data, this book certainly could not have provided readers with the range of information about the culture and practice of childbirth that it does.

For this project, I am especially aware of two of the many reasons I am grateful to David Shipley: as a stellar editor, and as the father of our children.

I also want to thank Maureen Rayson, CNM; Catherine Clark, CNM; and Julius Goepp, MD – for taking time from their patients to give the manuscript their thoughtful medical readings.

I am grateful to Powell's Bookstore, to Joan and John Shipley for their hospitality, and to Leonard and Deborah Wolf for their continuing help. Special thanks are also due to John Brockman and Katinka Matson for their steadfast encouragement; to Miren Lopategui for invaluable assistance with the British edition; and to the women who took time to share their birth stories and other experiences with me.

I am especially appreciative of the medical personnel I met – from midwives to obstetricians to researchers – whose example demonstrates their commitment to healing.

# Notes

## INTRODUCTION
### Being Pregnant . . .

1    **African proverb**

3    **Today's American pregnancy bible:** Arlene Eisenberg, Heidi F. Murkoff and Sandee E. Hathaway, *What to Expect When You're Expecting* (New York: Workman Publishing, York, 1991), 1996

4    **postpartum depression rate:** See Ann Dunnewold, Ph.D. and Diane Sanford, Ph.D., *The Postpartum Survival Guide* (Oakland, Calif: 1994 New Harbinger Publications).

4    **Jessica Mitford:** Jessica Mitford, *The American Way of Birth* (New York: Plume, York, 1991).

5    **Suzanne Arms:** Suzanne Arms, *Immaculate Deception: A New Look at Women & Children* (Boston: Houghton Mifflin 1975).

5    **Sarah Hrdy:** Sarah Blaffer Hrdy, *Mother Nature: A History of Mothers, Infants, and Natural Selection* (New York: Pantheon Books, New York, 1999).

## PART I: PREGNANCY
### First month

11    **'A dream tells the woman':** M. F. Ashley-Montagu, *Coming into Being Among the Australian Aborigines* (London: Routledge, 1905), p.131.

14    **In Britain:** Dr Foster survey, *Sunday Times*, 15 July 2001. **Jessica Mitford,** op. cit.

16    **Belizean midwife:** Audiotapes, New School Midwifery Conference, New York City, 2000.

16    **episiotomy:** Robbie E. David-Floyd, *Birth as an American Rite of Passage* (Berkeley, University of California Press, 1992).

16    **standard of care:** See, for instance, Robbie E. Davis-Floyd, op. cit., Chapter

3, 'Birth Messages', pp. 73–153; Thomas H. Strong, Jr, *Expecting Trouble: The Myth of Prenatal Care in America*, Chapter 1, 'Heresy: Sowing the Seeds of Change' (New York: New York University Press, 2000), pp. 82–143; also Henci Goer, *Obstetric Myths vs. Research Realities: A Guide to the Medical Literature*, Chapter 18; 'The Nature of Evidence: Why the Gap Between Belief and Reality', Bergin & Garvey, 1995), pp. 349–362.

17    **bikini cut:** Interview, Andra Armstrong, June 2000.

18    **emotional support:** see Sheila Kitzinger, *Your Baby, Your Way* (New York: Pantheon Books, 1987), 'Emotional Changes,' pp. 78–96.

## Second month

19    **Catharine MacKinnon:** Catharine MacKinnon, 'Can Fatherhood Be Optional?' *New York Times*, 17 June 2001, p. A15.

19    *What to Expect:* Eisenberg et al., op. cit.

20    **Best-Odds Diet:** ibid., pp. 80–98.

20    **Glass of Wine:** Eisenberg, ibid., p. 53.

## Third month

22    **The perceived need:** Thomas H. Strong, Jr. M.D. op. cit., p. 3.

25    **Lorna Sage:** Lorna Sage, *Bad Blood*, Fourth Estate, London, 2000.

26    **Western notions:** see John Stuart Mill, *On Liberty*, David Spitz (ed.) (New York: W.W. Norton, 1974), pp. 83–4.

27    **almost a quarter:** in 1996, an estimated 6.24 million pregnancies resulted in 1.37 million induced abortions. See: S. J. Ventura, W. D. Mosher, S. C. Curtin, J. C. Abma, and S. Henshaw, 'Highlights of Trends I: Pregnancies and Pregnancy Rates by Outcome: Estimates for the United States, 1976–96.' *National Vital Statistics Reports 47*, no. 29, (Hyattsville, Maryland, National Center for Health Statistics 1999).

29    **Bad news:** Barbara Katz Rothman, *The Tentative Pregnancy: How Amniocentesis Changes the Experience of Motherhood* (New York: W.W. Norton, 1993), p. 221. AFFT is sometimes called the MSAFP, which stands for maternal serum AFP. This test requires a sample of the mother's blood. The newer 'triple' (measuring human chorionic gonadotropin and estriol in addition to AFP) screen can come back low, normal or high. If a fetus has Down's syndrome, HCG levels are often higher than normal while estriol and AFP levels are often lower than normal. A combination of ultrasound and amniocentesis is necessary to diagnose chromosomal anomalies. The screening is said to identify pregnancies at higher-than-average risk of certain serious birth defects, including spina bifida and Down's syndrome.

Source: American College of Obstetricians and Gynecologists 'Maternal Serum Screening,' *ACOG Technical Bulletin*, no. 228 (September 1996), and J.F.X. Egan, P. Benn, A. F. Borgida, J. F Rodis, W. A Campbell, and A. M. Vintzileos, 'Efficacy of Screening for Fetal Down's syndrome in the United States from 1974–1997,' *Obstetrics & Gynecology*, 96, no. 6 (December 2000), pp. 979–85.

29 **Second World Congress:** 'Controversies in Obstetrics, Gynecology & Infertility' (September 9–9, 2001, Paris, France). A. Kurjak, K. Nicolaides, J. Thornton and R. Chervenak, 'Fetal Malformations: The Cost of Fetal Screening for Anomalies Is Not Optimized Yet'; and J. Thornton, 'Screening: Can We Still Increase Cost to Diagnose Down's Syndrome?'

30 **Marketing:** Rothman, op. cit., p. 263.

30 **Adds revenue:** Insurance Tables, *Health Insurance Association of America, Source Book of Health Insurance Data, 1999–2000* (Washington DC: Health Insurance Association of America, 2000), p. 113.

30 **major New York hospital:** Interview, December 2000.

30 **bonding:** Interview, Dr Michelle Asher-Dunne, mother–child bonding psychotherapist, March 2001.

30 **tens of thousands:** In 1990, more than 200,000 amniocentesis procedures were performed in the United States, See R. S. Olney, C. A. Moore, L. D. Edmonds, L. D. Boto 'Chorionic Villus Sampling and Amniocentesis: Recommendations for Prenatal Counseling', *CDC Morbidity and Mortality Weekly Report 44* (RR-9) (21 July 1995), pp. 1–12.

30 **nuchal fold test:** Interview Mary Stanton (Administration), Fetal Medicine Centre, London, June 2000.

31 **after quickening:** Many first-time pregnant women do not quicken until later. Scott et al. (1994), in a medical text, state, 'movement is generally perceived between weeks 16 and 18 in a multipara [woman who's already had at least one child] and several weeks later in a primpara [woman who's never had a child before.]' Source: J. R. Scott, P. J. Disaia, C. B. Hammond, W. N. Spellacy, *Danforth's Obstetrics & Gynecology* (Philadelphia: J.P. Lippincott Co., 1994,) p. 77.

31 **'How safe is it?':** Eisenberg et al., op. cit., p. 45.

32 **'bed rest':** ibid., p. 45.

32 **'still horrendous':** Ruth Wainer Cohen, *Open Season: Survival Guide for Natural Childbirth and VBAC in the 90s*, New York: Greenwood Publishing, 1991, p. 83.

32 **the risk of miscarriage:** Dr D. Barrere, www.EPREGNANCY.com.

32 **1996 study:** See S. G. Gabbe, J. R. Niebyl, and J. Simpson, *Obstetrics: Normal and Problem Pregnancies* (New York: Churchill Livingston, 1996), p. 227.

Risk of pregnancy loss secondary to amniocentesis: 0.5%

Risk of amniotic fluid leakage secondary to amniocentesis: 1% or fewer.

For an extensive report on the risks of amniocentesis and chorionic villus sampling, see R. S. Olney et al., op. cit.

32   **Caroline:** Interview, June 2001.

35   **Sarah:** Interview, February 2001.

37   **Marina:** Interview, February 2001.

40   **Dobson and Smith:** H. Dobson and R. F. Smith, 'What Is Stress and How Does It Affect Reproduction', *Animal Reproductive Science*, 60–61 (2 July 2000), pp. 743–52.

40   **stress:** R. H. Clarke, S. C. Klock, A. Geoghegan and D. E. Travossos, 'Relationship Between Psychological Stress and Semen Quality', *Human Reproduction*, 14, no. 3 (March 1999), pp. 753–85.

42   **global conference:** The Eleventh World Congress on In Vitro Fertilization and Human Reproductive Genetics, 13 May, 1999, Sydney, Australia.

42   **stress on families:** C. Chang, 'Raising Twin Babies and Problems in the Family', *Acta Genet Med Gemello*, 39, no. 4 (1990), pp. 501–5, and M. Garel, B. Blondel, 'Assessment at One Year of the Psychological Consequences of having Triplets', *Human Reproduction*, 7, no. 5 (May 1992), pp. 729–32.

45   **white couples:** Adam Pertman, *Adoption Nation: How the Adoption Revolution Is Transforming America* (New York: Basic Books, 2000), pp. 55–57, 157–61. 'Racial and ethnic minorities account for more than sixty percent of the children in "out-of-home care" . . . and forty-six percent of these boys and girls are black . . . Yet middle- and upper-income Americans eagerly spend large sums of money to adopt from other countries rather than seek sons or daughters from the United States for next to nothing.'

# Fourth month

50   **The cultural idiom of motherhood:** Sheila Kitzinger, *The Year After Childbirth: Enjoying Your Body, Your Relationships and Yourself in Your Baby's First Year* (New York: Charles Scribner's Sons), p. 116.

51   **whatever makes you feel contented:** Jennifer Louden, *The Pregnant Women's Comfort Book: A Self-nurturing Guide to Your Emotional Well-being During Pregnancy and Early Motherhood* (New York: Harper Collins 1995), p. 8.

51   **'My breasts can nourish life':** ibid., p. 60.

51   **'moments of stillness':** ibid., p. 55.

52   **50–80 percent:** Susan T. Blackburn and Donna Lee Loper, *Maternal, Fetal, and Neonatal Physiology: A Clinical Perspective* (Philadelphia: W. B. Saunders Co., 1992), p. 392.

52   **between one- and two-thirds:** Louden, op. cit., p. 90.

52   **stress of modern life:** Eisenberg et al., op. cit., p. 105.

52   **highly suggestible:** Eisenberg et al., op. cit. (1991 edition), p. 105.

52   **between five and twelve weeks:** Blackburn and Loper, op. cit., pp. 392–3.

52   **psychogenic in origin:** ibid., p. 392.

52   **more favourable outcome:** Gabbe et al., op. cit., p. 93 and Helen Varney, *Varney's Midwifery* (3rd ed.) (Boston: Jones & Barlett Publishers, 1997), p. 266.

52   **homeopathic:** R. Moskowitz, *Homeopathic Medicines for Pregnancy and Childbirth* (Berkeley: North Atlantic Books, 1992).

53   **more vulnerable:** S. M. Flaxman and P. W. Sherman, 'Morning Sickness: A Mechanism for Protecting Mother and Embryo', *Quarterly Review of Biology*, 75, no. 2 (June 2000), pp. 113–48.

57   **fear of the change:** Thomas Verny, M.D. with John Kelly, *The Secret Life of the Unborn Child* (New York: Dell Publishing, 1981), p. 134.

58   **Mary McCarthy's son . . . Anne Sexton's daughter:** Linda Gray Sexton, *Searching for Mercy Steet: My Journey Back to My Mother, Anne Sexton* (Boston: Little, Brown, 1994), p. 84: Carol Brightman, *Writing Dangerously: Mary McCarthy and Her World* (New York: Clarkson N. Potter, 1992), pp. 267–71; Linda Wagner-Martin, *Sylvia Plath: A Biography* (New York: Pelgrave, 1988), p. 243; Allan Massie, *Colette: The Woman, The Writer and The Myth* (London: Penguin, 1986), p. 86.

58   **preferring sweetness:** T. Verny and J. Kelly, op. cit., p. 37.

## Fifth month

62   **Beriba proverb:** Mararita A. Kay, *Anthropology of Human Birth* (Philadelphia: F. A. Davis), 1982, p. 198.

67   **birth with death:** Ina May Gaskin, *Spiritual Midwifery* (Summertown, Tenn: The Book Publishing Company, 1990), p. 476.

67   **'Fewer than 1 in 10,000':** Eisenberg et al., op. cit., p. 241. According to the National Center for Health Statistics, maternal mortality for 1998 was 7.1 deaths per 100,000 live births. See S. L. Murphy, 'Deaths: Final Data for 1998', *National Vital Statistics Reports*, 48, no. 11 Hyattsville, Maryland: National Center for Health Statistics, p. 13.

68   **state laws:** I. M. Gaskin, interview, Nov/Dec, 1999. See also Marsden Wagner, *Pursuing the Birth Machine: The Search for Appropriate Birth Technology* (Camperdown, NSW, Australia: ACE Graphics), 1994, p. 117.

68   **express their fears of dying:** R. W. Cohen, op. cit., p. 211.

70   **In the nineteenth century:** Adrienne Rich, *Of Woman Born: Motherhood as Experience and Institution*, (New York: W. W. Norton, 1005), p. 153.

## Sixth month

71 **Suzanne Arms**, *Immaculate Deception I: Myth, Magic & Birth* (Berkeley: Celestial Arts, 1996), p. 151.

71 **birth plan:** Eisenberg et al., op. cit., p. 225.

72 **Hospitals . . . encourage:** Interview 'on background' with midwife, January, 2001.

73 **Lamaze . . . gained momentum:** Barbara Katz Rothman, *In Labor: Women and Power in the Birthplace* (New York: W. W. Norton, 1982). For more on the history of childbirth education see S. Arms, *Immaculate Deception II*, op. cit., pp. 149–54, and Sheila Kitzinger, *Ourselves as Mothers: The Universal Experience of Motherhood* (New York: Addison-Welsley, 1995), pp. 88–93.

73 **Lamaze:** Childbirth education as it is most widely recognized in America (Lamaze), has its roots in France. Dr Fernand Lamaze, a French obstetrician, based his views of natural childbirth on Ivan Pavlov's work, who had developed a shallow breathing technique as a form of hypnosis to block the experience of pain perceived by the brain. Lamaze applied this breathing to childbirth. In 1960, the American Society for Psycho-prophylaxis in Obstetrics (ASPO or Lamaze) was founded in New York City. Over the years, this organization has fought for many developments in childbirth including discouraging drugs, anesthesia, and bottle-feeding. Although not as well known as Lamaze, the Bradley Method is another popular childbirth preparation method. Started in 1965 by Robert Bradley, this method gives fathers a key role in coaching birthing women, reducing the need for medication. For a comparison of Lamaze and Bradley childbirth classes, see M. A. Monto, 'Lamaze and Bradley Childbirth Classes: Contrasting Perspectives Towards the Medical Model of Birth', *Birth*, 23, no. 4 December 1996, pp. 193–201.

73 **'highly medicalized environment':** S. Kitzinger, *Ourselves as Mothers*, op. cit., p. 92. ' "My Lamaze instructor lied to me" is a frequent comment, for example, from women who underwent operative delivery and did not realize that the natural childbirth techniques were not designed for high-tech hospitals that place limits on the time allowed for labor before a cesarean is performed,' Richard W. Wertz and Dorothy C. Wertz, *Lying in: A History of Childbirth in America* (New Haven: Yale University Press, 1977), p. 252.

73 **epidurals:** Henci Goer, *The Thinking Woman's Guide to a Better Birth* (New York: Berkeley Publishing Group, 1999), p. 128.

76 **no euphemism:** Genesis 3: 16, Holy Bible, King James version (New York: Meridien, 1974), p. 11.

76 **most agonizing experiences:** R. W. Wertz and D. C. Wertz, op. cit., p. 113.

76 **Pain section:** Eisenberg et al., op. cit., p. 206–7.

77 **'discomfort' or 'pressure':** Gillian van Hasselt, M. D., *Childbirth: Your Choices for Managing Pain* (Dallas: Taylor Publishing Company, 1995), pp. xii, 1.

77   **Central-American midwife:** New School Midwifery Conference, op. cit., 1999.

78   **full stomach:** C. L. Mendelson, 'The Aspiration of Stomach Contents into the Lungs During Obstetric Anesthesia', *American Journal of Obstetrics and Gynecology*, 52, (1946), pp. 191–205.

78   **been discredited:** K. W. Elkington, 'At the Water's Edge: Where Obstetrics and Anesthesia Meet', *Obstetrics and Gynecology*, 77, no. 2 (February 1991), pp. 304–8. For more on oral intake in labour, see H. C. Scheepers, G. G, Essed, and F. Brouns, 'Aspects of Food and Fluid Intake During Labour: Policies of Midwives and Obstetricians in the Netherlands', *European Journal of Obstetrics, Gynecology, and Reproductive Biology*, 78, no. 1 (May 1998): pp. 37–40; L. M. Ludka and C. C. Roberts, 'Eating and Drinking in Labor: A Literature Review', *Journal of Nurse-midwifery*, 38, no. 4 (July–August 1993), pp. 199–207; S. A. O'Reilly, P. J. Hoyer and E. Walsh, 'Low-Risk Mothers, Oral Intake and Emesis in Labor', *Journal of Nurse-Midwifery*, 38, no. 4 (July–August 1993), pp. 228–35; and J. P. Rooks, N.L. Weatherby and E. K. Ernst, 'The National Birth Center Study, Part II: Intrapartum and Immediate Postpartum and Neonatal Care', *Journal of Nurse-Midwifery*, 37, no.5 (September–October 1992, pp. 301–30.)

78   **fetal monitors. . . IV drip . . . 1946 . . . episiotomies:** For the cumulative harmful effect of routine interventions, see H. Goer, *Obstetric Myths vs. Research Realities*, op. cit., pp. 157–293; M. Wagner, op. cit., pp. 140–94; and Christiane Northrup, M. D., *Women's Bodies, Women's Wisdom* (New York: Bantam Books, 1996), pp. 466–72; Dr Foster survey (UK), *Sunday Times*, 15 July 2001.

80   **hospital disclosure:** M. Wagner, op. cit., p. 117; Arthur Levin, interview, March 2001; and J. Mitford, op. cit., p. 139.

81   **midwives:** Eisenberg et al., op. cit., pp. 10–12.

# Seventh month

84   **Pregnant women:** D. V. Hart, P. A. Rajadhon, and R. J. Coughlin, *Southeast Asian Birth Customs: Three Studies in Human Reproduction* (New Haven: Human Relations Area Files, Inc., 1965), p. 41.

86   **Trobriand islanders:** Bronislaw Malinowski, *The Sexual Life of Savages in North-Western Melanesia* (New York: Horace Liveright, 1929).

86   **Cross-culturally . . . ceremony:** M. A. Kay, op. cit., pp. 150–250.

86   **rural Catholic Filipino:** D. V. Hart et al., op. cit., p. 21.

88   **treatise on PMS:** Janice Delaney, Mary Jane Lupton and Emily Toth, *The Curse: A Cultural History of Menstruation* (Chicago: University of Illinois Press 1988).

89   **turned their babies:** R. W. Cohen, op. cit., p. 47.

89      **Eighty-one per cent:** L. H. Mehl, M. D., 'Hypnosis and Conversion of the Breech to the Vertex Presentation', *Archives of Family Medicine*, 3, no. 108 (October 1994, pp. 881–7.

90      **Obstetrician Christiane Northrup:** C. Northup, op. cit., p. 451.

90      **some NHS hospitals:** Interview, head nurse, maternity unit, University College Hospital, interview, June 2001.

90      **Jacob produced speckled lambs:** Holy Bible, op. cit., pp. 32–37.

90      **Southeast Asian:** D. V. Hart et al., op. cit., p. 27.

90      **principle of caution:** M. A. Kay, op. cit., p. 150.

91      **Leonardo da Vinci:** T. Verny and J. Kelly, op. cit., p. 34.

91      **pass the placenta:** ibid., p. 57.

92      **active emotional life:** ibid., p. 12.

92      **see, hear, taste:** ibid., op. cit., p. 12.

92      **researchers were able to teach:** D. K. Spelt, cited in T. Verny and J. Kelly, op. cit., p. 19.

92      **A 2000 study:** Catherine Monk, William P. Fifer, Michael M. Myers, Richard P. Sloan, Leslie Trien, and Alicia Hurtado, 'Maternal Stress Responses and Anxiety During Pregnancy: Effects on Fetal Heart Rate', *Developmental Psychobiology*, 35, no. 1 (January 2000), pp. 67–77.

92      **Dr Michael Lieberman:** T. Verny and J. Kelly, op. cit., p. 20. See also Thomas Verny and Pamela Weintraub, *Nurturing the Unborn Child* (Ann Arbor: Sheridan Books, 2000), p. 126.

92      **intestinal rumblings:** Frederick Leboyer, *Birth Without Violence: The Book That Revolutionized the Way We Bring Our Children into the World* (Rochester: Healing Arts Press, 1974), pp. 17–18.

93      **mother's voice:** W. P. Fifer and C. M. Moon, 'The Role of Mother's Voice in the Organization of Brain Function in the Newborn', *Acta Paediatrica Supplement*, no. 397 (June 1994), pp. 86–93.

93      **fetus will literally jump in rhythm:** Dr Liley, cited in T. Verny and J. Kelly, op. cit., p. 39.

93      **transnatal learning:** J. P. Lecaunet and B. Schaal, 'Fetal Sensory Competencies,' *European Journal of Obstetrics, Gynecology, and Reproductive Biology*, 68, nos 1–2 (September 1996), pp. 1–23.

93      **Dr Henry Truby:** cited in T. Verny and J. Kelly, op. cit., p. 21.

93      **When the baby is born:** B. Schaal, L. Marlier and R. Soussignan, 'Olfactory Function in the Human Fetus: Evidence From Selective Neonatal Responsiveness to the Odor of Amniotic Fluid', *Behavioral Neuroscience*, 112, no. 6 (December 1998, pp. 1438–49.

93      **Studies by Israeli researchers:** M. Kaitz, A. Good, A. M. Rokem, and A. I. Eidelman, 'Mother's Recognition of Their Newborns by Olfactory Cues', *Developmental Psychobiology*, 20, no. 6 (November 1987), pp. 587–91.

93      **In a different study:** Dr Marcia Kaitz, interview, June 2001.

94      **mother's relationship with the father:** Lukesch, cited in T. Verny and J. Kelly, op. cit., p. 49.

94    **Dr Dennis Stott:** ibid., p. 49.

94    **E-poll:** 'Are Fathers the True-Heroes of Childbirth?' *The Times*, 22 March 2001.

94    **father's attention:** Lukesch, ibid., p. 131. For more on importance of father's relationship with mother to the mother's ability to bond, see K. C. Bloom, 'Perceived Relationship with the Father of the Baby and Maternal Attachment in Adolescents', *Journal of Obstetrical, Gynecological and Neonatal Nursing*, 27, no. 4 (July–August, 1998), pp. 420–30.

## Eighth month

96    **Before I was born:** M. F. Ashley-Montague, op. cit., p. 130.

97    **It is estrogen:** Blackburn and Loper, op. cit., p. 71–8.

97    **Deborah Sichel and Jeanne Driscoll:** Deborah Sichel and Jeanne Driscoll, *Women's Moods: What Every Woman Must Know About Hormones, the Brain, and Emotional Health* (New York: HarperCollins, 1999).

97    **'hormonal shifts':** ibid., p. 153.

97    **'When a woman':** ibid., p. 150–62.

97    **elevated levels of prolactin:** ibid.

98    **'feeling of meanness':** D. V. Hart et al., op. cit., p. 35.

98    **'From rodents to primates':** S. B. Hrdy, op. cit., p. 154.

99    **'messenger molecules':** C. Northup, op. cit., p. 30.

99    **Journalist and writer:** Isabel Fonseca, 'Mother's Superior', *Guardian*, 8 March 1999.

103   **psychologists Martin Daly and Margo Wilson:** S. B. Hrdy, op. cit., p. 458.

103   **resemblance to the father:** T. Verny and J. Kelly, op. cit., pp. 32–52.

## Ninth month

105   **'Many [cross-cultural]':** M. A. Kay, op. cit., p. 14.

105   **Sered and Abramovitch:** S. Sered and H. Abramovitch, 'Pregnant Dreaming: Searching for a Typology of a Proposed Dream Genre', *Social Science & Medicine*, 34, no. 12 (June 1992), pp. 1405–11. For more on dreams of pregnant women, see R. L. Blake, J. Reimann, 'The Pregnancy-Related Dreams of Pregnant Women', *Journal of the American Board of Family Practice*, no. 2 (March–April 1993), pp. 117–22. American College of Obstetricians and Gynecologists, 'Premature Rupture of Membranes: Clinical Management Guidelines for Obstetrician-Gynecologists', *ACOG Practice Bulletin*, no. 1 (June 1998), and B. P Tan and M. E. Hannah, 'Oxytocin for Prelabour Rupture of Membranes at or Near Term,'

(Cochrane Review), in *The Cochrane Library*, 2, 2001. Oxford: Update Software.

106 **In a 1993 study:** A. I. Eidelman, N. W. Hoffmann, and M. Kaitz, 'Cognitive Deficits in Women After Childbirth', *Obstetrics & Gynecology*, 8, no. 5, pt 1 (May 1993), pp. 764–7.

106 **A new study:** Dr Marcia Kaitz, interview, June 2001.

109 **Once nursing begins:** S. B. Hrdy, op. cit., p. 137.


# PART II: BIRTH
## Giving birth

115 **'To give birth':** Dr Michel Odent, *The Scientification of Love* (London, Free Association Books, 1999), p. 28.

115 **'nipple stim':** Hospital protocols, interview with head maternity nurse who asked not to be identified, February 2001.

116 **longer labor:** M. J. Keirse, H. P. Ottervanger and W. Smith, 'Controversies: Prelabor Rupture of the Membranes at Term: The Case for Expectant Management', *Journal of Perinatal Medicine* 24, no. 6 (1996), pp. 563–71.

116 **I could be paralysed:** 'If the epidural needle or catheter goes deeper than the epidural space, convulsions, respiratory paralysis, and/or cardiac arrest can occur. Tests are done to confirm proper placement before giving the full dosage.' H. Goer, *Obstetrics Myths vs. Research Realities*, op. cit., p. 250.

117 **mammals systems shut down:** R. P. Lederman, E. Lederman, B. A. Work and D. S. McCann, 'The Relationship of Maternal Anxiety, Plasma Catecholamines, and Plasma Cortisol to Progress Labor', *American Journal of Obstetrics and Gynecology*, 132, no. 5 (November 1978), pp. 495–500. See also C. Northrop, op. cit.: 'Is it any wonder that when you hook a vulnerable laboring woman up to three or four different tubes and wires, and then rupture her membranes, she, and subsequently her baby, might get a little scared–resulted in some fetal distress? . . . Biofeedback has documented the profound effect of thoughts on body systems such as blood pressure, pulse and skin resistance. The baby is *part* of a woman's body. She can tune in to it.' (p. 467).

120 **Studies in 2000 and 2001:** M. J. Renfrew, S. Lang, and M. W. Woolridge, 'Early Versus Delayed Initiation of Breastfeeding' (Cochrane Review). In *The Cochrane Library*, 2, 2001. Oxford: Update Software; A. B. Ransjo-Arvidson, A. S. Matthiesen, G. Lilja, E. Nissen, A. M. Widstrom and K. Uvnas-Moberg, 'Maternal Analgesia During Labor Disturbs Newborn Behaviour: Effects on Breastfeeding, Temperature and Crying', *Birth*, 28, no. 1 (March 2001), pp. 5–12. See also S. Kitzinger, *Ourselves as Mothers*, op. cit., pp. 170–2, for more on Caesareans and epidurals inhibiting bonding.

# Behind the birthing room

122 **Nurse-midwives:** Ina May Gaskin, interview, December 1999.

122 **Dianne:** Interview, November 1999. In fact, Dianne's hospital was not doing her baby any favours: hospital policies that keep mothers separated from new babies can harm the babies' ability to tolerate pain. One study found that skin-to-skin contact with the mother was a powerful pain reliever for the baby: L. Gray, L. Watt, and E. M. Blass, 'Skin-to-Skin Contact Is Analgesic in Healthy Newborns', *Pediatrics* 105, no. 1 (January 2000), p. e14. See also C. Northrup, op. cit: 'The cascade of adverse consequences of having your baby worked up for an infection include having your baby taken away from you and taken to the neonatal intensive care unit; more pain for the baby, because blood needs to be drawn and IV's started; the risks of antibiotics . . . increasing the risk of infection . . . increased anxiety for both mother and baby; and possible adverse effects on the establishment of successful breastfeeding' (p. 470).

124 **Teresa:** Interview, June 2001.

125 **Amanda:** Interview, 1999.

127 **Changing Childbirth**, British Government report, 1993, chaired by Baroness Cumberledge, Junior Minister for Health and Social Services. This report laid down guidelines for one-to-one support by midwives as well as 'choice, control and continuity' for women.

127 **Unlike their British counterparts:** Melanie Every (District Manager South), Royal College of Midwives, Interview, June 2001.

128 **the tiny fraction of nurse-midwives:** IN 1997, 96 per cent of CNM-attended deliveries occurred in hospitals, 4 per cent of CNM-attended deliveries occurred in freestanding birth centres and 1 per cent took place in the home. 'Basic Facts About Certified Nurse-Midwives' (Washington, DC; American College of Nurse-Midwives, 1999).

128 **as pathological:** Barbara Katz Rothman, *In Labor*, op. cit., p. 133.

128 **Strict guidelines:** 'Guidelines for the Incorporation of New Procedures into Nurse-Midwifery Practice', Washington, DC: American College of Nurse-Midwives.

128 **Holland and Denmark:** S. Arms, *Immaculate Deception II*, op. cit., pp. 48–9.

128 **infant and maternal deaths:** T. H. Strong, op. cit., pp. 12–16.

129 **'establish his identity':** R. W. Wertz and D. C. Wertz, op. cit., p. 64.

129 **'required . . . episiotomy':** ibid., p. 165.

129 **Before 1920:** ibid., p. 141.

130 **effective medically:** ibid., p. 144.

130 **Hospital . . . is the safest:** Eisenberg, et al., cit., p. 14.

130 **The United States is 21st in the world:** M. Wagner, op. cit., p. 14.

130 **in the United Kingdom:** Melanie Every, interview, June 2001.

130 **AIMS:** AIMS (Association for Improvements in Maternity Services): 21 Iver

Lane, Iver, Bucks SLO 9LH. Tel: 01753 652 781, 01865 55 22 70, www.aims.org.uk

130 **National Childbirth Trust:** National Childbirth Trust (NCT): Alexandra House, Oldham Terrace, London W3 6NH. Tel: 0870 444 8707, www.nct-online.org

131 **Research carried out:** Marjorie Tew.

131 **A 1994 study:** P. A. Janssen, V. L. Holt and S. J. Meyers, 'Licensed midwife-attended out-of-hospital births in Washington State. Are they Safe?' *Birth*, 21, no.3 (September 1994), pp. 141–8. For more on home birth, see P. A. Murphy and J. Fullerton, 'Outcomes of Intended Home Births in Nurse-Midwifery Practice: A Prospective Descriptive Study', *Obstetrics & Gynecology*, 92, no. 3 (September 1998), pp. 461–70; and C. Hafner-Eaton and L. K. Pearce, 'Birth Choices, the Law, and Medicine: Balancing Individual Freedoms and Protection of the Public's Health', *Journal of Health, Politics & Policy Law* 19, no. 4 (Winter 1994), pp. 813–35; and R. E. Anderson and D. A. Anderson, 'The Cost Effectiveness of Home Birth', *Journal of Nurse-Midwifery* 44, (1999), pp. 30–5.

131 **National Birth Center Study:** J. P Rooks, N. L. Weatherby, E. K. Ernst, S. Stapleton, D. Rosen and A. Rosenfield, 'Outcomes of Care in Birth Centers. The National Birth Center Study', *New England Journal of Medicine*, 321, no. 26, 28 December, 1989), pp 1804–11. In the United States, 77 birth centres are listed in the birth centre directory by the National Association of Childbearing Centers (2000).

131 **'high risk':** J. C. Carroll, A. J. Reid, J. Ruderman and M. A. Murray, 'The Influence of the High-Risk Care Environment on the Practice of Low-Risk Obstetrics', *Family Medicine* 23, no. 3 (March–April 1991), pp. 184–8. The care of 2,365 low-risk patients was examined in three different facilities. Two of the facilities cared for mostly high-risk patients, the third cared for mostly low-risk patients. Researchers found that the doctors in the two high-risk facilities performed more artificial rupture of membranes, epidurals, Pitocin administration, and episiotomies on low-risk patients than the doctors caring for similarly low-risk patients at the low-risk facility.

131 **Sydney Wolfe:** Public Citizen Health Research Group, 'Summary of Presentation by S. M. Wolfe, M. D.', Round Table on Hospital Reporting to the National Practitioner Data Bank, 29 October, 1996, Washington, DC, p. 1.

131 **Under-reporting:** D. O. Farley, T. Richards and R. M. Bell, 'Effects of Reporting Methods on Infant Mortality Rates Estimates for Racial Ethnic Subgroups', *Journal of Health Care for the Poor and Underserved*, 6, no. 1 (1995), pp. 60–75.

132 **Public Health Reports:** M. Gabay and S. M. Wolfe, 'Nurse-Midwifery: The Beneficial Alternative', *Public Health Reports*, 112 (1997), pp. 386–95.

132 **'an element of risk':** Eisenberg et al., op cit., p. 280.

133 **'A fetal monitor gauges':** ibid., p. 280.

133 **inaccurate up to 40–60% of the time:** S. Arms, *Immaculate Deception II*, op. cit., p. 95.

133 **The results of fetal monitor studies:** S. Arms, *Immaculate Deception II*, op. cit., p. 96. For a summary of the EFM literature, see Prentice and Lind, 'Fetal Heart Rate Monitor during Labor', 'Too Frequent Intervention, Too Little Benefit', cited in E. Davis-Floyd, op. cit., p. 10. For more on the unproven benefit of EFMs: L. A. Bracero, D. Roshanfekr, and D. W. Byrne, 'Analysis of Antepartum Fetal Heart Rate Tracing by Physicians and Computer', *Journal of Maternal and Fetal Medicine*, 9, no. 3 (May 2000), pp. 181–5.

133 **'Four rigorous studies':** Banta and Thacker; Haverkamp and Orleans, cited in Robbie E. Davis-Floyd, op. cit., p. 105.

133 **A bedrock of truth of EFM:** H. Goer, *The Thinking Woman's Guide to a Better Birth*, op. cit., p. 88.

133 **impatience and nervousness:** ibid., p. 106.

133 **A much larger study:** Leveno et al., ibid., p. 106.

133 **high-risk unmonitored women:** Shy et al., ibid., p. 106.

133 **One 1997 study:** R. A. Rosenblatt, S. A. Dobie, L. G. Hart, R. Schneeweiss, D. Gould, T. R. Raine, T. J. Benedetti, M. J. Pirani and E. B. Perrin, 'Interspeciality Differences in the Obstetric Care of Low-risk Women', *American Journal of Public Health*, 87 (March 1997), pp. 344–51.

133 **Continuously hooked up:** S. B. Thacker and D. R. Stroup, 'Continuous Electronic Heart Rate Monitoring for Fetal Assessment During Labor' (Cochrane Review), *The Cochrane Library*, 2, 2001. Oxford: Update Software.

134 **Even that benchmark:** M. G. Rosen and J. C. Dickinson, 'The Paradox and Electronic Fetal Monitoring: More Data May Not Enable Us to Predict or Prevent Infant Neurologic Morbidity', *American Journal of Obstetrics and Gynecology*, 168 (March 1993), pp. 745–51.

134 **If I didn't have a monitor strip:** C. Northrup, op. cit., p. 467.

134 **T. H. Strong:** T. H. Strong, Jr., op. cit., p. 83–4.

135 **routine monitoring be dropped:** American Academy of Pediatrics and the American College of Obstetricians & Gynecologists, *Guidelines for Perinatal Care* (4th ed. (1997), p. 101.

135 *Lying-In:* R. W. Wertz and D. C. Wertz, op. cit., p. 260.

135 **ACOG's own endorsement:** L. A. Haggerty, 'Continuous Electronic Fetal Monitoring: Contradictions Between Practice and Research', *Journal of OB/GYN and Neonatal Nursing*, 24, no. 4 (July–August 1999), pp. 409–16.

135 *Stanford Law Review:* Margaret Lent, *Stanford Law Review* 51, no. 4 (April 1999), pp. 807–37.

136 **United Kingdom:** National Health Service (UK) materials, Tracy Corrigan, interview, March 1999; Melanie Every, interview, June 2001; Dr Foster survey, *Sunday Times*, 15 July 2001. The World Health Organisation advises a Caesarean rate in developed countries of no higher than 10–15 per cent.

136 'natural position of women in labour': Robbie Pfeufer Kahn, *Bearing Meaning: the Language of Birth* (Chicago: University of Illinois Press, 1996). See also George J. Englemann (reprinted in 1977), *Labor Among Primitive Peoples* (New York: AMS Press, 1882), pp. 87–132; D. V. Hart et al., op. cit., and M. A. Kay, op. cit.

136 A nineteenth-century guide: G. Englemann, op. cit.

137 'The recumbent position': ibid., p. 4.

137 There is a reason: P. R. DeJong, R. B. Johanson, P. Baxen, V. D. Adrians, S. van der Wethuisen and P. W. Jones, 'Randomised Trial Comparing the Upright and Supine Positions for the Second Stage of Labour', *British Journal of Obstetrics & Gynaecology* 104, no. 5 (May 1997), pp. 567–71.

137 trauma: R. Olson, C. Olson, N. S. Cox, 'Maternal Birthing Positions and Perineal Injury', *Journal of Family Practice* 30, no. 5 (May 1990), pp. 553–7.

137 more 'bearing-down' pressure: S. Z. Chen, K. Aisaka, H. L. Mori and T. Kigawa, 'Effects of Sitting Position on Uterine Activity During Labor', *Obstetrics & Gynecology* 69, no. 1 (January 1987), pp. 67–73.

137 contractions more effective: C. M. Andres and M. Chrzanowski, 'Maternal Position, Labor and Comfort', *Applied Nursing Research* 3, no. 1 (February 1990), pp. 7–13.

137 lithotomy position . . . Louis XIV: C. Northrup, op. cit., p. 471. 'In the squatting position the anterior/posterior diameter of the bony pelvis (front to back) is increased by a half-centimeter or more . . . I've seen countless babies go into fetal distress in the delivery room simply because of the mother's position flat on her back' (ibid., p. 471).

138 'If we consider mammals': M. Odent, op. cit., p. 30.

138 'Friedman curve': Scott et al., op. cit., p. 106–7.

138 wide range of 'normal' responses to labour: L. L. Albers, M. Schiff, and J. G. Gorwoda, 'The Length of Active Labor in Normal Pregnancies', *Obstetrics & Gynecology*, 87, no. 3 (May 1996), pp. 355–9.

138 Is your patient still here?: Interview, May 2000.

139 'Arrested labour?': Ina May Gaskin, interview, December 1999.

140 Marshall Klaus and John Kennell: cited in S. Arms, *Immaculate Deception II*, op. cit., p. 162.

140 hands-on supporters: A. J. Gagnon, K. Waghorn and C. Covell, 'A Randomized Trial of One-to-One Nurse Support of Women in Labor', *Birth*, 24 (1997) pp. 71–7; J. Kennell, M. Klaus, S. McGrath, S. Robertson and C. Hinkley, 'Continuous Emotional Support During Labor in a U.S. Hospital: A Randomized Controlled Trial', *Journal of the American Medical Association*, 265 (1991), pp. 2197–2201; and K. Scott, G. Berkowitz and M. Klaus, 'A Comparison of Intermittent and Continuous Support During Labor: A Meta-analysis', *American Journal of Obstetrics and Gynecology*, 180 (1999), pp. 1054–9.

140 in an attempt to lower Caesarean delivery rates: OB-GYNs Issue

'Recommendations on Cesarean Delivery Rates' (Washington DC: American College of Obstetricians and Gynecologists, 2000), p. 2.

140 **epinephrine:** R. P. Lederman et al., op. cit.

140 **A 1997 Swedish:** B. Sjogren and P. Thowassen, 'Obstetric outcome in 100 women with severe anxiety over childbirth', *Acta Obstetricia et Gynecologica Scandinavica*, 76, no. 1 (November 1997), pp. 948–52.

140 **women's oxytocin levels:** R. A. Turner, M. Altemus, T. Enox, B. Cooper and T. McGuiness, 'Preliminary Research on Plasma Oxytocin in Normal Cycling Women Investigating Emotion and Interpersonal Distress', *Psychiatry* 62, no. 2 (summer 1999), pp. 97–113.

142 **Several European countries:** Sally Placksin, *Mothering the New Mother: Your Postpartum Resource Companion* (New York: New Market Press, 1994).

142 **'British mothers are visited':** Melanie Every, interview, June 2001.

142 **A 1 per cent rise:** Dr Foster survey, *Sunday Times*, 15 July 2001.

142 **The American system, too:** Public Citizens Health Research Group, 'Unnecessary Cesarean Sections: Curing a National Epidemic' (1994), pp. 1–3.

143 **severe perineal lacerations:** Julian N. Robinson, Errol R. Norwitz, Amy P. Cohen, Thomas F. McElrath and Ellice S. Lieberman, 'Epidural Analgesia and Third- or Fourth-Degree Lacerations in Nulliparas', *Obstetrics & Gynecology*, 94, no. 2 (August 1999), pp. 259–62.

143 **vacuum-assisted or forceps delivery:** Margaret Echt, M.D., Wallace Begneaud, M.D., and Douglas Montgomery, M.D., 'Effect of epidural analgesia on the primary cesarean section and forceps delivery rates', *Journal of Reproductive Medicine*, 45, no. 7 (July 2000), pp. 557–61.

143 **higher rates of Caesarean sections:** S. C. Morton, M. S. Williams, E. B. Keeler, J. C. Gambone and K. L. Kahn, 'Effect of Epidural Analgesia for Labor on the Cesarean Delivery Rate', *Obstetrics & Gynecology*, 83, no. 6 (June 1994), pp. 1045–52.

143 **11.8 to 28 per cent:** Ron Gonen, Roman Korobochka, Shimon Degani and Luis Gaitini, 'Association Between Epidural Analgesia and Interpartum Fever', *American Journal of Perinatology*, 17, no. 3 (2000), pp. 127–30.

143 **antibiotics:** E. Lieberman, J. M. Lang, F. Prigoletto, Jr., D. K. Richardson, S. A. Ringer and A. Cohen, 'Epidural Analgesia, Intrapartum Fever, and Neonatal Sepsis Evaluation', *Pediatrics*, 99, no. 3 (March 1997), pp. 415–19.

143 **'Epidural charges range':** H. Goer, *The Thinking Woman's Guide to a Better Birth*, op. cit., p. 128.

144 **Catherine Moore:** Interview, January 2001.

144 **Fifty to eighty per cent of women:** Mary J. Renfrew, Walter Hannah, Leah Albers and Elizabeth Floyd, 'Practices that minimize trauma to the genital tract in childbirth: a systematic review of the literature', *Birth*, 25, no. 3 (September 1998), pp. 143–60. UK data: Dr Foster survey, *Sunday Times*, 15 July 2001.

145 'minor surgical procedure': Eisenberg et al., op. cit., p. 284.

145 'traditional medical wisdom': ibid., p. 284.

145 **Kitzinger:** Sheila Kitzinger, *Year After Childbirth: Enjoying Your Body, Your Relationships, and Yourself in Your Baby's First Year* (New York: Oxford University Press, 1994), p. 70.

146 **Fewer than one new mother in ten:** ibid., p. 70.

146 **Fewer than one in five:** Dr Foster survey, *Sunday Times*, 15 July 2001.

146 **90 per cent:** Kitzinger, ibid.

146 **American first-time mothers:** Lisa Kane Low, Julia S. Seng, Terri L. Murtland and Deborah Oakley, 'Clinician-specific Episiotomy Rates: Impact on Perineal Outcomes', *Journal of Midwifery & Women's Health*, 45, no. 2 (March 2000), pp. 87–93.

146 **Dr Marsden Wagner:** M. Wagner, op. cit., p. 166.

146 **Six studies:** G. Carroli and J. Belizan, 'Episiotomy for Vaginal Birth' (Cochrane Review). In the Cochrane Library, 2, 2001. Oxford: Update Software.

147 **A 1994 study:** Michael C. Klein, Robert J. Gauthier, James M. Robbins, Janusz Kaczorowski, Sally H. Jorgensen, Eliane, D. Franco, Barbara Johnson, Kathy Waghorn, Morrie M. Gelfand, Melvin S. Guralnick, Gary W. Luskey and Arvind K. Joshi, 'Relationship of episiotomy to perineal trauma and morbidity, sexual dysfunction, and pelvic floor relaxation', *American Journal of Obstetrics & Gynecology*, 171, no. 3 (September 1994), pp. 591–8.

147 **Another study in 2000:** Low et al., op. cit., p. 87.

147 **women can labour and push longer:** S. M. Meticoglou, F. Manning, C. Harman and I. Morrison, 'Perinatal Outcome in Relation to Second-stage Duration', *American Journal of Obstetrics and Gynecology*, 173 (September 1995), pp. 906–12: and L. L. Albers, M. Schiff and J. G. Gorwoda, 'The Length of Active Labor in Normal Pregnancies', *Obstetrics & Gynecology*, 87, no. 3 (March 1996), pp. 355–9.

147 **'There is no evidence':** Erica Eason and Perle Feldman, 'Much Ado About a Little Cut: Is Episiotomy Worthwhile?', *Obstetrics & Gynecology*, 95, no. 4 (April 2000), pp. 616–18.

147 **In a study of 1,000 women:** J. Sleep, A. Grant, J. Garcia, D. Elbourne, J. Spencer and I. Chalmers, 'West Berkshire Perineal Management Trial', *British Medical Journal (Clinical Research Edition)*, 289, no. 6445 (September 1984), pp. 587–90.

147 **kneeling on all fours:** P. Aikins and J. B. Feinland, 'Perineal Outcomes in a Home Birth Setting', *Birth*, 25, no. 4 (December 1998), pp. 226–34.

147 **perineal massage:** M. Labrecque, E. Easno, S. Marcoux, F. Lemieux, J. J. Pinault, P. Feldman and L. Laperriere, 'Randomized Controlled Trial of Prevention of Perineal Trauma by Perineal Massage During Pregnancy', *American Journal of Obstetrics and Gynecology*, 180, no. 3, pt. 1 (March 1998), pp. 593–600.

147 **whirpool baths:** J. Rush, S. Burlock, K. Lambert, M. Loosley Millman, B. Hutchison and M. Enkin, 'The Effects of Whirlpool Baths in Labor: A Randomized Controlled Trial', *Birth*, 23, no. 3 (September 1996), pp. 136–43.

147 **highest rate of perineal trauma:** M. J. Renfrew et al., op. cit.

147 **your doctor's attitude:** Michael C. Klein, Janusz Kaczorowski, James M. Robbins, Robert J. Gatheir and Sally Helme Jorgensen, 'Physician's Beliefs and Behaviour During a Randomized Control Episiotomy: Consequences for Women in Their Care', *Canadian Medical Assocation Journal*, 153, no. 6 (September 1995), pp. 769–79; and M. J. Renfew et al., op. cit.

148 **a busy office:** E. Eason and P. Feldman, op. cit., p. 616.

148 · **Until the 1970s:** S. Arms, *Immaculate Deception II*, op. cit., pp. 91–2.

148 **The US Center for Disease Control:** Sally C. Curtin and Joyce A. Martin, 'Births: Preliminary Date for 1999', *National Vital Statistics Reports* 48, no. 14 (Hyattsville, Maryland: National Center for Health Statistics, 2000).

149 **Paris obstetrical conference:** Second World Congress on Controversies in Obstetrics, Gynecology & Infertility, Paris, 2001.

149 *Wall Street Journal:* Miriam Jordan, 'Many Brazilian Women Don't Choose to Give Birth the Old-Fashioned Way', *The Wall Street Journal*, 15 June, 2001, p. 1.

149 **Husarsky:** cited in R. W. Cohen, op. cit., p. 81.

149 **nearly as safe:** Eisenberg et al., op. cit., p. 244.

150 **two to five times more likely:** S. Arms, *Immaculate Deception II*, op. cit., p. 91. See also Bruce Flamm, M.D., Andrea Kabcenell, R. N., Donald M. Berwick, M.D. and Jane Rosessner, 'Reducing Cesarean Section Rates While Maintaining Maternal and Infant Outcomes' (Boston: Institute for Healthcare Improvement, 1997), p. xiv.

150 **more than 870,000:** S. C. Curtin et al., op. cit. According to the 1999 data, 22 per cent of 3, 957, 829 births in America were performed by C-section.

150 **Wolfe:** Public Citizens Health Research Group, 'Unnecessary Cesarean Sections: Curing a National Epidemic', op. cit.

150 **When midwives, rather than obstetricians:** R. A. Rosenblatt et al., op. cit; and L. G. Davis, G. L. Riedmann, M. Sapiro, J. P. Minogue and R. R. Kazer, 'Cesarean Section Rates in Low-Risk Private Patients Managed by Certified Nurse-Midwives and Obstetricians', *Journal of Nurse-Midwifery*, 39, no. 2 (March/April 1994), pp. 91–7. According to the Public Citizen's Health Research Group, in 1995, certified nurse-midwives had a cesarean section rate of 11.6 per cent and a VBAC rate of 68.9 per cent. During the same period, the national rates were 23.3 and 24.9 per cent, respectively. See 'Ensuring the Use of Nurse-Midwives' (Washington, DC: Public Citizen's Health Research Group, 1995). Other 'provider factors' have been linked to Caesarean rates. A study done in 1999 showed that young age of physician, graduation from a domestic medical school, group practice, and smaller volume of births were all significantly linked to lower Caesarean delivery

rates. See P. A. Poma, 'Effects of Obstetrician Characteristics on Cesarean Delivery Rates: A Community Hospital Experience', *American Journal of Obstetrics and Gynecology*, 180, no. 6, pt. 1 (June 1999), pp. 1364–72.

150 **your doctor's gender:** L. K. Mitler, J. A. Rizzo and S. M. Horwitz, 'Physician Gender and Cesarean Sections', *Journal of Clinical Epidemiology*, 53, no. 10 (October 2000), pp. 1030–5.

151 **Caesarean-Section rate break down by class:** S. Arms, *Immaculate Deception II*, op. cit., pp. 93–3.

151 **The same is true for Australia:** See James F. King, 'Obstetric Interventions Among Private and Public Patients, *British Medical Journal*, 321 (15 July 2000), pp. 125–6.

151 **The American College of Obstetricians and Gynecologists:** R. W. Wertz and D. C. Wertz, op. cit., p. 261. See also 'OB-GYNs Issue Recommendations on Cesarean Delivery Rates', American College of Obstetricians and Gynecologists (Washington DC: New York Times' followed by 'To avoid lawsuits' 2000).

151 *New York Times:* Dr Ibrahim I. Bolaji, cited in *The New York Times*, 1998.

151 **to avoid lawsuits:** For more on the impact of legal pressures on the Caesarean delivery rate, see A. Vimercati, P. Greco, A.Kardashi, C. Rossi, V. Loizzi, M. Scioscia and G. Loverro, 'Choice of Cesarean Section and Perception of Legal Pressure', *Journal of Perinatal Medicine*, 28, no. 2 (2000), pp. 111–7.

151 **demands of the clock:** For data supporting the argument that women suffer from an environment in which an artificial time pressure is placed upon the length of labour, see S. M. Menticoglou et al., op. cit; L. L. Albers et al., op. cit; and M. J. Keirse et al., op. cit.

151 **$1.1 billion:** R. W. Cohen, op. cit., p. 23.

152 **$175 million:** ibid., p. 25.

152 **Health Insurance Association of America:** Health Insurance Association of America, op. cit., p. 112.

152 **'Discuss the cesarean rate':** Eisenberg et al., op. cit., p. 246.

152 **Caesarean rate above 50 per cent for years:** Cohen, op. cit., p. 18.

152 **sutured:** S. Arms, *Immaculate Deception II*, op. cit., p. 89.

153 **the mother's attitude:** Eisenberg et al., op. cit., p. 242.

153 **high-profile women:** Libby Books, 'To Push Or Not To Push?' *Guardian*, 2 May 2000. See also David Charter, 'Caesarean Trend Blamed on Celebrities', *The Times*, 22 May 2001.

153 **'too posh to push':** Sheila Fitzsimmons, 'Too posh to push?' *Guardian*, 14 June 2001.

153 *The Times:* Mary Ann Sieghart, 'Forget Natural, Give Me Painless', *The Times*, 7 February 2001.

153 **normal course of events:** Susan Gilbert, 'Doctors Report Rise in Elective Cesareans', *New York Times*, 22 September, 1998.

153 **Department of Health figures:** Sheila Fitzsimmons, op. cit.; David Charter,

op. cit. See also Jo Revill, 'Caesarean Births on Demand', *Evening Standard*, 14 August 1998.

153 **another 2001 survey:** Dr Foster survey, *Sunday Times*, 15 July 2001.

154 **of £386 million:** Figures supplied by Litigations Office, Department of Health.

154 **national audit of maternity units:** News story published on website of Royal College of Midwives (www.rcm.org.uk), 27 August 2000. See also Libby Brooks, op. cit.

154 **'Maternal deaths':** Cohen, op. cit., p. 20; and B. Flamm, et al., op. cit., p.xiv.

154 **infant mortality:** B. Flamm et al, op. cit., p. xiv. 'Researchers who have looked at cross-national variations in cesarean section rates in the last ten years and compared these rates with perinatal mortality rates have failed to find any significant correlation . . . A study carried out by the National Centre for Health Statistics in the United States comments: "The comparison of perinatal mortality ratios with cesarean section and with operative vaginal rates finds no consistent correlation across countries" . . . A review of the scientific literature on this issue states: "a number of studies have failed to detect any relation between crude perinatal mortality rates and the level of operative deliveries."' See M. Wagner, op. cit., p. 178.

155 **labours of black women:** Emily Martin, *The Woman in the Body: A Cultural Analysis of Reproduction* (Boston: Beacon Press, 1987), p. 151.

155 **Scully:** cited in E. Martin, ibid., p. 153.

155 **New York City and Baltimore studies:** cited in E. Martin, ibid., p. 151.

155 **Goepp:** Interview, February 2001.

156 **one-to-one midwifery:** Melanie Every, Royal College of Midwives, interview, June 2001.

156 **a 2001 survey:** motherandbaby.co.uk website, cited in John Carvel, 'Women Dissatisfied With Care During Childbirth', *Guardian*, 22 March 2001.

156 **'old and filthy':** Lucy, interview, June 2001.

156 **had no soap or towels:** cited in *The Times*, 13 January 2001.

156 **In April 2000:** Information obtained from Department of Health website (www.chi.nhs.uk)

157 **Dick-Read:** Grantly Dick-Read, *Childbirth Without Fear: The Original Approach to Natural Childbirth* (New York: Harper and Row, 1993).

158 **Leboyer:** F. Leboyer, op. cit., pp. 101–11.

159 **women in the West:** R. W. Wertz and D. C. Wertz, op. cit., pp. 131–75.

159 **though supported by the earth:** Brigette Jordan, *Birth in Four Cultures: A Cross-Cultural Investigation of Childbirth in Yucatan, Holland, Sweden and the United States*, Prospects Heights, Illinois: Waveland Press, 1993. Also Megan Biesele, 'An Ideal of Unassisted Birth: Hunting, Healing, and Transformation among the Kalahari Ju/'hoansi', in Robbie E. Davis-Floyd and Carolyn F. Sargent (eds), *Childbirth & Authoritative Knowledge: Cross-*

*Cultural Perspectives* (Berkeley: University of California Press, 1997), pp. 474–492.

160 *Spiritual Midwifery*: I. M. Gaskin, op. cit.

162 **page that tallies:** I. M. Gaskin, op. cit., p. 473.

169 **a young mother:** interview, May 2001.

## PART III: NEW LIFE
## Joy and 'blues'

177 **'Even the mother':** Erica Jong, *Mothers: A Loving Celebration* (Philadelphia: Courage Books, 1977). p. 99.

177 **delayed bonding:** Dr Michelle Asher-Dunne, psychoanalyst specializing in restoring damaged mother-baby bond, interview, March 2001.

184 **50 per cent to 80 per cent:** Ann Dunnewold and Diane Sanford, *The Postpartum Survival Guide* (Oakland: New Harbinger Publications, 1994).

184 **'a transient state':** S. G. Gabbe et al., op. cit., p. 705.

185 **within 24 hours:** Deborah Sichel, M.D. and Jeanne Watson Driscoll, M.S., R.N., *Women's Moods: What Every Woman Must Know About Hormones, the Brain, and Emotional Health* (New York: HarperCollins, 1999). See also B. Harris, L. Lovett, R. G. Newcombe, G. F. Read, R. Walker, R. Riad-Fahmy, 'Maternity Blues and Major Endocrine Changes: Cardiff Puerperal Mood and Hormone Study II', *British Medical Journal*, 308, no. 6934 (9 April 1994), pp. 949–53.

185 **400,000 mothers:** C. T. Beck and R. K. Gable, 'Postpartum Depression Screening Scale: Development and Psychometric Texting', *Nursing Research*, 49, no. 5 (September/October 2000), pp. 272–82.

185 **hormonal changes women endure:** More sources point to a complex hormonal interaction. Even a purely biological analysis should nonetheless, it seems to me, lead the culture of birth and the social expectations around new motherhood to become far more supportive than they are now. See D. Sichel and J. W. Driscoll, op. cit.; and K. Berggren-Clive, 'Out of Darkness and into the Light: Women's Experiences with Depression After Birth', *Canadian Journal of Community Mental Health*, 17, no. 1 (spring 1998), pp. 103–20; and M. Bloch, P. J. Schmidt, M. Danaceau, J. Murphy, L. Nieman, D. R. Rubinow, 'Effects of Gonadal Steroids in Women with a History of Postpartum Depression', *American Journal of Psychiatry* 157, no. 6 (June 2000), pp. 924–30; and J. F. Buckwalter, F. Stanczyk, C. A. McCleary, B. W. Bluestein, D. K. Buckwalter, K. P. Rankin, L. Change and T. M. Goodwin, 'Pregnancy, the Postpartum and Steroid Hormones: Effects on Cognition and Mood', *Psychoneuroendocrinology*, 24, no. 1 (January 1999), pp. 69–84.

185 **conditions in hospital postnatal wards:** Kate Figes, *Life After Birth: What*

*Even Your Friends Won't Tell You About Motherhood* (London: Viking, 1998).

185   Jackie: Interview, June 2001.

186   **A randomized controlled trial:** J. M. Holden, 'A Randomized Controlled Trial of Health Visitors in the Treatment of Postnatal Depression', MPhil thesis, Faculty of Medicine, University of Edinburgh, 1989.

186   **'PPD is very common':** Karen R. Kleiman, M.S.W. and Valerie D. Raskin, M.D, *This Isn't What I Expected: Overcoming Postpartum Depression* (New York: Bantam Books, 1994). p. 2.

187   **'period of adjustment':** ibid., p. 3.

187   **Factors that contribute to PPD:** ibid., p. 7.

187   **Dunnewald . . . ashamed and even a little crazy:** A. Dunnewald and D. Sanford, op. cit., p. 5.

187   **isolation:** S. Kitzinger, *The Year After Childbirth*, op. cit., p. 139.

187   **40 days:** For a description of the cross-cultural period of 40 days in which new mothers are pampered and 'mothered' by other women, see S. Placksin, op. cit., p. 65.

188   **Greece, Guatemala . . . :** ibid., 64–7.

188   **In Malaysia the new:** M. A. Kay, op. cit., p. 98.

188   **altered psychological state . . . Winnicott:** cited in Kitzinger, *The Year After Childbirth*, op. cit., p. 8.

188   **India, Pakistan, Ecuador and Brazil:** Interview, Sakhina Jaffrey, referencing research by culinary writer Madhur Jaffrey.

188   **In Britain . . . Holland:** S. Kitzinger, *The Year After Childbirth*, op. cit., p. 124.

188   **in Japan the new:** M. A. Kay, op. cit., p. 113.

189   **Mary-Lou:** Interview, June 2001.

189   **This is a most atypical:** V. Evaneshlco, Ph.D., 'Tonawanda Seneca Childbearing Culture', in M. A. Kay, op. cit., pp. 395–411.

190   **Anthropologist Sarah Blaffer Hrdy:** S. B. Hrdy, op. cit., p. 91.

190   **isolated . . . virtual solitary confinement:** S. Kitzinger, *The Year After Childbirth*, op. cit., pp. 139–41.


## Calling it fair

191   **'The heart of a mother':** Honoré de Balzac in Tara Ann McFadden, op. cit., p. 121.

191   **The job market:** R. P. Kahn, op. cit.

193   **John M. Gottman and Nan Silver:** John Mordechai Gottman, PhD, and Nan Silver, *The Seven Principles for Making Marriage Work* (Three Rivers Press, 2000) (67 per cent of new mothers in a study of 130 couples said that their marriages had suffered after the baby's arrival).

193 **Solomon:** Then the king answered and said, Give her the living child, and in no wise slay it; she is the mother thereof.' The First Book of the Kings, 3:24–8, Holy Bible, op cit., p. 302.

194 **Tina:** Interview, June 2001.

195 **1993 Family and Medical Leave Act:** S. Kitzinger, *Ourselves as Mothers*, op. cit., p. 230.

195 **In Australia:** Jill Papworth, 'Lagging Behind in the Pregnant Pause', *Guardian*, 11 June 1999.

196 **most countries in Europe:** Ann Crittenden, *The Price of Motherhood: Why the Most Important Job in the World is Still the Least Valued* (New York: Metropolitan Books, 2001). See 'The Mommy Tax', pp. 87–109.

196 **A group of female MPs:** Interview, May 2001.

196 **another catch:** A. Crittenden, op. cit. For an analysis of the low status and difficult conditions of many child care centres and private care-givers, see her chapter, 'An Accident Waiting to Happen', pp. 219–32.

196 **National Building Museum:** Donald Albrecht (ed.), *World War II and the American Dream: How Wartime Building Changed a National* (Cambridge, Mass: MIT Press, 1995), pp. 126–7.

197 **needed their jobs back:** Betty Friedan, *The Feminine Mystique* (New York: Dell, 1984).

198 **the lion's share:** Arlie Russel Hochschild, *The Second Shift* (New York: Avon Books, 1997).

198 **Gottman and Silver's landmark research:** J. Gottman and N. Silver, op. cit.

198 **Gina:** Interview, October 1999.

200 **Dianne:** Interview, November 1999.

201 **Greta:** Interview, March 2000.

203 **Sarah:** Interview, May 2001.

206 **housework erotic:** J. M. Gottman and N. Silver, op. cit., pp. 205, 211.

206 **Barbara:** Interview, July 1997.

212 **Minnie:** Interview, July 1997.

215 **sitting on a bus:** Kate, interview, June 2001.

215 **In the United Kingdom:** *Mother and Baby* Magazine/BUPA Birth and Motherhood Survey 2000.

218 **£30 billion:** A. Crittenden, op. cit., p. 204.

218 **Kentucky Fried Child Care:** Kathy Modigliani, cited in ibid., p. 208.

218 **only one-third of day-care workers:** ibid., p. 205.

218 **Paul England:** cited in ibid., p. 205.

218 **rates near 50 per cent annually:** ibid., p. 208.

219 **'loss':** ibid., p. 208.

219 **'lax standards':** ibid., p. 231.

220 **Sharon:** Interview, June 1998.

223 **British research:** Charles Lewis, *What Good Are Dads?* Report based study of British and international papers on childhood, 1980–2000, cited in *Daily Telegraph*, 13 June 2001.

223   **Laura and Dan:** Interview, June 2000.

## Making Mothers

228   **A tree whose hungry mouth:** Joyce Kilmer and Marjorie Barrows (eds), *100 Best Poems for Boys and Girls* (Racine, WIIS: Whitman Publishing Co.,), p. 96.

229   **American Academy of Pediatrics:** M. Sara Rosenthal, *The Breastfeeding Sourcebook* (Lincolnwood Ill: Lowell House, 2000), p. xviii.

229   **Talmudic proverb:** Judith Goleman (Talmud scholar), interview, November 1999.

229   **living organism:** S. Kitzinger, *The Year After Childbirth*, op. cit., p. 80.

229   **a greater risk of allergies:** For a summary of the benefits of breast-feeding see American Academy of Pediatrics, 'Breastfeeding and the Use of Human Milk', *Pediatrics* 100, no. 6 (December 1997), pp. 635–9.

230   **benefits:** James W. Anderson, Bryan M. Johnstone, Daniel T. Remley, 'Breastfeeding and Cognitive Development: A Meta-analysis', *American Journal of Clinical Nutrition*, 70 (1999), pp. 525–35; M. J. Heinig, 'Host Defense Benefits of Breastfeeding for the Infant. Effect of Breastfeeding Duration and Exclusivity', *Pediatric Clinics of North America* 48, no. 1 (February 2001), pp. 105–23; and American Academy of Pediatrics, 'Breastfeeding and the Use of Human Milk', op. cit.

230   **A 2000 study:** S. Arora, C. McJunkin, J. Wehrer and P. Kuhn, 'Major Factors Influencing Breastfeeding Rates: Mother's Perception of Father's Attitude and Milk Supply', *Pediatrics*, 106, no. 5 (November 2000), p. E67.

# Bibliography

Abitol, M. M. "Supine Position in Labor and Associated Fetal Heart Rate Changes." *Obstetrics and Gynecology* 65 (1985): 481–86.

Arms, Suzanne. *Immaculate Deception*. New York: Bantam Books, 1975.

Arms, Suzanne. *Immaculate Deception II*.

Astbury, Jill. *Crazy for You – The Making of Women's Madness*. Oxford: Oxford University Press, 1996.

Bowen, Evlyn M. *Pre-Birth Bonding*. San Diego: HeartStart/LoveStart Publications, 1983.

Brazelton, T. B. "Effect of Maternal Expectations on Early Infant Behavior." *Early Child Development Care 2* (1973): 259–73.

Broach, Jeanine, and Niles Newton. *Food and Beverages in Pregnancy*. New York: Random House, 1988.

Cohen, Ruth Wainer. *Open Season: Survival Guide for Natural Childbirth and VBAC in the 90s*. New York: Greenwood Publishing, 1991.

Crowley Jack, Dana. *Silencing the Self – Women and Depression*. Cambridge, Mass.: Harvard University Press, 1991.

Curtin, S. C. "Recent Changes in Birth Attendant, Place of Birth, and the Use of Obstetric Interventions, United States, 1989–1997." *Journal of Nurse Midwifery* 44, no. 4 (July–August 1999): 349–54.

Curtin, S. C. and J. A. Martin. "Births: Preliminary Data for 1999." *National vital statistics reports;* vol. 48, no. 14. Hyattsville, Md.: National Center for Health Statistics, 2000.

d'Aquili, Egene G. "The Neurobiology of Myth and Ritual." In *The Spectrum of Ritual: A Biogenetic Structural Analysis*. New York: Columbia University Press.

Eckstein, K. L., and G. F. Marx. "Aortocaval Compression and Uterine Displacement." *Anesthesia* 40, no. (1) (1974): 92–96.

Ehrenreich, Barbara, and Deirdre English. 1973. *Complaints and Disorders: the Sexual Politics of Sickness*. Old Westbury, N.Y.: The Feminist Press, 1973.

—. *Witches, Midwives, and Nurses: A History of Women Healers*. Old Westbury, N.Y.: The Feminist Press, 1973.

# Bibliography

Entwisle, D. R., and S. G. Doering. *The First Birth: A Family Turning Point.* Baltimore: John Hopkins University Press, 1981.

Flaxman, S. M. and P. W. Sherman. "Morning Sickness: A Mechanism for Protecting Mother and Embryo." Q Rev Biol 75, no. 2 (June 2000): 113–48.

Gellhorn, E. "Central Nervous System Tuning and Its Implications for Neuropsychiatry." *Journal of Nervous and Mental Diseases* 147 (1968): 148–62.

—. "Further Studies on the Physiology and Pathophysiology of the Tuning of the Central Nervous System." *Psychosomatics* 10 (1969): 94–104.

—. "The Emotions and the Erogtrophic and Trophotropic Systems." *Psychologische Forschung* 34 (1970): 48–94.

Gellhorn, E., and W. F. Kiely. 1972. "Mystical States of Consciousness: Neurophysiological and Clinical Aspects." *Journal of Nervous and Mental Diseases* 154 (1972): 399–405.

Gabay, M., and S. M. Wolfe. "Nurse-Midwifery: The Beneficial Alternative." *Public Health Reports* 112 (1997): 386–95.

Goer, H. *The Thinking Woman's Guide to a Better Birth.* New York: Berkeley Publishing Group, 1999.

Haggerty, L. A. *Journal of Obstetrical, Gynecological and Neonatal Nursing* 28, no. 4 (July–August 1999): 409–16.

Hales, Dianne. *Just Like a Woman: How Gender Science is Redefining What Makes us Female.* New York: Bantam, 1999.

Hess, P. E., S. D. Pratt, A. K. Soni, M. C. Sarno, and N. E. Orio. "An Association Between Severe Labor Pain and Cesarean Delivery." *Anesth Alag 90*, no. 4 (April 2000):881–86.

Hodnett, E. D., M. E. Hannah, J. A. Weston, A. Ohlsson, T. L. Myhr, E. E. Wang, S. A. Hewson, A. R. Willan, and D. Farine. "Women's Evaluations of Induction of Labor versus Expectant Management for Prelabor Rupture of the Membranes at Term." *Birth* 24, no. 4 (December 1997): 214–20.

Kahn, Robbie Pfeufer. 1984. "Taking Charge of Birth." *Women's Review of Books,* December 1984, pp. 15–16.

Kitzinger, Sheila. *The Experience of Childbirth.* New York: Taplinger, 1972.

—. *Women as Mothers: How They See Themselves in Different Cultures.* New York: Vintage Books, 1980.

Kitzinger, Sheila. *The Year After Childbirth: Enjoying Your Body, Your Relationships, and Yourself in Your Baby's First Year.* New York: Oxford University Press, 1994.

Larson, E., S. Lunche, and J. T. Tran. "Correlates of IV phlebitis." *NITA* 7 (1984): 203–205.

Leach, Edmund. *Culture and Communication.* New York: Cambridge University Press, 1976.

Leboyer, Frederick. *Birth Without Violence.* Rochester, N.Y.: Healing Arts Press, 1974.

Lent, M., *Stanford Law Reveiw* 51, no. 4 (April 1999): 807–37.

Lex, Barbara. "The Neurobiology of Ritual Trance." In *The Spectrum of Ritual: A Biogenic Structural Analysis,* ed. Eugene d'Aquili, Charles D. Laughlin, and John McManus. New York: Columbia University Press, 1979.

Martin, Emily. *The Woman in the Body: A Cultural Analysis of Reproduction.* Boston: Beacon Press, 1987.

McKay, Susan, and Charles Mahan. "How Can Aspiration of Vomitus in Obstetrics Best Be Prevented?" *Birth* 15, no. 4 (1988): 222–29.

McKay, Susan, and Joyce Roberts. "Maternal Position During Labor and Birth: What Have We Learned?" *ICEA Review* 13, no. 2 (1989): 19–30.

Mendez-Bauer, C. J., C. Aroya, C. Garcia-Ramos, A. Menendez, M. Lavilla, F. Izquierdo, I. Villa Elizaga, and J. Zamariego. "Effects of Standing Position on Spontaneous Uterine Contractility and Other Aspects of Labor." *Journal of Perinatal Medicine* 3 (1975): 89–100.

Monto, M. A. "Lamaze and Bradley Childbirth Classes: Contrasting Perspectives Towards the Medical Model of Birth." *Birth* 23, no. 4 (December 1996): 193–201.

Morley, Gerald K., Arshag D. Mooradian, Allen S. Levine, and John E. Morley. "Mechanism of Pain in Diabetic Peripheral Neuropathy: Effect of Glucose on Pain Perception in Humans." *American Journal of Medicine* 77 (1984): 79–82.

Murphy, S. L. *Deaths: Final Data for 1998. National Vital Statistics Reports,* vol. 48, no. 11. Hyattsville, Md.: National Center for Health Statistics, 2000.

Needham, Rodney. "Percussion and Transition." In *Reader in Comparative Religion,* ed. William A. Lessa and Evon Z. Vogt. 4th ed. New York: Harper and Row, 1979.

Newton, Niles. *Material Emotions: A Study of Women's Feelings Toward Menstruation, Pregnancy, Childbirth, Breastfeeding, Infant Care, and Other Aspects of Their Femininity.* New York: Paul B. Hoeber, 1955.

Nolen-Hoeksema, Susan. *Sex Differences in Depression.* Stanford, Calif.: Stanford University Press, 1990.

Northrup, Christiane. *Women's Bodies, Women's Wisdom.* New York: Bantam Books, 1996.

Oakley, Ann. *Women Confined: Towards a Sociology of Childbrith.* New York: Schocken Books, 1980.

Odent, Michel. *Birth Reborn,* 2nd ed. Medford: Birthworks, 1994.

—. *The Scientification of Love.* London: Free Association Books, 1999.

Peterson, Gayle, and Lewis Mehl. *Pregnancy as Healing: A Holistic Philosophy for Pre-Natal Care,* vols. 1, 2. Berkeley, Calif.: Mindbody Press, 1994.@ep.

Rich, Adrienne. *Of Woman Born: Motherhood as Experience and Institution.* New York: Bantam Books, 1977.

Roberts, Joyce, C. Mendez-Bauer, and D. A. Woodell. 1983. "The Effects of Maternal Position on Uterine Contractility and Efficiency." *Birth* 10, no. 4 (1983): 243–49.

Rosenberg, Harriet. "Motherwork, Stress, and Depression: The Costs of Privatised Social Reproduction." In *Feminism and Political Economy: Women's*

*Work, Women's Struggles,* ed. H. J. Maroney and M. Luxton. Toronto: Methuen, 1987.

Rosenblatt R. A., S. A. Dobie, L. G. Hart, Schneeweiss, D. Gould, T. R. Raine, M. G. Rosen, J. C. Dickinson. "The Paradox of Electronic Fetal Monitoring: More Data May Not Enable Us to Predict or Prevent Infant Neurologic Morbidity." *American Journal of Obstetrics and Gynecology* 168 (March 1993): 745–51.

Rothman, Barbara Katz. "A Sociologic View of Birth: Physiologic Reality vs. People's Interpretations of that Reality." In *Compulsory Hospitalization or Freedom of Choice in Childbirth?* ed. David Stewart and Lee Stewart. Marble Hill, Mo.: NAPSAC, 1979.

—. "Awake and Aware, or False Consciousness? The Cooption of Childbirth Reform in America." In *Childbirth: Alternatives to Medical Control,* Shelley Romalis, ed. Austin: University of Texas Press, 1981.

—. *In Labor. Women and Power in the Birthplace.* New York: W. W. Norton and Co., 1982. (Reprinted in paperback under the title *Giving Birth: Alternatives in Childbirth.* New York: Penguin Books, 1985.)

—. *Tentative Pregnancy: Prenatal Diagnosis and the Future of Motherhood.* New York: Viking, 1986.

—. *Recreating Motherhood: Ideology and Technology in Patriarchal Society.* New York: W. W. Norton, 1989.

Seel, Richard. 1986. "Birth Rite." *Health Visitor* 59 (1986): 182–84.

Segal, B. S., and D. J. Birnbach. "Epidurals and Cesarean Deliveries: A New Look at an Old Problem." *Anesth Analg* 9 (2000): 775–77.

Segal, S., M. Su, and P. Gilbert. "The Effect of a Rapid Change in Availability of Epidural Analgesia on the Cesarean Delivery Rate: A Meta-analysis." *American Journal of Obstetrical Gynecology* 183, no. 4 (October 2000): 974–78.

Sichel, D., and J. W. Driscoll. (1999) *Women's Moods: What Every Woman Must Know About Hormones, the Brain, and Emotional Health.* New York: HarperCollins, 1999.

Sizer, A. R., and D. M. Nirmal. "Occipitoposterior Position: Associated Factors and Abstric Outcome in Nulliparas." *Obstetrics and Gynecology* 96, no. 5, Part 1 (November 2000): 742–52.

Tan, B. P., and M. E. Hannah. "Oxytocin for Prelabor Rupture of Membranes at or Near Term." *Cochrane Database Systems Review* 2 (2000): CDOOO157.

Taylor, Verta. *Rock-a-ByeBaby: Feminism, Self-Help, and Postpartum Depression.* New York: Routledge, 1996.

Thacker, S. B., and D. F. Stroup. "Continuous Electronic Heart Rate Monitoring for Fetal Assessment During Labor." *Cochrane Database Systems Review* 2 (2000): CDOOOO63.

Turner, R. A., M. Altemus, T. Enox, B. Cooper, and T. McGuinness. "Preliminary Research on Plasma Oxytocin in Normal Cycling Women Investigating Emotion and Interpersonal Distress." *Psychiatry* 62, no. 2 (summer 1999): 97–113.

Turner, Victor W. *The Forest of Symbols.* Ithaca, N.Y.: Cornell University Press, 1967.

—. *The Ritual Process: Structure and Anti-Structure.* Chicago: Aldine Publishing Company, 1969.

Ueland, K., and J. M. Hansen, 1979. "Maternal Cardiovascular Dynamics, II: Posture and Uterine Contractions." *American Journal of Obstetrics and Gynecology* 103, no. 1 (1979): 1–8.

Van Gennep, Arnold. *The Rites of Passage.* Chicago: University of Chicago Press, 1966.

Wagner, M. *Pursuing the Birth Machine.* Australia: ACE Graphics, 1994.

Whybrow, Peter, *An Unquiet Mind. The Female Malady. Women, Madness, and English Culture 1830–1980.* New York: Pantheon Books, 1985.

Zain, H. A., J. W. Wright, G. E. Parrish, and S. J. Diehl. "Interpreting the Fetal Heart Rate Tracing. Effect of Knowledge of Neonatal Outcome." *Journal of Reproductive Medicine* 43, no. 4 (April 1998): 367–70.

Zhang, J., M. K. Yancey, M. Klebenoff, J. Schwartz, and D. Schweitzer. "Effects of epidural analgesia on the course of labor and delivery: a natural experiment." *Obstetrics and Gynecology* 95, no. 4. Suppl. 1 (April 2000): S45.

# Index